Social Approval as an Incentive

Institutional and Socio-Economics

Edited by Wolfram Elsner,
Wilfred Dolfsma, Arne Heise, Helge Peukert and Werner Schönig

Volume 17

PETER LANG
Frankfurt am Main · Berlin · Bern · Bruxelles · New York · Oxford · Wien

Matthias Greiff

Social Approval as an Incentive

The Voluntary Provision of Public Goods in Social Production Communities

PETER LANG
Internationaler Verlag der Wissenschaften

Bibliographic Information published by the Deutsche Nationalbibliothek
The Deutsche Nationalbibliothek lists this publication in the Deutsche Nationalbibliografie; detailed bibliographic data is available in the internet at http://dnb.d-nb.de.

Zugl.: Bremen, Univ., Diss., 2011

D 46
ISSN 0948-6178
ISBN 978-3-631-63016-7

www.peterlang.de

Contents

List of Figures

List of Abbreviations

ACM	Association for Computing Machinery
AIC	Akaike Information Criterion
ALLC	All Cooperate (Strategy)
ALLD	All Defect (Strategy)
ASF	Apache Software Foundation
AT&T	American Telephone and Telegraph Company
BSD	Berkeley Software Distribution
CD	compact disc
CVS	Concurrent Version System
DVD	digital versatile disc
e.g.	exempli gratia (for example)
EPO	European Patent Office
FSF	Free Software Foundation
FTP	file transfer protocol
GDP	gross domestic product
GE	General Electric
GNU	GNU is not Unix
GPL	General Public License
HP	Hewlett Packard
i.e.	id est (that is)
IBM	International Business Machines
MC	marginal cost
MIT	Massachusetts Institute of Technology
MPCR	marginal per capita return
NE	Nash equilibrium
OS	Operating System
OSS	open source software

PG	public good
SPNE	subgame perfect Nash equilibrium
TFT	Tit For Tat
US	United States
WSLS	Win-Stay, Loose-Shift (Strategy)

List of Symbols

A	set of action profiles
A_i	set of actions for player i
a	acion profile in a repeated game
$a_i \in A_i$	action for player i
b	benefit of a reward or punishment
C	contribute or to cooperate (strategy)
CN	strategy (contribute in first stage, do not give rewards in second stage)
CR	strategy (contribute in first stage, give rewards in second stage)
c	cost of contributing to the public good
$c(i)$	individual contributions in treatment i
c_i	contribution of player i
c_i^*	morally ideal contribution of player i
c_{-i}	average contribution of all other players except player i
$\mathbf{c}$	contribution profile
D	defection (strategy)
d	discount parameter for reinforcement learning
E	expectation operator
e	parameter for assortative matching
e_i	endowment of player i
e_{-i}	endowment of all players except player i
F	F-test statistic
f_i	player i's function for determining the value of social approval (T1)
G	Gini coefficient
g_i	player i's function for determining the value of social approval (T2)
$\mathcal{G}$	game
h	cost of giving a reward or cost of punishing
$h^t \in \mathcal{H}^t$	one possible history

$\mathcal{H}$	set of all possible histories in a repeated game
$\mathcal{H}^t$	set of possible histories of the game up to period t
I_i	individual i's self-image
K	number of control questions answered correctly
L_i	individual i's leisure time
$\bar{L}_i$	total time available to individual i
l	size of a set
MC	marginal cost
m	number of rewards
m_i	number of actions available to player i
$\bar{m}$	product of m_i over all players i
N	sample size
NN	strategy (do not contribute in first stage, do not give rewards in second stage)
NR	strategy (do not contribute in the first stage, give rewards in the second stage)
n	number of players or subjects
$\mathbf{N}$	set of players
P	payoff (prisoner's dilemma)
PG	amount of the public good supplied
p	price
$\tilde{p}$	player's belief
$p_{i,j}$	probability of player i interacting with player j
p_C	probability of being matched with a cooperator
p_D	probability of being matched with a defector
$p(s_x\|s_y)$	probability that a player with strategy y is matched with a player with strategy x
$\mathcal{P}$	proposition
$\mathbf{P}$	matrix of probabilities
q_{SP}	parameter in utility function with social preferences
$\mathbf{Q}$	set of *Contributors* and *Enforcers*
$\mathbf{Q}_i$	set of *Contributors* and *Enforcers* selected by player i
R	payoff (prisoner's dilemma)
$\bar{R}^2$	adjusted R-square
r	time preference

r_{SP}	parameter in utility function with social preferences
rc_i	relative contribution of player i
rc_{-i}	average relative contribution of all other players except player i
$\mathbb{R}^n$	n-dimensional space of real numbers
S	payoff (prisoner's dilemma)
S_i	set of player i's strategies
s	vector of strategy shares
s_i	share of strategy i
$\dot{s}_i$	time derivative of share of strategy i
s_{SP}	parameter in utility function with social preferences
$\mathbf{S}_{CR}$	set of players with strategy CR
$\mathbf{S}_{CN}$	set of players with strategy CN
$\mathbf{S}_{NN}$	set of players with strategy NN
T	payoff (prisoner's dilemma)
T0	Treatment 0 (Control Treatment)
T1	Treatment 1
T2	Treatment 2
t	time
$\bar{t}$	repetitions of a game
U	set of utility functions
u_i	utility function player i
$u(X)$	utility from playing strategy X
$u(X, Y)$	utility from playing strategy X against an opponent who plays strategy Y
$u(X_1X_2)$	utility from playing strategy X_1 in the first and X_2 in the second stage
$u(X_1X_2, Y_1Y_2)$	utility from playing strategy X_1 in the first and X_2 in the second stage against an opponent who plays Y_1 in the first and Y_2 in the second stage
$\underline{\mathrm{v}}_i$	player i's minimax payoff
w	propensity
$\mathbf{W}$	adjacency matrix
$\mathbf{X}$	payoff matrix
X, X_1X_2	strategy

x_i	private consumption player i
x	population state
Y, Y_1Y_2	strategy
α	probability of changing the strategy
β_i	parameter for reinforcement learning (if action i is chosen)
γ_i	parameter for reinforcement learning (if action i is chosen)
$\delta, \delta_1, \delta_2$	discount factors
$\hat{\delta}$	probability that the game continues
η	mutation probability
θ_{SP}	parameter in utility function with social preferences
κ	parameter for reinforcement learning (if logistic response rule is used)
λ	share of cooperators
$\dot{\lambda}$	time derivative of share of cooperators
$\bar{\lambda}, \bar{\bar{\lambda}}$	stable and unstable state
ν	marginal per capita return (MPCR) from the public good
Π_i	payoff player i in a repeated game
π_i	payoff player i
$\pi(X)$	payoff from playing strategy X_1 in the first and X_2 in the second stage
$\pi(X, Y)$	payoff from playing strategy X against an opponent who plays strategy Y
$\pi(X_1X_2)$	payoff from playing strategy X_1 in first and X_2 in the second stage
$\pi(X_1X_2, Y_1Y_2)$	payoff from playing strategy X_1 in the first and X_2 in the second stage against an opponent who plays Y_1 in the first and Y_2 in the second stage
$\bar{\pi}$	average payoff
ρ_{SP}	parameter in utility function with social preferences
σ	strategy profile
σ_i	strategy player i
σ_{-i}	strategy of all other players but player i
σ_i^*	Nash equilibrium strategy player i

σ^*	Nash equilibrium strategy profile
$\sigma_{i\|h^j}$	player i's continuation strategy induced by history h^j
σ_{SP}	parameter in utility function with social preferences
ϕ_i^1	number of stars received by subject i (in treatment 1)
ϕ_{-i}^1	sum of stars received by all other subjects but subject i (in treatment 1)
ϕ_i^2	number of stars received by subject i (in treatment 2)
ϕ_{-i}^2	sum of stars received by all other subjects but subject i (in treatment 2)
χ^2	Chi-square test statistic
$\bar{\omega}$	a constant
ξ	positive constant in the function for self-image
$\emptyset$	empty set

Foreword of the Editor

In times of fragmented value-added chains ('outsourcing'), being spread out globally and at the same time clustered locally, with hierarchies combining with inter-firm net-relations, and ubiquitous 'net-technologies' involved, much information, information generation, innovation, and even physical production, in this 'new economy' has become public in some sense. The ubiquity of coordination- and dilemma-game type decision problems, e.g., the increased relevance of net-externalities on the 'problem side', and of technical standardization and behavioural institutionalization, knowledge sharing, and forms of networking and related proper learned governance systems on the 'solution' side are indications of major changes in the 'deep structure' of the 'new economy'.

The present book lies at the heart of the modern reactions of economics in response to these changes – as represented by today's most dynamic areas of 'complexity economics' and 'behavioural economics', using different evolutionary, institutional, and experimental approaches. Most dynamic areas of economic research have been defined and pushed forward by those approaches in the last, say, three decades.

The present book starts from related empirical phenomena, particularly, what is called 'user-led innovation', 'user-generated content', and 'open-source' production of digital microelectronic content, particularly software. This is introduced here as forms of social production, which makes much sense since here we are dealing with complex and genuinely multi-personal decision structures that represent direct interdependencies and require interactively learned forms of common and collective 'governance' (i.e., coordinated and cooperative forms of behaviour).

This book, in its Chapter 2, provides a short and stringent history of 'open source' as well as an appraisal of the principles and rules of organisation and governance in related (what is called here) 'social production communities', among others. Its empirical résumé clearly indicates that while such social production is characterized not only by non-rivalry but most importantly by

non-excludability, channels of selective social approval appear to become a critical factor to establish and maintain systems of voluntary contribution to public goods.

Chapter 3 reflects public-good problems through game theory, particularly public-good and social dilemma games. While, basically, there are game-theoretic settings when supergames, played in populations and in evolutionary modelling with replicators and strategy change, may lead to emerging 'self-organizing' communities that sustainably may produce the relevant collective good through learned stable institutions of cooperation, this very result mostly is feasible only under very restrictive conditions. Selective partner encountering is mostly one of the devices required here to attain a cooperative equilibrium. But, still, this generally will remain one out of multiple equilibria (if at all), particularly in an exploding strategy space (in supergames with memory and strategy updating). Another way out here is the switch to evolutionary game theory with a given and small set of strategies, as pursued in Chapter 4.

It is a major contribution of this book that it connects empirics, complex game-theoretic modelling, some simulation, and, last not least, experimental, lab-related 'behavioural economics'. The results of the latter test a simplified version of the theoretical model and provide important 'heuristic' information for further theoretical research. The book takes a decision to focus on a second-stage social-approval dilemma and to solve this by some selective mechanism of social approval.

The review of what experimental economics has to offer covers the different motivations suggested in the literature for agents to voluntarily contribute to the first-stage public-good production. Among them, this thesis investigates individual use-values, intrinsic motivation, and social preferences, such as altruism, fairness norms, reciprocity norms, and inequality aversion. It becomes obvious that experimental/behavioural economics still is far from being 'settled' on a clear set of logically related crucial factors. Since the field is hardly 20 years old, still many new studies offer different (or differently conceptualized) critical factors. Thus, there also are many different ways available to sort and relate the theoretical conceptions or factors offered (those mentioned above).

The book provides a good connection between the 'intrinsic' approach and the later lab treatment (Chapter 6), which uses an anonymous group and in this way generates a relation to intrinsic value, as no particular in-

formation on who contributes and who approves whom, is known to the individual.

Chapter 5 further elaborates on the theme by developing a public-good game on a dynamic network with reinforcement learning – a changing neighbourhood/proximity/ distance topology, a related 'assortative matching' and strategy updating in the final extension of the model.

This all together is at the cutting-edge of current complexity-economics research. Together with the second-stage selective social approval 'module', this all definitely sums up to a considerable net contribution to the frontier of current economic research.

One important outcome here is the 'eternal' trade-off between diversification (strategy updating in this case) and selection (network adaptation in this case). For the model's systems to attain a rest point, strategies should not be changed too fast relative to the adaptation of social distance.

A general caveat against the explicatory power of experimental economics, as pursued in Chapter 6, would be that we deal with real-world agents who introduce their whole full-fledged culture into the lab process. This would basically have to be controlled for, i.e., first test the more or less cooperative habits and norms the agents bring along to the lab, as these would already explain much or most of their behaviour during the experiment. For instance, 'norms of modesty' may make social approval unobservable, which, thus, are underreported in much of the existing studies on voluntary contributions to social production. Particularly, if agents come to the lab with a high disposition to contribute (given the relatively low rewards to be gained there), they might contribute anyway, independently of any rewarding, i.e., even if remaining fully anonymous, as in this case. In a word, lab experiments should control for the systems of dispositions, habits, and norms that real-world agents bring to the lab. However, in this case, a control treatment controls for such dispositions, habits, and norms, since the difference between the control treatment and the regular treatments is exactly the social approval.

The general results of the lab treatments indicate a confirmation of the general theoretical thrust of the book, and particularly the relevance of visibility or what is called in original institutional economics, 'recognized interdependence'.

Finally, in chapter 7, the book offers a well-reflected discussion of implications and further research perspectives. This includes implications of the conditions of self-sustaining 'open' social production, elaborated here for

practical governance and management of social production communities – be the final motivation intrinsic or extrinsic.

Practical implications also touch ongoing and unsolved questions of intellectual property rights and the main thrust of policies of the last fifteen years to establish ever higher walls around intellectual property, which may have become counterproductive for information flow and the amount and speed of innovation in general. Which way to go is the 'natural' one and which the 'artificial' one: Is safeguarding private profit by policy and public bureaucracies under all circumstances the 'natural way?

To sum up, the present book is high-level and cutting-edge in its field. It is so by elaborating a model, and identifying critical factors, of sustainable social production communities, combining empirics, theory, modelling, and lab experiments. The work has excellent introductions to every chapter, meaningful upshots at the end of every chapter. The overall argument, thus, is well thought-through and easy to follow.

Bremen, June 2011

W. Elsner

Acknowledgements

The writing of this dissertation was a long and sometimes solitary journey. It required not only patience, discipline and sacrifice but also the help of many people. Given this, I wish to thank all those who permitted me to pursue my journey.

The research presented in this book would not have been possible without the excellent academic guidance by my supervisor Wolfram Elsner. He gave me the freedom to pursue my own way and I am very grateful to him for intellectual support and encouragement. I am also very grateful to Stefan Traub, who was on my dissertation committee. He was an excellent advisor to me whenever I asked him for help and support.

Over time, I have benefited from intense and inspiring discussions with many people. Special thanks go to Jürgen Bitzer, Christian Cordes, Simon Deichsel, Rogier De Langhe, Stephen Kinsella, Ulrich Krause, Edward J. Nell and Fabian Paetzel. Invaluable support has also been provided by Shuanping Dai, Torsten Heinrich and Henning Schwardt, my colleagues at the Institute for Institutional and Innovation Economics at the University of Bremen.

The Centre for Philosophy of Natural and Social Science at the London School of Economics invited me in 2009. Although my dissertation was at an early stage at that time, I am grateful for the feedback and discussions I enjoyed there. Special thanks go to Christian List, Jason McKenzie Alexander and the members of the LSE Choice Group.

The expenses of this publication have been partly met by the "Verein zur Förderung des Fachbereichs Wirtschaftswissenschaft der Universität Bremen und dessen Zusammenarbeit mit der Wirtschaft" (wiwib e.V.). I am very grateful for this generous financial support and appreciate the coordinating work done by Maren Hartstock.

Last but not least, there are personal debts. I wish to express my deepest gratitude to Renate Greiff, Leonhard Greiff and Frauke Prothmann. I doubt that I would have finished this dissertation without their support.

Chapter 1

Introduction

Why do thousands of individuals collaboratively work on the Linux kernel which is at the core of the most successful computer operating systems? Why do thousands of individuals contribute to the Wikipedia encyclopedia? What motivates thousands of individuals to write cooking recipes, make them publically available at AllRecipes.com, and comment on others' recipes? These questions are extremely puzzling because the vast majority of these individuals receive no monetary compensation and the finished product is placed in the public domain. Most contributors are not paid and the product is given away for free. These individuals are engaged in *social production communities*, large groups of individuals who collaboratively and successfully produce information and digital products and make them freely available to everyone. What makes this form of mass-collaboration even more puzzling is the fact that the members of social production communities are scattered around the globe and most of them never meet each other face-to-face.

Members of social production communities contribute to the *voluntary provision of public goods*. They produce information and digital goods which can be replicated almost costlessly, and which everyone can use for free. In economic theory, the decision to contribute to a public good is equivalent to the decision to cooperate in a dilemma game. In small groups of humans cooperation can be explained by kinship-structures (Trivers, 1971), team identity (Eckel and Grossman, 2005), and altruism (Andreoni, 1990). The ability to cooperate, however, extends to large groups of unrelated individuals, for which social production is a prime example, but cooperation in large groups of unrelated individuals cannot be explained by kinship-structures, team identity, and altruism alone. *Social institutions* are crucial in order to achieve cooperation in large groups. In this thesis we will show how the voluntary provision of public goods is a social dilemma which is solved by

social institutions controlling the temptation to free-ride and enhancing contributions to the public good.

Social institutions play a crucial part for the conduct of human affairs by providing prescriptions on how to deal with each other. They regulate human affairs by coordinating individual behavior. Only a small part of social institutions are formal institutions. The majority of institutions are informal institutions which are neither written down as laws nor enforced by the government. Informal institutions emerge out of the interactions of interdependent individuals rather than being designed by some external authority. Nonetheless, these informal institutions must be enforced.

The importance of social institutions as problem-solving devices becomes obvious in *social dilemma problems*. Social dilemma problems are recurrent decision problems of direct interdependence (i.e., the outcome for A depends on B's decision) in which individually rational behavior results in a Pareto-inferior outcome. In such situations social institutions are problem-solving. If individuals behave in accordance with the habituated prosocial behavior, society will end up at the Pareto-optimal outcome. Hence, a social dilemma is a decision problem where, if everyone behaves individually rational, everyone is worse off compared to the situation in which everyone would behave prosocially. Examples for social dilemmas are the prisoner's dilemma (Luce and Raiffa, 1957; Hardin, 1968), the voluntary provision of public goods (Samuelson, 1954; Stiglitz, 1999), the use of common pool resources (Ostrom, 1990), problems of collective action (Olson, 1965) and team production (Alchian and Demsetz, 1972).

In order to dicuss the link between social dilemmas and institutions, we have to be precise in how we use the term institution. Following the game-theoretic definition (Schotter, 1981; Elsner, 2011), we define institutions as *habituated decision rules in social dilemma problems*. More precisely, institutions are habituated decision rules resulting in a Pareto-optimal outcome if a critical proportion of the population conforms to the institution. Through a process of social learning an institution gains general approval, hence an institution is not only a decision rule for players' own behavior but also informs players' expectations about other players' behavior, resulting in mutually consistent expectations. Moreover, the institution informs about the fact, that if anyone deviates, some or all other players will also deviate, resulting in an outcome which is worse for all players. Since players know that unilateral deviation triggers more deviation in the future, resulting in a situation in which each player will be worse off, the institution has an endogenous

sanctioning mechanism. The size of the sanction is the payoff difference between the situation in which all players behave prosocial and the situation in which all players free-ride.[1] Viewed from a game-theoretic perspective the following two questions come to mind immediately. First, how do institutions emerge and survive? And second, how are institutions enforced in a population of players?

In this thesis we are concerned with the instrumental, problem-solving character of institutions in relation to public good games. We will discuss emergence, stability, and enforcement of institutions because understanding emergence, stability, and enforcement enables us to understand and explain the voluntary provision of public goods by social production communities. By *emergence* we refer to a process in which a population of selfish players arrives at a situation in which the large majority of players contributes to the public good. *Stability* refers to the persistence of a situation in which the large majority of players contributes to the public good, and by *enforcement* we refer to the mechanism by ensures that the community's members behave in accordance with the institution. Since the enforcement of institutions in social production communities is closely related to the exchange of social approval, which is a reward given to contributors, we will investigate social approval as a selective incentive. The specific research questions which we will answer throughout this thesis are the following:

1. What are the selective incentives for contributors in social production communities?
2. Who provides selective incentives for contributors, and what are the institutions that ensure the provision of selective incentives for cooperation?
3. How can an institution emerge from and survive in a population of selfish individuals?
4. How is the institution enforced?

---

1 Ethical standards or morals can also be described as habitualized decision rules that solve dilemma problems. Ethical standards and morals, however, are based on a system of ethical or moral values and can remain in place even if the habitualized behavior has lost its problem-solving capacity. Old institutionalists would speak of ceremonial encapsulation and argue that the social institution changed into an abstract norm (Bush, 1987; Bush and Tool, 2001). Since our primary concern is the instrumental, problem-solving character of institutions we do not discuss ethical standards and morals.

5. Can we find empirical evidence for the claim that the exchange of social approval increase voluntary contributions to a public good, even if social approval does not lead to delayed benefits?

We use social production to illustrate the voluntary provision of public goods. A public good is a good or service that, once it is provided, can be used by all members of a society. As nobody can be excluded from using them, public goods cannot be provided for private benefit, and competitive markets will fail to provide public goods. One possible solution is state intervention, but often public goods are voluntarily supplied by *self-organizing communities* (Ostrom, 1990). Self-organizing communities solve the public good problem through the design and enforcement of formal and informal institutions inducing individuals to contribute to the public good. *User-led innovation*, *user-generated content*, and *open source software* are instances of social production, in which a self-organizing community supplies a public good. Production in social production communities is radically different from both markets and firms because monetary incentives (i.e., wages and prices) and strong hierarchies are absent. Social production communities achieve high levels of cooperation because they rely on a system of social institutions. But exactly what are these institutions and how are they enforced?

Several explanations have been proposed in order to understand the voluntary provision of public goods by social production communities. Among the explanations are use value, intrinsic motivation, social preferences (altruism and reciprocity), and social approval including signaling and reputation. These explanations delineate different incentives which operate simultaneously with some incentives being more salient than others. In the literature there is agreement that social approval is important in social production communities. Social approval is the expression of opinion and an evaluation of others' behavior but has no direct effect on monetary payoffs. One function of social approval is to facilitate coordination among decentralized but interdependent individuals (Manzini et al., 2009; Dugar, 2010). Viewed from this perspective the exchange of social approval is a form of non-binding communication (cheap-talk) facilitating coordination. We, however, argue that individuals have a preference for social approval, i.e., we argue that social approval is a nonmonetary payoff. The exchange of social approval not only facilitates coordination but is an incentive for the mobilization of effort and the voluntary provision of public goods. Individuals have a preference for social approval for two reasons. They care about social approval because it is

valued on its own, and because it gives rise to delayed benefits. We speak of the intrinsic value of social approval if social approval is valued on its own, and we speak of the extrinsic value of social approval if social approval is valued because it increases future income. One argument, developed in this thesis, is that the intrinsic value of social approval is a major incentive in social production communities.

A better understanding of social approval as an incentive has implications for social production, team productivity, efficiency wage models, and, more general, for the enforcement of institutions. Social approval can enhance efficiency in team production settings which are ubiquitous in economic and non-economic organizations (Alchian and Demsetz, 1972). If it is possible for team members to monitor others' effort levels, and high effort can be rewarded by social approval, the benefit from social approval can compensate for the cost of monitoring, thus increasing team productivity. This is particularly relevant since recent findings suggest that increasing monetary incentives does not necessarily increase performance (Hennig-Schmidt et al., 2010), and sometimes even leads to a deterioration in performance (Ariely et al., 2009a,b). Other studies show that individuals do not only care about their own monetary benefit, but also about fairness (Falk et al., 2008) and nonmonetary rewards (Frey and Neckermann, 2008; Frey, 2010). By taking into account the motivational effects of social approval employers can induce employees to increase effort. This is closely related to the literature on efficiency wages (Akerlof, 1982) in which recent research revealed that the introduction of nonmonetary rewards can lead to larger increases in effort than wage increases (Kube et al., 2010).

Social approval does not only facilitate coordination and increase effort levels but can also explain the stability of institutions because exclusion from social approval is an efficient mechanism for the enforcement of institutions. We consider social approval to be a reward which is given to contributors to a public good. If rewards are given conditional on contributions, individuals have an incentive to contribute to the public good and hence the public good will be provided. But why should individuals behave in accordance with the institutionally prescribed behavior and give rewards? How is the social institution "give rewards to contributors" enforced?

To understand how institutions are enforced *social networks* play an important role. In a group of individuals some individuals are closer together than others. Those who are closer tend to interact more often. How A interacts with B depends not only on B's characteristics but also on the relation be-

tween A and B. In order to take interpersonal relations into account we combine network theory and evolutionary game theory and show that if rewards are given based on contributions and *interpersonal relations* (social distance in our case), free-riders will be gradually excluded from rewards and the institution is enforced by exclusion. On a theoretical level this thesis furthers the understanding of the voluntary provision of public goods by self-organizing communities and the enforcement of institutions.

1.1 Research Objectives and Expected Contribution

The research objective of this thesis is threefold: *First*, we discuss social production as an example for the voluntary provision of public goods by a large group of individuals and argue that social approval is a crucial incentive; *second*, we present an evolutionary game-theoretical model illustrating how a social institution emerges in, and is enforced by, a population of selfish players; and *third*, we empirically test the intrinsic value of social approval as an incentive for increasing contributions to a public good.

We define social production as the production of information and digital goods by groups of individuals operating outside the market and without monetary incentives. Since the information and digital goods produced by social production communities are not protected by intellectual property rights and can be copied infinitely often, they are nonexcludable and nonrival, hence they are public goods. Although some social production communities produce physical products, we are concerned with the information that is embedded in these physical products because only the information but not the physical product itself is nonrival in consumption.[2] Social approval is a strong incentive in social production communities because of open communication, the necessity and simplicity of monitoring individual contributions, and the large number of channels through which social approval can be expressed. We argue that the exchange of social approval affects interpersonal relations by creating a bond of loyalty and increases intrinsic motivation and team identity at the same time. Since the mechanisms for the exchange of social approval are designed by the community itself, social production communities are self-organizing communities in which the exchange of social approval is institutionalized and explains large-scale cooperation.

2 Since our definition of social production is confined to information and digital goods, we exclude other forms of production which take place outside the market, like voluntary community work, for example.

In the game-theoretic model we consider social approval as a reward given to contributors. In public good games the provision of the public good is also possible without rewards. For example, consider the situation in which all players contribute to the public good provided that all others contribute. If one player defects, all other players will defect in all remaining rounds of the game. This strategy is called a grim-trigger strategy. If all players use this strategy, the efficient provision of the public good is possible but very fragile. By adding a second stage in which players have the opportunity to give rewards to contributors we combine two dilemmas: (i) the decision to contribute to the public good, and (ii) the decision to give a reward to contributors. If players give rewards to contributors there is a selective incentive for contributors and the public good will be supplied. But how can we be sure that players give rewards? By explicitely modeling social distances between players as a dynamic network we show that the institution ("give rewards to contributors") is enforced by exclusion. The crucial aspect of the model is the dynamic network without which exclusion would not be possible. Our model illustrates institutional emergence, stability, and enforcement. Emergence means that, starting from a population of selfish players, players learn and habituate the decision rule, and a critical mass of players behaving in accordance with the institution comes into existence. The size of the critical mass is such that the critical mass is large enough to achieve an almost efficient provision of the public good. By explicitly modeling social distance between players as a network, our model contributes to the small but growing literature on evolutionary games played on dynamic networks.

Unfortunately, the effect of social approval is difficult to observe in empirical survey studies, either because it is underreported or because it is unobservable. The lack of empirical evidence for social approval as an incentive led us to conduct an empirical analysis in the laboratory. Using an anonymous public good game we test the claim that people care about social approval. If true, we observe higher contributions to the public good. In our experiment we test the intrinsic value of social approval. Actually, a small number of experiments on social approval exists in the literature, but since there are many different ways in which social approval can be expressed (e.g., awards, verbal feedback, written messages) and the distinction between the intrinsic and instrumental value of social approval is not always clear-cut, our experiment constitutes an addition to the literature because – to our best knowledge – it is the first experiment combining real effort and the intrinsic value of social approval in a public good game. Hence our exper-

iment contributes to the existing literature on nonmonetary incentives and provides empirical support for our claim that social approval is an important incentive in social production communities.

1.2 The Structure of the Thesis

The structure of this thesis is as follows. Together with this introduction, chapter 3 provides the background by reviewing the literature on social production communities. Chapters 4 and 5 discuss different motives which are used to explain voluntary contributions to public goods. Most attention will be paid to social approval as a reward for increasing contributions to the public good social production. In chapter 6 we set up an evolutionary game theory model and shows how the social institution "give rewards to contributors" can be enforced by exclusion. Chapter 7 gives the results from a laboratory experiment, empirically testing whether social approval is valued on its own, before chapter 7 concludes.

This thesis started out of the desire to understand the individual motives for the provision of public goods, in particular the voluntary provision of information and digital goods that are placed in the public domain. We choose the term social production in order to emphasize the difference between market production and social production. While market production relies on wages, prices and contracts, these elements are absent in social production. In social production information and digital goods are supplied by a group of heterogeneous individuals collaborating successfully without formal hierarchies, as in firms, and without flexible wages and prices, as in markets. The relations between individuals are governed as a network, which has been identified, besides markets and hierarchies, as a third form for the governance of economic organizations (Powell, 1990; Sydow and Möllering, 2009; Elsner et al., 2010). In chapter 3 we will explain different forms of social production, emphasizing the importance of information and digital goods in the New Economy. We use several examples from user-led innovation, user-generated content, and open source software to illustrate our argument.

In the third chapter dilemma problems are looked at from a game-theoretical perspective and different solutions are discussed. One possible solution is the introduction of an outside authority which has the power

to change the payoffs.[3] This is not the route that we take. We are concerned with self-organizing communities, i.e., communities which are able to set up and enforce institutions for cooperation, because social production communities are self-organizing communities. Since no attempts are made to exclude free-riders, the institutionalized behavior gives rise to private benefits which accrue only to contributors. These private benefits are what Olson (1965) calls *selective incentives*. We review empirical studies on social production communities and identify use value, intrinsic motivation, social preferences, and social approval as selective incentives. These selective incentives are not mutually exclusive and most of them operate simultaneously. We discuss use value, intrinsic motivation, and social preferences in chapter 3 and show how they transform the structure of the underlying public good game. Although there is evidence that use value, intrinsic motivation, reciprocity, and impure altruism explain contributions to social production, we argue that social approval is an important incentive which has not yet received adequate attention.

Since we hope that a detailed discussion of social approval increases our understanding of social production communities and the voluntary provision of public goods chapter 4 starts with a discussion of social approval and distinguishes between the intrinsic and extrinsic value of social approval. The focus will be on the intrinsic value which we discuss in general and in relation to social production communities. Our argument is that the intrinsic value of social approval is an important incentive for explaining contributions to social production communities because the organization of social production communities is such that the intrinsic value of social approval is likely to be high. The intrinsic value of social approval, however, has not received adequate attention yet because it is underreported in empirical studies (Lerner and Tirole, 2002; Bitzer et al., 2007; Bitzer and Geishecker, 2010) and closely intertwined with intrinsic motivation, social preferences, and the extrinsic value of social approval. The extrinsic value of social approval can be divided into signaling and reputation which we discuss also. Then, we

3 We use the term self-organizing community for referring to a community which establishes a social institution for solving a particular dilemma problem (e.g., voluntary contributons to the public good social production). In this sense the state emerged in response to the problem of the "war of all against all" (Hobbes, 1984/1651), and later was transformed into a formal institution or social contract. Here we distinguish between outside authority and self-organizing community, and we use the term outside authority for referring to a formal institution that emerged in the past in response to another dilemma problem and which might be inappropriate for solving the original problem.

introduce social approval as a reward in a nonrepeated and repeated prisoner's dilemma and argue that evolutionary game theory is the appropriate method for modeling the exchange of social approval and the emergence of a social institution in a population of boundedly rational players.

Chapter 5 presents a theoretical model and asks: *Given that social approval is a reward, under which conditions can a self-organizing community achieve the stable provision of a public good?* The model presented in chapter 5 is an evolutionary game theory model of a public good game with rewards. It illustrates that the introduction of rewards alone cannot achieve the provision of the public good. "Giving rewards to contributors" can be understood as institutionally prescribed behavior, but as the model makes clear, the institution has to be enforced. If the game is played on a dynamic network the institution can be *enforced by exclusion*. The core idea is to let the network structure evolve endogenously. Here it is assumed that the exchange of rewards creates a bond of loyalty and reduces social distance between giver and receiver so that "successful" social relations are maintained and "unsuccessful" social relations are cut off. Players, who behave in accordance with the institutionally prescribed behavior, will, on average, receive a higher payoff while free-riders will be excluded from the benefit of the institution. The model analyzes the conditions which are necessary for *emergence and stability of a social institution of cooperation*. On a theoretical level the model shows that structure, i.e., the underlying *interpersonal relations between players* modeled as a dynamic network, is crucial in determining the outcome of the game. While with random matching evolutionary stable strategies are a subset of the set of Nash equilibria, this relation does not hold any more if the game is played on a dynamic network. This means that a model of an evolutionary game played on a dynamic network is able to explain and predict outcomes different than the Nash equilibrium of the underlying game.

Chapter 6 presents results from a laboratory experiment testing the hypothesis that the exchange of social approval induces higher contributions to a public good even if social approval does not lead to future benefits. Chapter 6 is a test of a simplified version of the full-blown model from chapter 5, testing whether social approval is valued on its own. In the simplified version of the model the effect of changes in social distance (or interpersonal relations) is absent because the experiment relies on stranger matching and anonymity. While the main aim of the full-blown model is to investigate the conditions for emergence, stability, and enforcement of social institutions given that individuals are motivated by social approval, the focus of the sim-

plified model (and experiment) is on social approval as a nonmonetary incentive. Although social approval is ubiquitous in human life, its role as an incentive has rarely been investigated in the economics literature. Chapter 6 tries to fill this gap by providing empirical evidence for a deeper understanding of nonmonetary incentives in general and social approval in particular.

The thesis ends with a conclusion (chapter 7), summarizing chapters 1 to 6 and pointing out how they relate to each other. Finally, we derive some implications and directions for further research.

Chapter 2

Social Production in the New Economy

During the past decade the role of social production has increased dramatically. In the popular literature social production has been labelled by different neologisms like "Smart Mobs" (Rheingold, 2002), "Wisdom of the Crowds" (Surowiecki, 2004), "Wikinomics" (Tapscott and Williams, 2008), "Crowdsourcing" (Howe, 2008), and "We-Think" (Leadbeater, 2009). In the academic literature social production has been discussed by Eric von Hippel's work on user-led innovation (von Hippel, 1988, 2005; von Hippel and von Krogh, 2006), Yochai Benkler's work on commons-based peer production (Benkler, 2003, 2006; Benkler and Nissenbaum, 2006) and in the literature on open source communities (Ljungberg, 2000; Lerner and Tirole, 2001, 2002; Weber, 2004; DiBona et al., eds, 2006; Lerner et al., 2006).

In this chapter we focus on three particular forms of social production, namely user-led innovation supplying innovations, user-generated content supplying information, and open source software supplying software. Two explicit features of social production are *open access* and *immateriality*. Open access means that the product is placed in the public domain where everyone has access to the product. The products are immaterial, can be stored as digital products, and can be copied costlessly, making them *nonexcludable*. This implies *nonrivalry* since innovation, information, and software do not deplete with use. Hence social production is an example for the voluntary provision of public goods.

In contrast to proprietary production no property rights are used and individual contributors do not receive any monetary compensation. From the viewpoint of innovation economics social production represents a puzzle. Why do thousands of indviduals voluntarily contribute to the production of a public good? How do social production communities solve the problem of underprovision of public goods? This question lies at the core of this thesis.

This chapter presents social production as a new form of economic or-

ganization. The chapter's structure is depicted in figure 2.1. With the IT revolution and the New Economy, to be described in section 2.1, the role of social production increased dramatically. We lay down the characteristics of the New Economy focusing on innovation, information, and digital goods. Thereafter, we explain important general features of social production in section 2.2 before we describe three typical examples of social production (user-led innovation, user-generated content, and open source software) in detail (section 2.3). Before we conclude this chapter, we delineate the different mechanisms which are used for organization and coordination in social production communities in section 2.4. As we will see, there are various institutions ensuring open communication, facilitating monitoring of individual behavior and the exchange of social approval. These institutions are important because there are interdependencies between organization of production and the effectiveness of different incentives which motivate individuals to contribute to the public good social production.

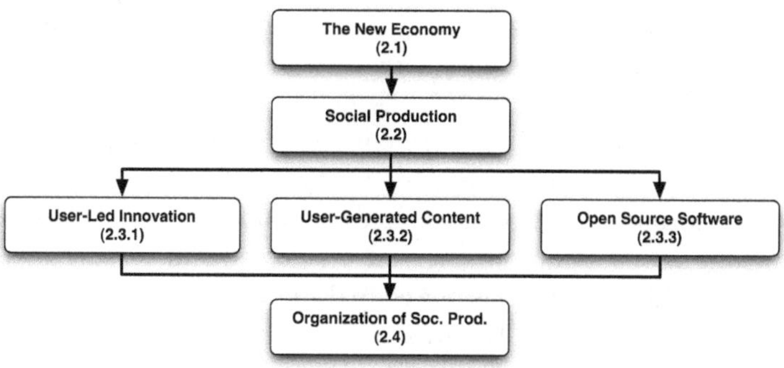

Figure 2.1: The Structure of chapter 2.

2.1 The New Economy

The *New Economy*, or sometimes called the *Economy of Information Technology*, came into existence with the dramatic decline in costs and the widespread

availability of computers and internet connections in the 1990s.[4] The availability and power of personal computers increased rapidly while prices declined. The number of internet users increased sharply, from worldwide 61 million in 1996 to 320 million in 2000 (Huberman, 2001, p.14). This shift on the supply side (i.e., the availability of computers at low prices) had an immense influence not on any industry in particular but on all industries. IT technology is a *General Purpose Technology* since it affects all industries (Helpman, ed, 1998; Jovanovic and Rousseau, 2005; Lipsey et al., 2005). In the New Economy information goods have a strong influence on aggregate economic performance (Quah, 2003). Between 1995 and 1998 the IT sector accounted for about eight percent of US GDP but was responsible for about 35 percent of the growth in real GDP (Huberman, 2001, p.84).[5]

In addition to the heightened importance of digital goods for production there is a shift in consumption patterns. Immaterial information goods, knowledge and culture in form of writings, music, videos, software, rather than material goods, increase as a fraction of total consumption (Quah, 2001; Huberman, 2001). A growing fraction of total consumption is devoted to digital goods, just think of your consumption of the Wikipedia encyclopedia or the Google search engine.

A topic which has received much attention in the literature on the New Economy discusses the production of information goods and digital goods which have high fixed costs and close to zero marginal costs. Average costs

4 Note that some authors (for example Elsner, 2004, and Elsner et al., forthcoming) emphasize increasing complexity because of the fragmentation of value-added-chains in addition to the increased importance of IT technology. Since we are concerned not with private companies operating in fragmented value-added-chains but with users who produce public goods, our emphasis is on the increasing importance of IT technology for social production. Nonetheless, social production communities are special kinds of networks (as we will see in section 2.1.2), which can be considered to be a reaction to increasing complexity, fragmented value-added-chains, and increasing importance of information and knowledge. The key difference between value-added-chains as networks of private companies and social production communities as a network of individuals, however, is the relative importance of money and social approval. While for private companies the profit-motive is crucial and social approval is relatively unimportant, the reverse holds for members of social production communities, for whom social approval is one of the main motivations and monetary incentives are relatively unimportant.

5 From a macroeconomic perspective the term *New Economy* is associated with higher productivity growth, lower unemployment, and low inflation due to technological advances associated with IT technology which reshaped the economy in fundamental ways (see Gordon, 1998, and Jorgensen et al., 2000). With the collapse of the (overvalued) stock markets in 2000 and the recession that followed it became clear that hugh productivity growth, low unemployment, and low inflation is not sustainable.

decline with the scale of production. A technology characterized by falling average costs is said to have increasing returns to scale, meaning that production sets are non-convex. In the New Economy increasing returns come from demand and supply. On the supply side the cost structure results in increasing returns since digital goods are indefinitely expandable (to be defined in a moment). Once the first copy is produced it is very cheap to reproduce additional copies. For example, the first copy of Microsoft Windows 97 cost fifty million dollars but the second copy cost only three dollars.[6]

On the demand side network effects, also called network externalities, are the source of increasing returns. With network effects the value of a good increases with the number of users. Famous examples are the telephone and the VHS video system. Increasing returns due to network effects are well-known due to the work of Brian Arthur and colleagues (David, 1985; Katz and Shapiro, 1986; Arthur et al., 1987; Arthur, 1989). If network effects are present individual choices are path-dependent eventually resulting in a lock-in. In a lock-in individuals have made a choice which is not necessarily efficient from an ex post perspective. Due to the nature of the lock-in individuals have no incentive to reverse their decision because once you have chosen a certain path switching can be very expensive. Network effects and lock-ins are particularly relevant with respect to technological standards. Technological standards ensure compatibility, interoperability, and enable data exchange and communication among different devices. Standards, like the Microsoft Office file format, exhibit increasing returns to scale because of network effects. The more users use Microsoft Office, the more sense it makes for me to use Microsoft Office because this allows me to work with the documents created by other users. Increasing returns can lead to lock-ins where users are locked-in into an inferior standard. Changing to another (superior) standard is associated with high switching costs, thus preventing users from using the superior alternative. Open source, especially open standards in contrast to proprietary standards, reduces switching costs. A standard is open if any party can implement the standard without payment. If the standard, in our example the Microsoft Office file format, would be open, competing software applications could use the same standard so that compatibility would be ensured. Switching costs would be reduced and it would

6 See Ethan Zuckerman's article "Samuel Bowles Introduces Kudunomics", available at http://www.ethanzuckerman.com/blog/2009/11/17/samuel-bowles-introduces-kudunomics/2010.

be easier to switch from a suboptimal standard (the lock-in) to a superior standard.

2.1.1 Information Goods and Digital Goods

Let us pause for a moment to get clear on some terminology. We are concerned with the increasing importance of information goods and digital goods in the New Economy. Information goods and digital goods are not identical but share some important characteristics. Information goods are goods whose value derives from the information they contain. Using ink and paper you can produce a poem, but the value of the poem does not derive from the value of those materials. In this case ink and paper are just the materials which carry the poem but the same poem could be displayed on the screen of my mobile phone. In either case the value of the poem derives from the particular arrangement of the words and phrases and is consumed through reading. Other definitions define information goods more broadly as "anything that can be digitized" (Shapiro and Varian, 1999, p.4).

Digital goods are a subset of information goods. Digital goods are information goods that are actually digitized. Digital goods also derive their value from the information they contain, but with digital goods the information is encoded in bitstrings (sequences of 0s and 1s). The information which is contained in digital goods has economic value. A poem might not have economic value, but information regarding new production technologies or information about the financial market certainly has economic value. Digital goods can be stored (on disks, memory-sticks, hard-drives), transmitted (internet, email, FTP) and manipulated electronically.

Printed and leather-bound, an encyclopdia might be of decorative value because it looks nice in the bookshelf. According to our definition the books belonging to the encyclopedia are not information goods because the user derives her main value from the physical characteristics of the leather-bound encyclopedia and not from the information.

Information and digital goods contain knowledge. If knowledge gets codified in such a manner that others can understand it, it becomes a public good. The knowledge contained in a digital good is codified knowledge, in contrast to tacit knowledge which is embodied in economic agents. Think of a cooking recipe which lists all ingredients and instructions on how to combine them. The list of ingredients and the instructions are codified knowledge which can be understood by readers of the recipe, but in order to pre-

pare a delicous meal you also need tacit knowledge. That is why excellent chefs can publish their recipes and people will still go to their restaurants.

For what follows it is useful to delineate the key characteristics of digital goods. Following Quah (2003) there are five key characteristics of digital goods, which also apply to information:

1. **Nonrivalry:** A good is considered to be nonrival if consumption by others does not limit my own consumption of the good. Examples are cooking recipes, mathematical theorems and software.

2. **Infinitely expandable:** A good is considered to be infinitely expandable if "its quantity can be made arbitrarily large arbitrarily quickly at no cost" (Quah, 2003, p.13). Digital goods like music and images are good examples of infinitely expandable goods since they can be replicated with just a single click. The cost of replication is low since marginal costs are close to zero. With digital goods production is reproduction; and every copy is a perfect copy and hence a perfect substitute for the original.

3. **Discrete / indivisible:** The first creation of a digital good is called *instantiation*. Digital goods come always in integer quantities and are instantiated to quantity one. Instantiation of the first copy of the good requires considerable investment (e.g., writing the first copy of the software). The cost of creating the first copy of a software is known as *first-copy-cost*. First-copy-costs are indivisible in the sense that there is no half idea or no half software (Arrow, 1959; Quah, 2003).

4. **Aspatial:** Digital goods are aspatial because they are nowhere and everywhere at the same time (Quah, 2003, pp.18-19). The internet allows for instantaneous distribution of digital goods, i.e., the costs of distributing the good are virtually zero.

5. **Recombinant:** Weitzman (1998) describes recombinant growth as new ideas arising "out of existing ideas in some kind of cumulative interactive process" (p.332). In the creative process innovation comes from the hybridization of existing ideas. Much earlier this was also mentioned in Schumpeter: "As a rule, the new combinations must draw the necessary means of production from some old combinations (...) development consists primarily in employing existing resources in a different way, in doing new things with them" (Schumpeter, 1934, p.68). Digital goods

are recombinant since a new digital good emerges from the combination from different digital goods. In the process of recombination digital goods are both input and output. This is clearly observable in modular programming where one module can be reused in different applications, and in sampling where parts of existing songs are reused to create a new song, to mention just two examples.

Because of the just-mentioned characteristics digital goods are sometimes said to be weightless or massless. An economy in which the importance of digital goods is high is sometimes called the weightless or massless economy (Huberman, 2001; Quah, 2002). The five points mentioned above did not discuss the use of intellectual property rights. This, however, is an important issue since social production communities supply digital goods that are not protected by intellectual property rights. Since these unprotected digital goods are nonrival, infinitely expandable, and aspatial, the digital goods supplied by social production communities are *pure global public goods* (Samuelson, 1954; Stiglitz, 1999).

Digital goods are global public goods since on a worldwide scale everyone can use them without having to pay. Digital goods are pure public goods since the individual benefit from using the good does not diminish as more people use the product. However, the problem that has to be overcome first is the provision of the public good. With respect to digital goods provision is equivalent to the instantiation of the digital good. Since first-copy-costs, the costs of instantiation, are private, no-one has an incentive to contribute to the provision of the public good. In social production communities the public good problem is solved through selective incentives i.e., incentives that only accrue to contributors.

The public goods that are produced by social production are information and digital goods. Ocassionally, especially when writing about user-led innovation, we refer to innovation. In user-led innovation the term innovation refers to incremental innovations in which an existing product is customized and to the production of new products (von Hippel, 2005). Although there are a few examples in the literature in which new products have been the result of innovation by users (Brost and Uchatius, 2009; Faulkner and Runde, 2009), most innovations are incremental. Since we are concerned with public goods we use the term innovation to refer not to the product itself but to the information that the customized or newly developed product carries.

2.1.2 Networks

In the preceeding sections we explained the characteristics of the New Economy and described digital goods in detail. In this section we discuss the organization of production in the New Economy. The shift from physical products towards digital products and the increased importance of information that occured with the IT revolution resulted in a change in the organization of production, affecting not only the production of digital products. Value-added chains became more fragmented reducing the degree of vertical integration (Elsner, 2004, 2005; Sydow and Möllering, 2009). The role of markets and hierarchies became less important as production is organized in networks. As a system of governance and organization, a network is different from both the ideal type market and the ideal type hierarchy. A network is not a hybrid between market and hierarchy, although a network contains elements of markets and hierarchies (Powell, 1990; Sydow and Möllering, 2009; Elsner et al., 2010). In a network, firms interact with each other using not only prices, competition, and contracts to govern interactions. Relations between members of a network are characterized by direct interdependencies, reciprocal patterns of exchange, and a rapid flow of communication. In contrast to market transactions, the interactions among the members of a network are non-ephemeral but recurrent and durable, facilitating the transfer of knowledge. In contrast to both markets and hierarchies, networks involve commitment and personal involvement, and according to Powell (1990) "embedding of business relations in moral and social concerns does not reduce economic vitality" (p. 312). Although networks exhibit a tension between collaboration and competition, members often forego the right to pursue their own interest at the expense of others and cooperation can be achieved. Due to the open-ended nature of the relation between members of the network mutually supportive actions are taken and the network can be seen as institutionalized, multilateral cooperation (Elsner, 2005).

A social production community is a special form of a network. The network's members are not private companies but individuals. The members of the network are both users and producers of information and digital goods. In fact, there is no clear distinction between user and producer, and terms like *prosumer* are sometimes used instead (Blättel-Mink and Hellmann, eds, 2010). The boundaries of the network are not clearly defined, making it easy for individuals to enter or leave the network. Although the membership structure is flexible, interactions between network members are recurrent

and networks exist for long periods of time. Transactions between members are not governed by prices or contracts, and in fact, money is not used as a medium of exchange. Instead, transactions are governed by formal and informal rules and norms (to be described below) and social production communities can be understood as an extreme form of networks in which prices and contracts are completely absent. Hierarchical governance structures are not completely absent, but usually the existing hierarchies are flat and based on merit. Referring to the Linux network Elsner et al. (2010) argue that "[t]he network seems to have triggered fast exchange, joint learning, effective routinization, and institutionalization of cooperation, emerging from "dense" repeated interaction" (p.15). The loose and flexible structure of the network allows for an efficient transfer of kowledge and often, social production communities are a valuable source of innovation.

2.1.3 "Open" and "Closed" Production

Having elaborated on the nature of digital goods and the organization of production in the New Economy we are now in a position to distinguish "open" (non-proprietary) and "closed" (proprietary) production. As we have mentioned above, digital goods are public goods if unprotected by intellectual property right. This raises the question of how to achieve an efficient provision of public goods since the dominant strategy in public good problems is to free-ride. Regarding digital goods the question is: *Who instantiates the public good and pays for the first-copy-cost?*

The "closed" solution uses intellectual property rights which transform the public good into a private good. The private company who supplies the product can charge a higher price in order to recover the costs it incurred for instantiation. The "open" solution is the provision of public goods by social production communities. What is of particular interest to us is that in the New Economy an increasing proportion of digital goods are produced in social production communities operating outside the market.

Under proprietary production private companies hire workers and compete in a market. Perfect competition will result in equilibrium prices, p, being equal to marginal costs, MC, and the resulting allocation is Pareto efficient (First Welfare Theorem). In the digital economy this does not hold any longer. If $p = MC$ Microsoft would never be able to recover the initial investment which was necessary to obtain the first copy of Windows. If private companies cannot recover their initial investment they have no incentive to

innovate and instantiate the digital good. Property rights are a solution since they allow private companies to charge a price above marginal costs so that they can recover the cost of their initial investments. Property rights create incentives for private companies to innovate and create dynamic efficiency, i.e., the improvement of efficiency over time. However, since $p > MC$ the First Welfare Theorem will not hold and the resulting allocation will be statically inefficient. There exists a tradeoff between static and dynamic efficiency which can be altered by varying the length of the property rights protection. A problem with digital goods is that the protection of property rights is very costly and ineffective since copying costs are low. Private companies pay much money to protect CDs and DVDs, but illegal copies are still available (Peitz and Waelbroeck, 2006).

"Open" production in social production communities is radically different from "closed" production. In social production communities there is no central authority coordinating individual activities. A few individuals start a project, for example the production of an operating system as an alternative to Windows. They use their personal computers and internet connections and work mostly in their spare time. They make the production process open and actively invite everyone to participate. Through various mechanisms individual contributions are aggregated into a finished product which can, as in the case of Linux, be of high quality. Instead of having to make a large investment at the beginning, they use their existing equipment to set up a decentralized infrastructure. The high fixed costs for physical inputs (e.g., computers, internet connection) are distributed among a large number of contributors so that each individual contributor only has to bear a small part of it. Since individuals do not receive monetary compensation there are no wage costs. No intellectual property rights are used, meaning that no single individual owns the product. The product is in the public domain and free in the sense that everyone is allowed to use, modify, and redistribute it. This is similar to the openness of information required by net-structures and fragmented value-added-chains, to which networks as a form of institutionalized cooperation are a solution. However, there are two differences. First, in networks of private companies information is not a public good but a club good since it is available only to the network's members. Second, in fragmented value-added-chains the actors are private companies are driven by the profit motive while in social production communities the actors are

individuals not driven by monetary compensation.[7] Since social production will be discussed throughout this thesis, we describe it in more detail in the remainder of this chapter.

2.2 Social Production

A key characteristic of social production projects is that individuals interact decentralized and collaboratively engage in the production of public goods. As has been described in section 2.1.2, collaboration is a key element in networks. Social production, however, can be considered to be an extreme type of a network, because the key elements of markets (prices) and firms (wage-contracts) are completely absent.[8] Social production can be characterized as a loose, flexible, decentralized arrangement of a large number of people who coordinate their efforts, often with the use of modern IT technology, into large and coherent projects. Social production is mass collaboration in a cooperative network of volunteers.

The production process is open, meaning that everyone is invited to participate. This requires openness in design, i.e., the products are designed in such a way as to allow contributors to engage in the production process by investing only limited time and effort. The rest of section 2.2 discusses general features of social production before specific forms of social production are discussed in more detail in section 2.3.

2.2.1 Users as Producers as a Source of Value

The members of a social production community are users and producers at the same time. The fact that users are a source of value does not imply that every user automatically creates value. Rather it is the case that value comes from users, defined as individuals who benefit from using the product, as opposed to manufacturers, who benefit from selling the product (von Hippel, 2005). Since social production communities are characterized by free reveal-

7 For a detailed discussion of the dilemmas which private companies face in a decentralized economy characterized by fragmened value-added-chains, net-technologies, and strategic interdependencies, and how clusters and networks can be seen as a reaction to these dilemmas, the reader is referred to Elsner (2005) and chapter 2 in Elsner et al. (forthcoming).

8 There are some private software companies paying part of their employees for working on open source software. Such companies sell complementary products and hence have a clearly defined interest in open source software. We will neglect employees of private companies and focus on contributors who are not paid.

ing / open access (to be described in section 2.2.4) the value that is created is accessible for everyone.

In user-led innovation the innovation itself and the information about users' needs contained within the innovation is of value and is often used by manufacturing firms. Users not only buy a product, they also customize the product to better fit their needs. By modifying existing products, or inventing new products, users reveal information about their specific needs. In user-generated content valueable information in the form of writings, music, and videos is supplied. By aggregating contributions of individual users, social production communities are able to supply information, like the AllRecipes.com cookbook[9] , the Wikipedia encyclopdia[10] , or Last.fm's customized radio stations.[11] And in open source software, software is supplied. Software that is produced through individuals' collective efforts can be used by everyone, like the R-software for statistical computing[12] , or the Python programming language.[13] Not only can the software be used by end-users, but also, and this is a crucial aspect, the software's source code is available, allowing everyone to modify, customize, and extend the software. The core idea of open source software is that by making the source code available, interested users are attracted to contribute to the software's development.

In all cases the information that is supplied by engaging in social production is not protected by intellectual property rights. Manufacturing firms can incorporate the new information stemming from users into the innovative process. The recognition of users as a potential source of value can help firms to develop new products more quickly and inexpensively than with their internal design teams.[14] Wikipedia can be used by every user,

9 http://allrecipes.com/
10 http://www.wikipedia.org/
11 http://www.last.fm/
12 http://www.r-project.org/
13 http://python.org/
14 A similar but not identical concept is *Open Innovation*, developed by Chesbrough (2003). Open Innovation emphasizes the the interrelatedness of the process of innovation. To advance its innovative capacity a company should open up its process of innovation. The focus is on the strategic exchange of knowledge, meaning that companies should use knowledge from suppliers and users instead of relying on knowledge generated within the company (outside-in-process). Also, the company should sell knowledge, for example by licensing knowledge which is not crucial for the company's core business (inside-out-process). This is in contrast with the use of the term open in open source, where the emphasis is on the openness of the process of innovation, meaning that everyone is invited to participate and no barriers are erected by using intellectual property rights.

whether or not the particular user has contributed by writing a Wikipedia article. And open source software can be used by every user, whether or not the user contributed to the software's development.

While in user-led innovation users are part of the value-added chain and form a symbiotic relation with producing firms, in user-generated content the distinction between users and producers disappears. Members of social production communities producing user-generated content take both roles as user and producer simultaneously. They contribute content and read the content contributed by others. But why do users produce in the first place, instead of buying from firms?

2.2.2 Persistent Information Asymmetries between Users and Producers

The main reason why users start to contribute to social production is a persistent information asymmetry between users and manufacturers. The prevalence of user-led innovation suggests that users have a need for customized products. As von Hippel (2005) argues, users have heterogeneous needs and derive large benefits from products which exactly fit their personal needs. Products available on the market are mostly mass manufactured and do not fulfill users' personal needs.

While users exactly know their personal needs manufacturers do not know the users' personal needs. In fact, the act of using a product can lead to innovation, for example if the product is used in extreme or novel contexts (Shah, 2006; Faulkner and Runde, 2009).

The information asymmetry is persistent since information about users' personal needs is sticky, generated in the context of use, and because manufacturers have limited absorptive capacity. Information about users' needs is sticky if it involves tacit knowledge which cannot be codified. Because of the sticky character of information, transferring the information might be costly or even impossible. Another reason for the persistence of the asymmetry is that the information about users' personal needs is generated in the context of use. For example, if an existing product is used in novel contexts new information about its use-value is generated, and this new information is not readily acessible to manufacturers (Ogawa, 1998; von Hippel, 2005). The third reason for the persistence of the information asymmetry is manufacturers' limited absorptive capacity (Cohen and Levinthal, 1999). Manufacturers might not have sufficient absorptive capacity if they lack prior, more basic knowledge which is needed to absorb the new information. All

three reasons, the stickiness of information, the relation between information and context-of-use, and manufacturers' insufficient absorptive capacity are reasons to believe that the information asymmetry will persist over time, suggesting that manufacturers' products do not fulfill users' personal needs.

2.2.3 Low Cost of Contributing

The existence of the information asymmetry described in the last paragraph cannot explain social production since it is a necessary but not a sufficient condition for the success of social production communities. What is needed in addition is the expertise that is necessary to modify an existing product or to invent a new product which fulfills users' personal needs. The members of social production communities need to have the necessary skills and capital to supply an innovation.

Since collaborating is the norm in user communities, innovating users can expect to receive help from a large set of users with heterogeneous abilities (von Hippel, 2005; Bravo, 2010). Each user draws on the knowledge she has from her job and previous experience. In this way, pre-existing knowledge is combined and the power of diversity of perspectives is used in order to innovate. Innovation is supported by web-based communication systems (to be described below). In user led innovation the users that are mainly responsible for innovations are called lead users and in open source they are referred to as core users (von Hippel, 2005). Lead users and core users are defined as users who are at the leading edge and currently experience needs that will be experienced later by other users. They anticipate the high benefits that can be obtained from an innovation, i.e., lead users are more likely to innovate because their expected benefit is high. The opportunity costs for coming up with an innovation are low because users draw on skills from their job (instead of acquiring new skills) and because they can expect assistance from other users.

For digital goods supplied in user-generated content and open source software, the capital requirement boils down to a personal computer and a connection to the internet, which users have already. Although the investment required to equip every member of the Linux community with personal computer and internet connection would be tremendously high, this investment is not necessary since every member already made this investment in the past. In fact, these costs are declining reducing capital costs per capita even further. Only for innovations in capital-intensive products which require

huge indivisible capital investments, manufacturers have an advantage since they have access to large amounts of capital.

2.2.4 Free Revealing, Open Access, and Open Source

Users innovate because they have more information about their needs. They freely reveal their innovations and the information embedded therein instead of trying to appropriate the returns from their innovative activity. Free revealing appears paradoxical because it reduces individual income. Free revealing means that the innovating user gives up all property rights and the information becomes a public good (von Hippel, 2005; Shah, 2006). The term free revealing is common in the literature on user-led innovation. In the literature on user-generated content the equivalent term is open access, meaning that the content that is generated is free for everyone to use. In open source, the term open source refers to open access to the software's source code. Free revealing, open access, and open source implies that the product becomes part of the public domain, but this does not imply that the information is accessible to others at no cost. It can be costly for somebody to acquire the information because she needs to invest in absorptive capacity at first. In open source, for example, users must make an investment and learn the programming language before they can understand the source code. The key feature of free revealing, open access, and open source is that the members of the social production community do not profit since property rights are given up voluntarily. Free revealing, open access, and open source imply that the innovation becomes a public good. The use of property rights which would transform the public good into a private good is explicitely rejected. This represents a puzzle to economists since by using property rights the innovators could reap the benefits from selling their innovation, while the giving up of property rights means that innovators do not receive any monetary compensation.

We argue that in social production communities the benefits from free revaling exceed the benefits from copyright protection. In terms of payoffs this means that $\pi(\text{public domain}) > \pi(\text{private})$ (see equations 2.1 and 2.2).

$$\pi(\text{public domain}) = \text{customized product} - \text{effort} + \text{attracting more contributors} \tag{2.1}$$

$$\pi(\text{private}) = \text{customized product} - \text{effort} + \text{royalties} - \text{cost of legal protection} \tag{2.2}$$

In many cases of user-led innovation, von Hippel and von Krogh (2006) argue, free revealing is the best practical option. Innovating users face the

choice between free revealing and trying but fail to protect the innovation. Legal protection by patents and copyrights does not work effectively since patents and copyrights do not exclude imitators. Keeping the monopoly control over the innovation-related information is hard since others often know something close to your "secret" (von Hippel, 2005). Moreover getting a patent is costly in terms of time and money; these costs are small for private firms but can be quite large for individuals.[15] Hence the main reasons why patent protection is not used in user-led innovation are the ineffectiveness of patents and the high costs for obtaining a patent.

The literature on social production suggests that there are nonmonetary benefits which individuals derive from contributing to social production. Contributing, however, is only possible if the production process is open. Finding a bug in Microsoft Word I cannot correct it because the source code is not available to me. Finding a bug in Open Office, an open source alternative to Microsoft Office, I can correct it since the source code is placed in the public domain. The point is that if production takes place in the public domain everyone can participate but whereas production takes place in private only employees can contribute. Taken for granted that individuals will contribute if given the opportunity to do so, production that takes place in the public domain will attract more contributors. Since social production has efficient mechanisms to avoid negative effects on quality from increasing the number of contributors, attracting more contributors will improve the quality of the product (for Wikipedia as an example see Wilkinson and Huberman, 2007).

Lastly, it remains to be mentioned that there is a positive externality associated with "open" production. By putting the innovation in the public domain the innovation and the information contained therein diffuses and becomes available to others who might use it. Free revealing helps innovations to spread and fosters re-use since information from within the public domain will be used as a building block for new products. Resources are not wasted because multiple individuals do not have to invent the same thing again, avoiding the duplication of effort. Since the innovation process is open, others are free to copy the product and modify it further, thus benefiting from the information that is available in the public domain. In principle,

15 The average cost for obtaining a European patent are about five thousand euros. Additional costs might be charged to obtain validity of the patent in individual states of the European Union. After three years additional payments are necessary to maintain the patent. Source: http://www.epo.org/metanav/help/faq_de.html#a4.

this benefit is available to everyone since both social production communities and private companies can re-use existing information taken from the public domain.

2.3 Three Forms of Social Production

In the following sections 2.3.1 to 2.3.3 we describe user-led innovation, user-generated content, and open source software, three particular types of social production in more detail. In all three forms of social production a public good is supplied by users taking the role of producers.

User-led innovation, our first example, can be seen as an early form of social production. User-led innovation originates in user-communities, i.e., communities of users who share their experiences with a certain product and customize it collaboratively. In discussing user-led innovation the importance of *lead users*, i.e., users who use the particular product intensively becomes clear. Also, the literature on user-led innovation emphasizes the information asymmetry between users and producers and the *importance of use value* as a driving force for starting customization of existing and innovation of new products. Since the use of web-based communication is absent in early examples of user-led innovation, most communities are either geographically concentrated or geographically dispersed and meet only infrequently.

This is in sharp contrast with user-generated content and open source software, in which users are geographically dispersed and use *web-based communication*. In fact, the IT revolution led to a sharp increase in social production by drastically facilitating communication and collaboration across large distances. Digital goods became more important and so-called *virtual communities*, supplying information, knowledge and culture, emerged. A virtual community is defined as a community of people sharing common interests, ideas, and feelings over the internet. The members rarely meet each other personally and have no common past or future (Jarvenpaa and Leidner, 1999). User-generated content and open source software are two particular examples of virtual communities.

User-generated content reveals the importance of *modularity* and *granularity* since individual contributions can be very small (e.g., a correction of a Wikipedia entry). Individual contributions are easily aggregated into a coherent product. In many cases of user generated content there are no in-

terdependencies between contributions and aggregation of individual contribution is equivalent to adding a contribution, like adding a new recipe to AllRecipes.com. In some cases, however, there are interdependencies, for example if many authors collaborate on the same entry in the Wikipedia encyclopedia. In open source software the interdependecies are more pronounced. Although modularity reduces interdependencies, the remaining *interdependencies are a potential source of conflict.* This becomes apparent in open source software and there are various mechanisms for dealing with conflicting interests.

Although there is a large number of projects especially in user-generated content and open source, the projects vary greatly in size. Measured by the number of contributors, a small number of projects is very large and the majority of projects is rather small. Within projects, the number of contributions per individual follows a similar pattern. While most individuals make very few contributions, a small number of contributors is responsible for a large number of contributions. In other words, both the *size distribution of projects* as well as the *number of contributions per individual* is skewed (van Wendel de Joode, 2005; Lerner et al., 2006). Using the Gini coefficient to describe contribution patterns within Wikipedia, Ortega Soto (2009, p.106) finds that the distribution of revisions in Wikipedia has a coefficient of $G = 0.93$ (December 2007 data from English-language Wikipedia). In open source projects, for example the Apache projects, the Gini coefficient for the distribution of aggregate contributions is $G = 0.91$. However, by distinguishing contributions into different categories (e.g., improvement of source code, documentation, bug-reporting) it can be shown that the distribution of contributions which require less time, effort, and skills is close to uniform. For example, the Gini coefficient of contributions which report bugs is $G = 0.21$ (Asundi et al., 2005).

2.3.1 User-Led Innovation

In user-led innovation a small group of people, called lead users, have a particular problem that they try to solve (von Hippel, 1988, 2005). Most innovations come from lead users who are "ahead of the majority of users in their populations with respect to an important market trend, and they expect to gain relatively high benefits from a solution to the needs they have encountered there" (von Hippel, 2005, p.4). Often it is the case that there is no appropriate solution available on the market. Lead users start inventing

a new product or modifying an existing product with the goal of coming up with a viable solution to their problem. Users ask others for help and accept contributions from what comes to be a community. Since the users have a common interest centered around a specific product we call them a community. Users who innovate themselves or assist others who do so can be called contributors; those users who use the customized products (the public good) without contributing can be called free-riders.

By creating a new prototype product the user-community reveals information about their needs, information which is not protected by intellectual property rights. Users disseminate their ideas and others pick them up, creating positive feedback loops. Users are organized in communities consisting of loosely-affiliated users with a common interest. Due to the absence of a hierachical structure there is a relatively free flow of information. Open communication together with heterogeneity of individual needs and diversity of individual skills fosters collaboration and innovation.

The mountain bike, for example, emerged from the activities of a group of cycling enthusiasts (lead users) determined to race downhill off-road, initially using traditional bikes but repeatedly modifying them until they became the heavy-duty variant we know today (Bünstorf, 2003). Although today mountain bikes are supplied by commercial manufacturers, the initial idea emerged from a community of voluntary contributors. The public good which is supplied is not the mountain bike itself but the information on how to build it.

User-led innovation is distinct from all other forms in that it does not necessarily use the internet for communication, organization and collaboration. User-led innovation is a form of social production which existed before the advent of the internet but has received a huge boost with the IT revolution. Members of user innovation communities meet each other personally more or less frequently. Some communities also use web-based communication in addition to their meetings. For example, the sporting communities which we discuss below meet at up to ten competitions per year where they spend considerable time in assisting each other and developing their equipment (von Hippel, 2005).

Many examples of user-led innovation come from sporting communities.[16]

16 We focus on innovations by individual users not firms. Firms, however, also collectively modify and improve the products that they use, as has been shown by Allen (1983). For more recent examples see von Hippel (2005, p.20) and the references therein.

Above we sketched the history of the mountain bike. Other examples from sporting communities are kiteboarding (von Hippel, 2005), sailplaining, canyoning, boardercross and handicapped cycling (Franke and Shah, 2003) and windsurfing, skateboarding and snowboarding (Shah, 2000, 2006). Using questionaire studies Franke and Shah (2003, Section 4) found that about a third of the community members, mostly lead users, innovated, and that a quarter of the innovations is now produced by commercial manufacturers. Their studies reveal that innovation is a joint effort in which many users collaboratively exchange information and give assistance. Another finding that is illustrated by these examples is that the public goods supplied by social production communities can lead to the development of private goods. If there is effective demand for a public good supplied by a social production community, private companies have an interest to appropriate the public good, sell it, and increase their profits. We will see this pattern again in the conflict between Berkeley and AT&T (section 2.3.3.a).

The innovations developed in sporting communities were innovations in form. But as Faulkner and Runde (2009) show, innovation in function is also possible. Faulkner and Runde use turntablism to illustrate how a community assigns a new function (musical instrument) to an existing product (the turntable) without modifying its physical form. Innovations in function for existing products are likely when the product that would normally be used for some task is either unavailable, defective, or considered inappropriate (Faulkner and Runde, 2009). Most innovations are a mixture of changes in form and function. For example, the run bike (or balance bike) is a bike without pedals (change in form) that helps children learn balance and steering (change in function). The first run bike was developed by Rolf Mertens whose son wanted to have a bike but was too small for existing bikes (Brost and Uchatius, 2009). Mertens initially developed the run bike because there was no bike which was appropriate for his son. Since then the demand for run bikes surged and Mertens started a company. The examples of the mountain bike and the run bike illustrate that social production, the collaborative development of a public good through voluntary contributions, can give rise to the development of a private good. This is similar to precompetitive research in which private companies collaboratively engage in research and development (sometimes supported by the government) but compete in the market in which they sell their goods (Allen, 1983; Quintas and Guy, 1995; Lipsey et al., 2005).

The just-mentioned examples of user-led innovation reveal three impor-

tant patterns which are typical in user-led innovation communities. First, the need for a new product, i.e., use value is (in most cases) the driving force for inventing a new or customizing an existing product. Second, innovations get started by a relatively small number of lead users who then receive assistance from a large number of other users. Third, social production can lead to the development of private goods. As the reader might expect, we will see these three patterns again in user-generated content and open source software.

2.3.2 User-Generated Content

User-generated content is a form of social production that uses Web 2.0 technologies to aggregate indvidual contributions.[17] The OECD defines user-generated content as "i) content made publicly available over the Internet, ii) which reflects a 'certain amount of creative effort', and iii) which is 'created outside of professional routines and practices' " (OECD, 2007, p.4). Although there are user-generated content projects in which contributors get paid, or in which users have to subscribe in order to access the content, such projects are rare and we will focus on projects which rely on voluntary contributions and put the content in the public domain. Although contributors are not paid there might be overhead costs which can be covered by revenues from advertisements, donations, or (in the case of private companies) by revenues from selling complementary products.

As we can see in figure 2.2 the percentage of internet users who engage in Web 2.0 activities, like chat rooms, newsgroups, fora, file sharing, and creating webpages is relatively high, especially among younger users. Although not depicted in figure 2.2 the most prominent examples of Web 2.0 technologies are social networks services like Facebook[18] and MySpace[19] , blogs like AllRecipes.com, collaboration platforms like Wikipedia, and platforms for sharing videos, like YouTube.[20] Another example, where user-generated content is only part of a larger, commerical project, is Amazon's system of book reviews, allowing everyone who has an Amazon account to write book reviews.

In social network services each member is represented by her profile and

---

17 Other terms that are used instead of user-generated content are consumer-generated media and user-created content. The term Web 2.0 is usually used to describe web applications that allow users to actively interact with others and to contribute content, instead of being a passive user. For a detailed survey see (OECD, 2007).

18 http://www.facebook.com

19 http://www.myspace.com

20 http://www.youtube.com

her relations to other members of the same social network service are visible. Social network services allow members to contribute and share their ideas, activities, events, etc. Blogs are usually centered around a specific topic. Contributors provide information, state their opinion, and discuss with others about the subject. The blog's community consists not only of all contributors but includes contributors and readers. Some user profiles in social network services and some blogs have only restricted access, i.e., it is only possible for registered users to view the content. In this case we do not have a public good but a club good.

In user-generated content it is the norm that there is open access to the content, i.e., the information supplied by contributors. Wikipedia, for example, is a system of mass collaboration allowing millions of individuals to create an encyclopdia by writing, correcting and improving the encyclopdia's entries. AllRecipes.com is a good example of an internet platform specialized on a particular topic, in this case cooking recipes. The virtual community which "meets" on this online platform consists of individuals who never meet each other personally but who all share a common interest. Members of the community produce the content of AllRecipes.com consisting of

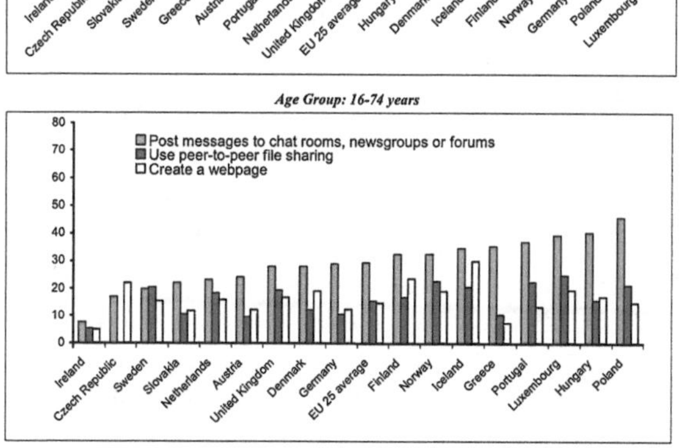

Figure 2.2: User-generated content in the EU as percentage of the number of internet users. Source: OECD (2007, p.10).

thousands of recipes for cooking and baking organized in various categories. In addition to recipes there exists the opportunity to upload photos and to create a profile (visible to all others) telling something about yourself (e.g., cooking level, cooking interest, hometown). Members can give feedback and indicate their preference by voting for the recipes they like best. Members receive no monetary compensation for making their recipes publically available or for commenting and voting on others' recipes. They simply enjoy cooking, want to learn about new recipes and share their recipes with like-minded people. In user-generated content the use value that is the driving force for starting for example a blog varies widely. In many instances the information that is shared on the web takes the form of instructions providing detailed and practical advice on literally all kinds of subjects. For many social network services and blogs in which users share more personal information (e.g., photos and videos) the use value can be considered to be the joy of sharing information, engaging in communication with others (e.g., in chats), or even finding new friends.

All instances of user-generated content have in common that different kinds of digital content are produced by users and made publically available. In addition to active contributors there are users who consume without contributing. Considering user-generated content as a public good it becomes obvious that active contributors' behavior is equivalent to cooperation, and the behavior of the passive audience corresponds to free-riding.

The Web 2.0 has opened up new ways in which individuals can share their ideas with others in a way that is cheaper, easier, and faster than before the Web 2.0 (Huberman, 2001; Benkler, 2006). By posting a recipe on a blog the recipe is immediately available to the largest audience possible (i.e., everyone with access to the internet). Before the internet only a few newspapers and broadcasters had the possibility to reach a large audience because large capital investments were required. The Web 2.0 allows each individual to run her own online newspaper or broadcasting channel. Websites like Wikipedia or AllRecipes.com provide a platform for individual self-expression. They have the power to unite small contributions from individuals and aggregate them into a coherent product. In the case of Wikipedia the emerging product is an encyclopedia, and in the case of AllRecipes.com it is a cookbook. Both are probably superior or come close to any encyclopedia or cookbook supplied by a private company (Giles, 2005).

Unfortunately, user-generated content comes with two downsides which we mention for the sake of completeness. The first problem is the loss of con-

trol once a contribution is made. After a contributon is made, the contributor has little or no control over her contribution which can become a problem especially if the contribution involves private data. The second problem is with quality since contributions are not produced or edited by professionals. A discussion of these problems is beyond the scope of this thesis, but can be found in Espejo (2007) and the articles therein.

2.3.3 Open Source Software

Open source is a form of social production and an approach for developing software. It relies on the collaborative efforts of a large number of contributors working voluntarily, decentralized and without monetary compensation. Information and software are both digital goods but in contrast to information, software is more complex. While information is expressed and can serve as an input (e.g., the information from a Wikipedia can serve as an input for writing a paper) a piece of software is more like a tool that is used to transform input into output (e.g., the R-software takes data as input and produces regression results as output).

Open source software is software which is distributed under open source standards. Most importantly open source standards imply that not only the software but also the source code of the software can be obtained freely ensuring that everyone has access to the source code. "Free" does not mean at zero cost, contributors still have to pay the cost for acquiring the relevant skills and buying the tools (e.g., computer, internet connection). "Free" means that the source code is open and that there are no restrictions on reuse of the code. Nobody is restricted from taking the source code and modifying the program or from taking the source code and reusing parts of it in other programs.

Open source software spreads rapidly because software is a digital product which can be copied at virtually zero cost. Since no restrictions are placed upon the source code copying is not illegal, as it is with proprietary software.[21] Because open source software is the most complex and fascinating form of social production we describe it in more detail in the following sections. In particular, we sketch the history of open source using Unix and Linux as main examples. We emphasize some core principles of open source,

21 In contrast to the commons, open source software is nonrival in consumption since there are no negative external effects from adding additional users. If there are external effects (network effects), they are positive, for example if the software is adopted by a large number of users and becomes a standard.

such as listing contributors, modularization, the importance of licenses, and forking. After sketching the history we describe the enormous success that open source software had during the last twenty years. As the success of various open source applications shows, open source is not just a side issue but a phenomenon having a great impact on the whole economy.

2.3.3.a The History of Open Source

From the beginnings of software development in the 1950s there was a tradition of sharing and collaboration (Lerner and Tirole, 2002). Computers were very expensive and only a few companies and universities could afford them. Sharing computing time between different research groups was common (Weber, 2004). After the first commercial electronic computer (the IBM 701 costing $ 150,000 a month) came out in 1952 it soon became clear that getting the instructions into the machine is the hard part. There was the need for software, and writing the software would be much easier if a compiler could be used (Weber, 2004). A compiler would allow developers to program in high-level languages and use the compiler to translate it into executable machine code. PACT, the Project for the Advancement of Coding Techniques, brought together software engineers from different companies whose task it was to collaboratively write a compiler, a task that could not be solved by one company alone. The need for collaboration arose out of the requirement to solve a technical problem that was of interest to all but could not be solved by one of them working alone.

The next step was multiprogramming/multitasking, i.e., how to overlap several jobs on a single machine. For this, MIT, Bell Labs, and GE started the Multics project (Multiplexed Information and Computing Service) but the project was too ambitious and failed in 1969. Bell Labs withdraw from the Multics project but two of its software developers, Ken Thompson and Dennis Ritchie, still felt that they had to solve the problem. They wrote what was to be the first version of Unix in 1969. Unix spread and was used by sixteen developers inside AT&T (Bell Labs was part of AT&T at that time) in 1973. As the number of contributors increased there was pressure to write a documentation. The first Unix documentation came out in 1971. "The first edition of the programmer's manual established another important Unix cultural tradition: listing each subprogram with an "owner," the person principally responsible for writing and maintaining that particular block of code" (Weber, 2004, p.27). As we will see later in more detail, the need for a doc-

umentation and the informal ownership structure are crucial for the success of open source projects.

The next major innovation in Unix was the pipe. A pipe transforms output from one program into the input of another program. It is the key element of modularization since it allows to combine and recombine different programs to build more complex software. This was a major breakthrough since modularization is key to the success of open source, as we will see in section 2.4.6.

In 1973 Thompson and Ritchie presented a paper on Unix at the ACM Symposium on Operating Systems which marked the beginning of the spread of Unix outside Bell Labs / AT&T. Bell gave out copies of Unix at a nominal charge since because of the consent decree no commercial use was allowed. There was no email protocol available for Unix so the transmission was via tapes and disks. The first Unix license stated that AT&T provides no support, giving users an incentive to share support and bug fixes with one another (Weber, 2004). At that time the community of Unix-enthusiasts consisted of researchers from various university departments and from commercial firms. "So Unix spread in the most traditional of ways – scholars on sabbatical and research fellows going back and forth between BTL, Xerox, PARC, and university departments. There was a physical community of Unix users long before anything like a virtual community could have been imagined" (Weber, 2004, p.29). In many ways the Unix community was similar to user-innovation communities.

In 1974 Robert Fabry installed Unix at the University of Berkeley, and in 1975 Ken Thompson spent his sabbatical there. Together with two graduate students, Chuck Haley and Bill Joy, the Berkeley group developed a set of tools called the Berkeley Software Distribution, BSD. The first version came out in 1978. Of course it was given out in source code which promted users to make improvements which they shared back with the community. At this point is was becoming clear that both AT&T and Berkeley had great interest in Unix. For Berkeley, Unix was not just a free operating system, it was a flourishing research project. AT&T recognized the growing demand for Unix and tried to find ways to monetize it. The divergent interests led to legal quarrels between Berkeley and AT&T. Eventually AT&T created a division for Unix and licensed Unix for large fees (Weber, 2004). The source code was appropriated by AT&T and was not open any more. As a consequence Berkeley was not allowed to distribute the BSD since it contained

Unix source code which now belonged to AT&T. In section 2.4.7 we will see how licenses protect source code from appropriation.

Although Unix now was proprietary software, the parts developed at Berkeley without the help from AT&T were still open. These parts were put together and distributed openly as Networking Release 1. Networking Release 1 was licensed then under extremely liberal terms that would later become the BSD-style license (Weber, 2004). Since Network Release 1 was no full operating system the next step was to take the BSD and replace any parts that came form AT&T. The leader of this project was Keith Bostic who actively tried to convince others to participate in this collective effort. The following quote illustrates two rules which became institutionalized in open source communities: listing projects or sub-projects with an owner who is responsible, and giving credit to contributors.

> It was Keith Bostic who led the way in putting together a consciously designed, public, decentralized, voluntary mass involvement, Internet-based development effort to write software. (It didn't always feel so voluntary to Bostic's friends: Bostic was known for pressuring them in all sorts of ways to take on one or another task.) Beyond this circle of friends, Bostic solicited contributors at Unix user group meetings, in public speeches, and over the net. He promised in return one thing only: Each contributor would have his name listed in the credits, specifying the utility that he wrote. (Weber, 2004, p. 41)

Poor network communication and insufficient bandwith complicated the collaboration but in 1991 Networking Release 2, now a standalone operating system whose source code contained no parts developed by AT&T, was distributed. Networking Release 2 was immediately picked up by Bill Jolitz who adapted the operating system for the newly emerging Intel x86 chip architecture.[22] Jolitz's 386/BSD was the first complete operating system to be distributed over the internet. Thousands of users adopted 386/BSD, dived into the source code and send bug fixes, modifications and improvements back to Jolitz who incorporated them into future versions (Weber, 2004).

In the following years it came to a project fork. Forking occurs if software developers take the source code of an existing project and independently de-

22 Unix was originally written to run on the DEC Alpha chip architecture, at that time (1991) the cutting edge. Intel's x86 chip architecture was just getting started but would evolve and spread rapidly over the next years.

velop a new, distinct piece of software, often as a consequence of an unresolvable conflict. The 386/BSD Unix distribution forked into NetBSD, OpenBSD and FreeBSD, each project having a slightly different focus.

Also noteworthy is a movement in the 1970s at MIT which led to the creation of the Free Software Foundation (FSF). Richard Stallman, then at graduate student at MIT, promoted the idea that proprietary software is morally wrong. Software is not just a tool, rather it is en expression of human creativity and it exists to solve problems together for the common good. With this ideological position Stallman left MIT in 1984 and started the Free Software Foundation. The FSF came up with the General Public License (GPL). The GPL, also known as "copyleft" requires that all works that are derived from GPL software are licensed under the same terms. This viral clause ensures that derivative works are not appropriated but remain in the public domain.

Under the umbrella of the FSF Stallman pushed the GNU-Project.[23] GNU is a collection of several smaller tools which were developed as part of the GNU-project, which should become a free alternative to the Unix operating system. The acronym GNU stands for "GNU is not Unix", however, GNU is compatible with Unix, making it possible for Unix developers to integrate GNU tools. The development of GNU Hurd, the kernel which belongs to the GNU project, was somehow problematic, so developers used the Linux kernel together with GNU tools. Such operating systems are known as GNU/Linux. Both the GNU tools and the Linux kernel are licensed under the GPL.

Linux illustrates that a project which was started mainly for fun can become quite powerful, and, although licensed under the GPL license, can become quite interesting for private companies. Linux was started in 1991 by Linus Torvalds who was dissatisfied with the slow progress of Minix, a open-source version of Unix created for educational purposes. In August 1991 Torvalds posted the following message on the Minix discussion group:

> I'm doing a (free) operating system (just a hobby, won't be big and professional like gnu) for 386(486) AT clones. This has been brewing since april, and is starting to get ready. I'd like any feedback on things people like/dislike in minix, as my OS resembles it somewhat (same physical layout of the file-system (due to practical reasons) among other things).

23 This paragraph on GNU and the Linux kernel is based on Iannacci (2005); Weber (2004); Benkler (2003) as well as the Linux homepage http://www.linux.org/info/.

> I've currently ported bash(1.08) and gcc(1.40), and things seem to work. This implies that I'll get something practical within a few months, and I'd like to know what features most people would want. Any suggestions are welcome, but I won't promise I'll implement them :-) (Torvalds and Diamond, 2001, p.85).

In 1992 Linux was licensed under the GPL, and from thereon, it started to spread rapidly. Linux has attracted a large community of users and developers. Although Linux market share in personal computers is still below five percent, it is used more widely as operating system for web servers (market share slightly above forty percent) and it is used on almost all supercomputers.[24] The most impressive fact, however, is that not only individual users but also governments and a large number of private companies have adopted Linux. For example, the city of Munich[25] and the US Department of Defense[26] use Linux as operating system (Varian and Shapiro, 2007). Many private companies in the IT sector use Linux and many of them, like Dell, IBM, HP, Oracle, Sun and Novell, actually contribute to the development of Linux.[27] The widespread adoption and the decision to contribute shows that Linux, despite the fact that the GPL is a quite restrictive license, attracts large interest among private companies. These companies benefit not directly from Linux but from selling complementary products, like the provision of user support, the specialization of Linux distributions, or by combining Linux with proprietary software packages.

Today, there are literally hundreds of operating systems based on the Linux kernel. The Linux kernel provides the core of the operating system and is complemented by different software packages. A Linux distribution then is a collection of system software and applications which together represent a coherent operating system. Technically, a distribution consists of different software packages. A distribution is maintained by an individual, a group of individuals, or private companies. Different distributions are not always a result of conflict but often a result of heterogenous and specialized interests. The availability of a large number of different Linux distributions illustrates the importance of parallel development and forking.

---

24 The data is taken from Wikimedia, hhttp://stats.wikimedia.org/archive/-squid_reports/2010-10/SquidReportOperatingSystems.htm (accessed in January 2011) and Netcraft's SSL Survey, https://ssl.netcraft.com/ssl-sample-report// (accessed in June 2010).

25 http://www.muenchen.de/Rathaus/dir/limux/english/147197/index.html

26 See Jack Wallen's article at http://blogs.techrepublic.com.com/opensource/?p=347 and Tom Adelstein's article at http://www.linuxjournal.com/article/7644.

27 http://en.wikipedia.org/wiki/Linux

2.3.3.b The Success of Open Source

As we saw in the previous section, the internet allowed geographically dispersed individuals to collaborate, and it enabled software to spread rapidly. This section shows the enourmous success of open source software in terms of quantity and quality. We show that software produced in open source communities is a high-quality product. In fact, in some sectors open source software replaced commercial alternatives and came to dominate the market.

SourceForge is a centralized, web-based source code repository which empowers the open source movement. It is the largest single repository where developers store their open source projects and users can download them. As of November 2009, SourceForge.net lists 380,214 projects in total. Unfortunately this number is not a good indicator for the size of the open source movement since many projects are abandoned or have no significant development. Of all projects listed on SourceForge only 9.2 percent have an activity index between ninety and one hundred percent and at least one file release in the last year.[28] These estimates can be considered to be a lower bound since most but not all projects are listed on SourceForge. Setting the activity criterion to eighty percent also leads to underestimation. Projects which have no recent release because they are completed or have no known bugs are not included.

Besides there being a large number of open source projects, open source is also growing fast. Deshpande and Riehle (2008) analyze detailed data about more than five thousand active and popular projects from 1990 to 2006. They find that the number of open source projects is growing at an exponential rate. Figure 2.3 shows the total number of open source projects (left) and the number of projects added (right). According to this sample it takes 13.9 month for doubling the number of open source projects.

The growth in the total number of projects is only a rough proxy since many projects are inactive or abandoned, as mentioned above. A better indication for the growth of open source software can be obtained by looking at the source code. By counting total lines of source code (omitting empty and commented lines) Deshpande and Riehle (2008) show that the amount of source code grows exponentially.

Open source software is not only growing at an exponential rate, it is also

28 See Carlo Daffara's article "Estimating the Number of Active and Stable FLOSS Projects" at
http://robertogaloppini.net/2007/08/23/estimating-the-number-of-active-and-stable-floss-projects/.

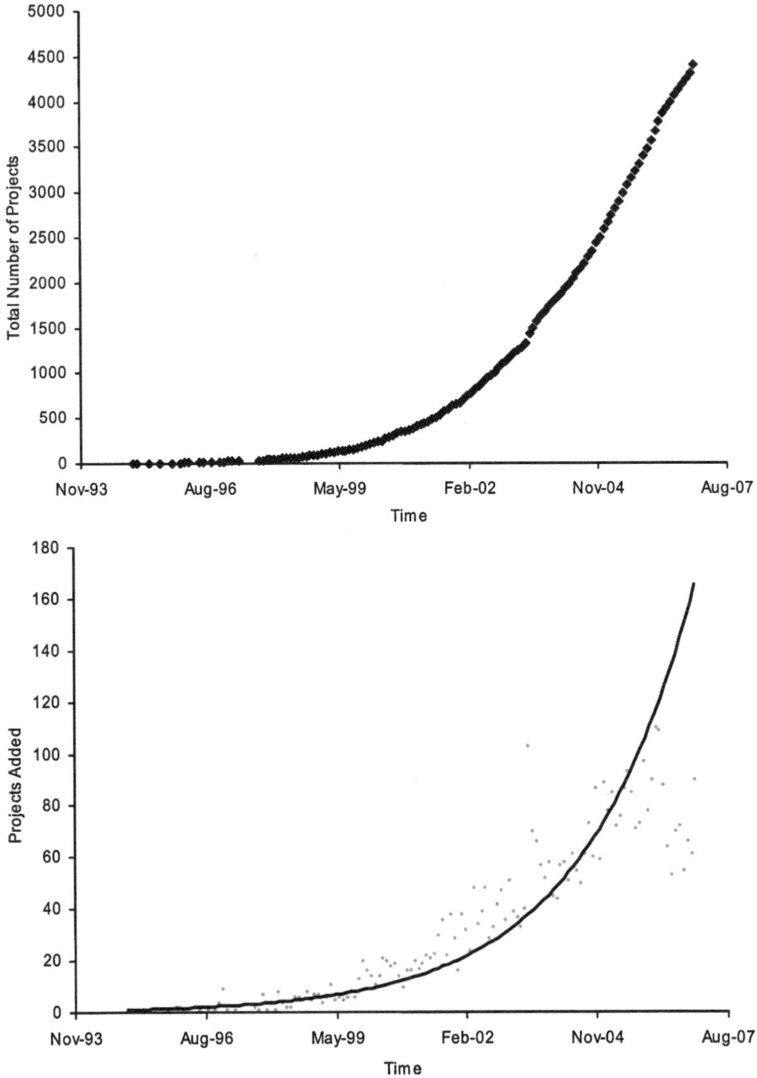

Figure 2.3: Total number of open source projects (top) and number of open source projects added (bottom). Source: Deshpande and Riehle (2008).

successful in terms of quality. The success of open source software over commercial software can be seen by looking at web browsers. Microsoft's Internet Explorer can be downloaded and used without having to pay, but the source code is not available because it is proprietary. The Internet Explorer has lost its dominant market position and its market share is steadily declining. Microsoft's largest competitor in the market is Mozilla Firefox, an open source project which was started by the Mozilla Foundation in 2004. Since then, Mozilla's market share has increased above forty percent while the Internet Explorer's market share has fallen below thirty percent (see figure 2.4). Although Microsoft gives its Internet Explorer away for free it still looses market share to the Mozilla Firefox browser.

If the proprietary software is not freely available, as it is the case with most proprietary software, the position of open source software is further strenghtened. This can be seen by looking at the market for web server software. Among the top servers from all domains Apache has increased its market share to almost sixty percent and dominates the market (see figure 2.5, top). This picture becomes even more evident if we look at the web server software that is used for the million busiest sites. Here, Apache has a market share close to seventy percent while its closest competitor, Microsoft's

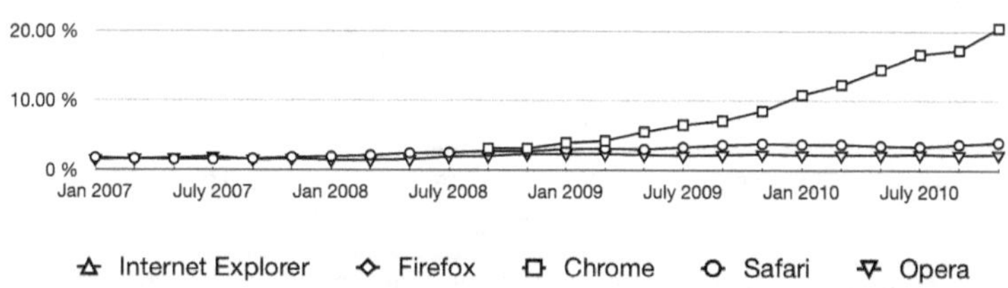

Figure 2.4: Usage share of web browsers. Own graphic, data taken from W3Schools.com, http://www.w3schools.com/browsers/browsers_stats.asp, accessed January 6th, 2011. (Other websites have slightly different statistics in which the share of Microsoft's Internet Explorer is higher. This is especially the case for US data since Internet Explorer's usage share is still higher than Firefox's usage share in the US.)

IIS, has a market share of roughly twenty percent, as can be seen in figure 2.5 (bottom).

If we look at what operating system the web servers use, the success of Linux becomes apparent. The market share of Linux as an operating system for servers varies between twenty and seventy-five percent across coun-

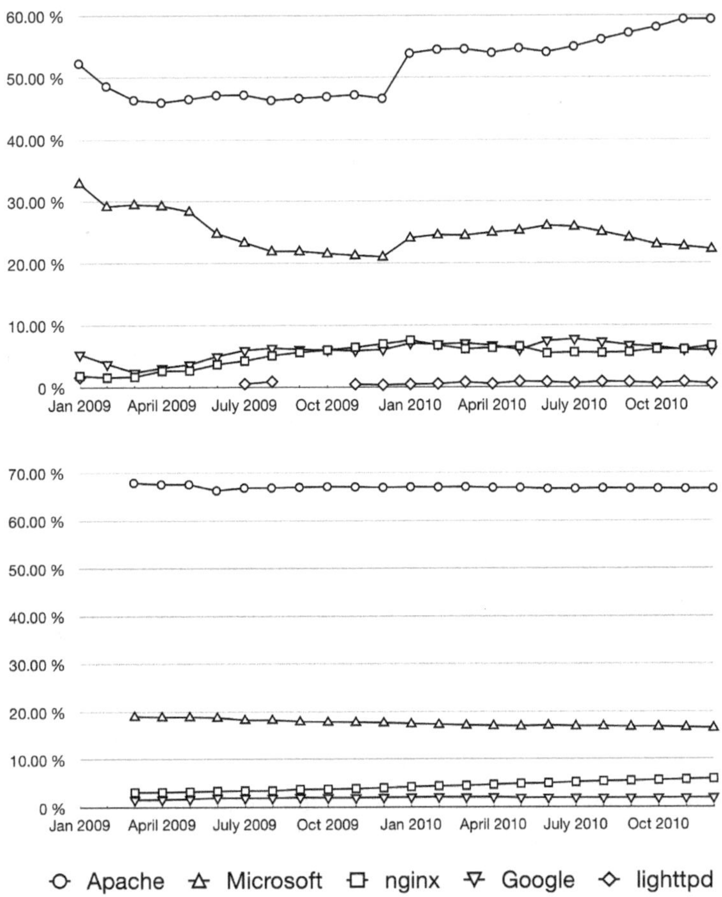

Figure 2.5: Market share for top servers across all domains (top) and market share for top servers across the million busiest sites (bottom). Own graphic, data taken from Netcraft's Web Server Survey, http://news.netcraft.com/archives/category/web-server-survey/, last accessed January 8th, 2011.

tries. In 2009 the Linux share in the global server market was slightly above forty percent, and Linux' market share had just surpassed Microsoft Windows Server, which dominated the market until 2009.[29]

Of course, not all open source projects are as successful as Mozilla or Apache. In fact, there are many small open source projects which die after a short while. However, the sheer number of open source projects and its tendency to grow suggest that the importance of open source will increase even more. In the next section we will lay out the organization of open source projects and social production communities in order to understand their success.

2.4 Organization of Social Production

The two main challenges facing social production communities are (i) the mobilization of effort and (ii) the allocation of effort. Although we are concerned primarily with the mobilization of effort, we discuss the problem of allocating effort in this chapter because the strength of the incentives which are used for the mobilization of effort depends, at least partly, on how the allocation of effort is handled.

By allocation of effort we refer to the problem of organizing and coordinating the production process in such a way that a coherent product emerges. Individuals not only have to work on something, they have to work on the right tasks. Let us neglect the problem of motivating effort for the moment so that we can illustrate the role of social approval for the allocation of effort. For example, suppose an open source community has to decide which of several competing tasks it should implement next. Call the two tasks A and B and assume that task A is more important from the community's perspective. This can be thought of as the community setting-up a poll in which members can indicate their preference. The poll aggregates individual preferences and signals the members' preferences. Assume that the quality of individual contributions is observable and that contributions to task A will receive more social approval than contributons to task B. Support for this assumption can be found in Raymond (2001) arguing that contributions are rewarded based on novelty and necessity. If contributors have a preference for social approval they will contribute to task A. If contributors have no preference for social approval they will be indifferent between contributing

29 Data from the Netcraft SSL Survey, http://news.netcraft.com/ssl-survey/.

to task A or B. In this situation social approval works as a social cue, signaling the importance of tasks A and B. By observing this signal contributors will allocate their efforts on task A.[30]

In the rest of this chapter we analyze how social production communities organize themselves and allocate the efforts of individual contributors. Organization in social production communities is characterized by various institutions which ensure open communication, facilitate the monitoring of individual behavior and the exchange of social approval. Although the question of how social production communities organize themselves is not the central topic of this thesis, a discussion of this question is necessary because, as we will argue in section 4.1.1.b, the organization of social production communities explains why social approval is a strong incentive for the mobilization of effort.

In social production communities it is not unusual that many thousands of developers voluntarily and collaboratively work on a project. Categorizing the community's members into different roles provides a natural starting point for our discussion of organization, as section 2.4.1 argues. Since all contributors work on the same project there is the need for governance. Each social production community has to make decisions, for example about the quality of the product or about how to aggregate individual contributions. Sections 2.4.2 and 2.4.3 reveal that governance in social production communities is characterized by a high degree of mental proximity (to be explained below) and a weak, informal hierarchy based on merit and informal property rights. Since in mental proximity the deliberative process is crucial, section 2.4.4 illustrates the particular mechanisms and tools that are used in order to facilitate discussion and collective choice. Unfortunately, not all differences can be resolved through deliberation and differences in opinion are a potential source of conflict. Section 2.4.5 describes parallel development and forking, two mechanisms designed to mitigate the negative sides of conflict and to resolve conflict eventually. Lastly, we discuss modularity, a technical feature of open source software reducing the need for coordination (2.4.6) and licenses, a legal feature governing the legal aspects between social production communities and users of their products (2.4.7).

2.4.1 The Different Roles in Social Production Communities

The different roles in user-led innovation communities and user-generated content communities are visualized in in figure 2.6 (left). At the core there are lead users (user-led innovation) and users who contribute regularly (user-generated content). Next, there are users and contributors who contribute only occasionally. Finally, there are users who never contribute but use the product or the information that is supplied. In open source software the roles are more differentiated. While most contributors are software developers, different developers have different roles within a community. The structure of a typical open source community is often visualized as an onion which layers correspond to the different roles, as depicted in figure 2.6 (right). Often the roles of individuals overlap but the onion model provides a good starting point for understanding the organization of open source communities. In the outside layer there are *passive users* who just download the software and use it. They never look at the source code and have no intention to develop the software. If they find a bug they do not write a bug report. This is different with *active users* who are situated on the next layer. Active users perform relatively simple tasks like reporting bugs and providing help by answering questions on mailing lists. Moving inwards we find *developers*. Developers are mainly occupied with the maintenance of old code and the development

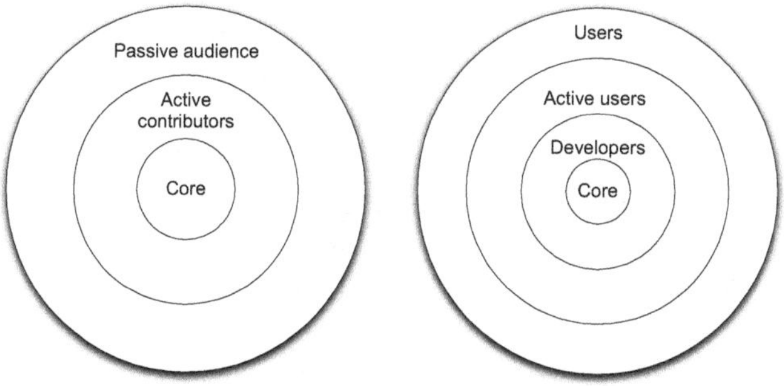

Figure 2.6: The different roles in social production communities (user-led innovation and user-generated content on the left, open source communities on the right, based on van Wendel de Joode, 2005).

30 For experimental evidence on social cues as coordination devices see Manzini et al., 2009, and Dugar, 2010.

of new code. At the center of the onion is the *core*. The core consists of core contributors and the project leader or owner.

If we view open source as a public good, it is not entirely clear whether passive users contribute or not. Passive users do not actively or intentionally contribute to the public good open source software. But the software industry is a network industry where the value of a product depends not only on the product itself but also on the rate of adoption. As more users adopt the software it becomes more interesting for other users, so passive users contribute to the success of open source software without contributing to the public good open source software.[31]

2.4.2 Anarchy or Hierachy?

Social production communities can be described as a network of individuals (see section 2.1.2). Since individuals have to coordinate their decisions there is the need for a system of governance. This section discusses governance in open source communities. Since open source software is a complex product and the interdependencies between individual decisions are high, there is a strong need for governance. Governance in user-led innovation and user-generated content is similar to governance in open source communities but since there are fewer interdependencies, they only use a subset of the mechanisms for governance that are used in open source communities. Analogous to our distinction between firms, markets, and networks we can distinguish three ideal types of governance (following Sacchetti and Sugden, 2009, and Elsner et al., 2010). The three ideal types are markets, hierarchies, and mental proximity.

- **Markets:** Interactions in markets are governed by flexible prices. Power is assumed to be absent in perfectly competitive markets, but is present if competition is imperfect. Following this definition of market power, power is measured by the deadweight loss resulting from market power compared to the Pareto optimal situation (i.e., the distance from total welfare at the hypothetical optimum characterized by perfect competition). When referring to power Sacchetti and Sugden (2009) do not mean market power and its impact on market efficiency but economic power. Economic power is a broader concept and takes into account the

31 A similar division of members into roles is made by the Apache Software Foundation and can be found at http://www.apache.org/foundation/how-it-works.html.

interests of the publics.[32] Following Dewey (1927) the publics are defined as everyone who is significantly affected by the consequences of the decision.

- **Hierarchies:** A hierarchy is a directed system of governance. People at the higher levels of the hierarchy have the power to decide without taking into account the interests of those at lower levels of the hierarchy. Mathematically, a hierarchy is a partially ordered set, in which the relation between each pair of elements is transitive, meaning that there are no circular relationships.
- **Mental Proximity:** Mental proximity is an ideal type situation in which a decision is made as the result of a deliberative process involving the publics. It is best illustrated with the following quote: "There is mental proximity amongst a complex of people in the organization of production when they each seek compatibility with the interests of publics through jointly embracing the procedural rule of democratic deliberation based on its necessary values, including: the rejection of controlling influences; positive freedom; inclusion on equal terms; informed participation; the desire to reach a consensus; sympathy; mutual respect; reciprocity; continuous learning" (Sacchetti and Sugden, 2009, p. 301).

Markets, hierarchies, and mental proximity are three mechanisms of governing economic or social systems. In the real world all three mechanisms are present in varying degrees. In a private company, for example, there is mental proximity (e.g., deliberation between the employer and her employees), hierarchy, and there are prices in the form of wages. In social production, however, markets are absent and the system of governance is combined of a flat hierarchy and mental proximity.

Governance through mental proximity is characterized by the availability of different mechanisms for communication, coordination, and conflict resultion. This ensures that the process of deliberation is open to publics and that there are mechanisms enabling debate, discussion, and persuasion. By using these mechanisms preferences and opinions are shaped, and mutual understanding can be reached. Power is rarely used and controlling influ-

32 For example, a private firm uses its economic power to prevent a local government from raising taxes although raising taxes would be beneficial for the local community as a whole.

ences are absent.[33] Discussions are based on rational arguments, sympathy, reciprocity, and respect, and there is a high willingness of reaching consensus. The rest of this section and the following two sections describe the mechanisms that ensure a high degree of mental proximity in open source communities.

Open source projects are often portrayed as anarchic where everyone gabbles around like in a bazaar (Raymond, 2001; van Wendel de Joode, 2005). Upon closer inspection it becomes clear that open source is far from anarchic. There are well-defined roles and the community's members are ordered hierarchically. In very small projects the hierarchical structure might be absent but as soon as the project grows there is an indespensable need for a minimal hierarchical structure. The existence of a hierarchy is not incompatible with mental proximity but requires that power is not abused to impose decisions despite the interests of others. At the top of the hierarchy is the owner of a project. Large projects are often divided into sub-projects, each sub-project having its own owner. The Linux operating system employs this model. Torvalds has the power to decide which patches get accepted in the official Linux distribution, but he rarely uses his power. Instead, Torvalds is willing to accept decisions that are preferred by many developers even if they are not preferred by him (Torvalds and Diamond, 2001; van Wendel de Joode, 2005). Although Torvalds is the founder and owner of the project there are a couple of lieutenants each being responsible for a Linux sub-project. In the case of Linux, the hierarchy has evolved naturally as Linux grew. Core contributors became lieutnants because of their skills and past contributions. In other open source projects lieutnants are democratically elected by the community, e.g., the Debian project[34] or the Apache Foundation.[35] The lieutnants receive contributions from developers working on the particular sub-project, and their main task is to accept or reject contributions. This kind of leadership structure does not restrict individual behavior a lot since owners and lieutenants have no formal authority over developers. In fact, project leaders or lieutnants rarely use their power to end a conflict (van Wendel de Joode, 2005, p.108) but ignore the conflict or let the community decide. The differ-

33 An example for the absence of controlling influences is a norm, prescribing not to use words like "help" or "urgent" when posting a question in user support forums. The reason for this norm is to avoid any pressure on contributors so that they do not feel compelled to contribute (for a concrete example: http://www.golatex.de/kann-man-tabellen-im-querformat-darstellen-t2003.html).

34 See http://www.debian.org/intro/organization and http://www.debian.org/vote/.

35 http://www.apache.org/foundation/

ent ways to coordinate production are discussed in the next section, and the different ways of resolving conflicts are discussed in section 2.4.5.

2.4.3 Informal Property Rights

In the conventional sense property is the right of the owner to exclude others from using her property. The conventional structure of property rights is absent in open source software. In open source nobody owns a project in the conventional sense and the licenses explicitely make sure that there will be no exclusion.

An informal theory of property rights for the open source domain has been introduced by Eric Raymond (2001). It can be considered to be an informal institution. In contrast to conventional property right the owner of an open source project does not have the right to exclude others. According to Raymond (2001) the founder of a project automatically becomes its owner.[36] The right of ownership is recognized by the community although it is not legally binding. The owner is responsible for the project and maintains the official version of the program. She is the only person who has the right to distribute modified versions of the official program. Developers working on the project send their improvements to the owner who then decides whether to incorporate them into the next release of the official version. If a CVS (to be explained in the next section) is used, source code can be uploaded by any developer who has the committer status which is granted (and withdrawn) to developers by the project owner. In some projects, however, the decision about incorporation of new patches is made differently, for example by a voting system.

If the owner of a project loses interest, the property right has to be transferred. Ideally, the owner finds someone who is interested and hands over the ownership. If no new owner can be found, either because there is no-one interested in becoming the owner or because the old owner is not actively searching for a new owner, the project becomes an orphan. An orphaned project has no owner. Ownership for an orphaned project can be acquired by announcing the intention. The prospective owner tries to contact the last owner to ask her for permission. If the old owner can be found she can transfer the property right to the new owner. Otherwise the new owner becomes

36 This is similar to priority of discovery as a form of property right in science (Stephan, 1996).

the owner if there is no resistance in the community (e.g., no developers with similar claims for ownership).

2.4.4 Mechanisms for Deliberation and Collective Choice

Although the need for coordination is reduced by a modular architecture (to be explained in section 2.4.6 below) the need for coordination is not eliminated completely. In this section we discuss various tools which are used in the process of deliberation. All these tools support discussion and debate, thus facilitating governance through mental proximity.

The internet provides several tools facilitating coordination by minimizing time and money developers have to spend on coordinating their efforts. Consequently, barriers are very low and everyone has access to the deliberative process. In contrast to one-to-one communication, like email, the deliberative process is visible to everyone. In this form of one-to-all communication individual contributions (e.g., an entry in the bug-tracking system) are accessible to everyone. This does not imply that everyone participates in the deliberative process, but it means that joining the discussion is easy. Members of open source communities are able to actively participate in the deliberative process and can affect the community's operational rules. The discussion and deliberation about a particular open source software is a special form of user-generated content, where the users are users of the software and the content is information about the particular software.

According to Ostrom (1990) participation and communication are essential for the success of self-organizing communities. The importance of participation and communication is reaffirmed in several empirical studies on open source communities (Weber, 2004; Iannacci, 2005; van Wendel de Joode, 2005; Bates and Stone, 2006). In his study of the Linux kernel development Iannacci (2005) emphasizes communication and users personal interest as crucial and argues that "[i]nteraction patterns in general and dialogic negotiations in particular are the hallmark of the Linux kernel development process and allow it to escape the traditional division of labor typical of conventional software development based on a clear separation between job requirement and personal interests" (p. 13). The tools which are used most frequently for communication and deliberation are documentations, mailing lists, bug

tracking systems, to-do lists, concurrent version systems (CVS), coding style guides, and credit files. Consider these seriatim.[37]

- **Documentations:** As the size of the project and the number of developers working on it increase, the software gets more complex because there are more interdependencies. The need for a documentation arises. Documentations are used to describe the interfaces linking different modules so that others know how their modules can communicate with other modules.
- **Mailing Lists:** In mailing lists email technology is used to disseminate information to a large number of recipients. A mailing list contains a single email address called *reflector* and a list of email address of all recipients, called *subscribers*. Mailing lists are partially or fully automated. In partially automated mailing lists, an email that is send to the reflector is forwarded to all subscribers after the email is approved by the mailing list's moderator. In fully automated mailing lists an email that is send to the reflector is automatically forwarded to all subscribers.
- **Bug Tracking Systems:** A bug tracking system is a database keeping track of all bugs that are reported by users. Using a bug tracking system software users and developers can communicate. The bug tracking system allows to keep track of the users who reported the bug, the conditions under which the bug appeared, and the developers that are working to fix the bug. Not only developers but also users without any knowledge of software development can report bugs by describing under which conditions the bug occurs. In open source software development the bug tracking system is usually accessible for everyone and represents a centralized database listing the software's bugs. A bug's life cycle is tracked by assigning different statuses to the bug. If the bug is solved, its status is changed or the bug is deleted from the database. The bug tracking system is useful since it allows users to report bugs and enables developers to see who else is working on the same bug.
- **To-Do Lists:** To-do lists provide a marketplace where demand for new features is signaled to others who might have the knowledge to implement the feature. They are similar to bug tracking systems but the difference is that users report requests for new features instead of reporting

37 The following descriptions are based on Weber (2004),van Wendel de Joode (2005), and DiBona et al., eds (2006).

bugs. Both bug tracking systems and to-do lists provide important feedback for further improvement of the software.

- **Concurrent Version Systems:** Concurrent version systems (CVS) store the current version of a software project and its history (i.e., changes and previous versions) on a server. Using a CVS ensures that developers always have access to the latest version of the software. They can download a so-called working copy in which they can make changes. Then, the modified files are uploaded into the CVS and the version numbers of all files that were changed are updated automatically. This ensures that all developers are working on the latest version, reducing duplications of effort. The CVS also automatically stores old versions of the source code, making it easy to revert changes if necessary. Thus the CVS not only reduces the time spend on coordination individual contributions but also ensures that damages can easily be repaired.

- **Coding Style Guides:** Coding style guides consist of code standards or code conventions prescribing how developers should write the source code. Coding style guides are specific for a project or a programming language. The main object of coding style guides is the appearance of the source code. Coding style guides specify the use of spaces, tabs, and looping techniques (and more) with the goal of minimizing the effort required to read and understand the source code.

- **Credit Files:** In open source projects it is the norm that the names of individual developers are attached to modules (if they created the module) or improvements (if they improved the module). This is either done by writing the names in the source code itself, in credit files, or listing the names with the associated contributions on a website. For Linux there even exists a virtual Hall of Fame[38] , listing institutions and individuals who made valueable contributions. By attaching developers' names to contributions developers get recognition for their effort and their responsibility increases. Looking at credit files, others know whom to contact if they have questions or find bugs concerning this particular contribution. Due to credit files and information about contributors is made available. The names of the contributors are distributed with the software making it possible to identify individual contributors, which is

38 http://linux-vserver.org/Hall_of_Fame

crucial for the exchange of social approval, as we will argue in chapter 4.

In addition to the just-mentioned mechanisms for web-based communication open source communities interact personally. There are frequent conventions of specific communities where commercial firms, core developers from the open source community as well as interested users get together and exchange information. On a smaller level there are numerous regional user groups where users meet in person.[39]

2.4.5 Conflict Resolution

The mechanisms described in the last section facilitate discussion in open source communities and ensure a high degree of mental proximity. Nonetheless, there might be issues in which no consensus will be reached. In particular, the contributors' heterogeneous backgrounds and the interdependencies between different parts of the software can give rise to unresolvable conflict. Conflict has both positive and negative sides. Conlict can lead to higher levels of productivity, for example when a contributor tries to convince others that her solution is better than a competing alternative. On the other hand, conflict can give rise to negative feelings, inaction, or even aggression.

In open source conflict can arise, for example, if two developers work on patches to fix the same problem. If such a conflict occurs, it is the norm that the conflict is resolved according to functionality and elegance of the source code. If patch A solves the problem better than patch B does, patch A should be included. So the first thing that a patch (and more general any submission of source code) has to do is to successfully solve the problem. If patches A and B work equally well in the sense that both produce the same solution to the posed problem, patches are judged by the elegance of the code. Elegant code reduces the need for coordination and eases the implementation of changes by reducing the time participants have to invest in order to understand the software, thus making it easy to develop the software further.

The functionality and elegance of competing solutions will be discussed among the members of the community. During discussion attacks on contributor's personality and competence should be avoided and the discussion should focus on the source code. Since most contributors are anonymous it is often impossible to attack the contributor's personality or to judge her

39 According to http://www.linux.org/groups/germany.html there were 73 Linux user groups in Germany in November 2010.

competence. All information that is available about the contributor is contained in the source code. Discrimination, i.e., judging two contributions of the same quality differently, is almost impossible since personal information about the contributor is rarely available. Hence, the opinions that are voiced within the discussion accurately reflect the quality of the contribution. Moreover, if each member of the community is more likely to be right than wrong, the probability that the opinion of the community's majority is the right opinion converges towards one as the size of the community grows.[40]

If the rules of discussion are ignored, there are *graduated sanctions* (Osterloh et al., 2001). Contributors can be excluded from a community, as it happened, for example, with Theo de Raadt, a core developer in the NetBSD project. De Raadt had repeatedly harassed and abused users and developers who in turn complained about de Raadt's behavior (Weber, 2004). Since de Raadt did not change his behavior after several warnings from NetBSD's core contributors, they took away his committer status and asked him to resign. This was the starting point of a flame war in which numerous emails, often hostile and insulting, were exchanged between de Raadt and NetBSD's core contributors.[41] At the beginning of this flame war, the participants tried to resolve the conflict but did not succeed. A couple of month after the flame war broke out, de Raadt started a new fork of NetBSD which he labelled OpenBSD. OpenBSD specialized in security, attracted new developers, and helped to solve several security problems. The story of Theo de Raadt and NetBSD illustrates how a the negative sides of conflict (e.g., the insulting discussions) can be transformed into the positive sides of conflict (the project fork and the resulting new product OpenBSD). Moreover, it illustrates the use of graduated sanctions (warnings, taking away committer status, exclusion from the community) which according to Ostrom (1990) are essential for the success of self-organizing communities.

If a conflict cannot be resolved on the basis of functionality and elegance, differences in opinion can also lead to commit wars. In a commit war developers override changes that they disagree with, only to find that they are over-written again by developers advocating competing approaches. Commit wars are a serious threat because they can destabilize the community. In

40 This result is known as the Condorcet Jury Theorem, stating that a majority is more likely to select the better alternative if the probability that each member of the group votes for the better alternative is larger than one half. Here it is assumed that one solution is objectively better than the alternative (Condorcet, 1785; Gaertner, 2009).

41 A record of the emails can be found at de Raadt's homepage: http://www.theos.com/deraadt/coremail.

such cases the project leader could intervene and try to resolve the conflict, but that does rarely happen. Project leaders do not want to spend their time debating conflicts, they actually want to write source code (van Wendel de Joode, 2005).

Since leaders do not use their authority to mitigate conflicts, conflicts can continue for quite a long time. If a debate cannot be solved it can come to parallel development. Parallel development means that one software project splits up into two development lines, each line implementing the patches that they consider to be best. Conflict is transformed into competition where each developement line tries to get more contributors than the other. The initial conflict, however, is not resolved, but its negative sides (inactivity) are avoided while its virtues (autonomy, perfectionism, stimulating creativity) are promoted (Benkler and Nissenbaum, 2006). Eventually, the better performance and elegance of one development line is acknowledged and a consensus is reached. Otherwise, the open source project forks into separate development lines which have irreconcilable differences.

We saw that in open source communities there are institutions which reduce the negative sides of conflict. Parallel development allows contributors to demonstrate that they are right by implementing their patches and building a release which attracts lots of developers and users. In parallel development competition avoids excessive debate and lets participants focus on what they want to do: write good code that works. If parallel development does not work out participants can still take the source code and start their own release, resulting in a fork of the project. This means that the hierarchy and the community's institutions for conflict resolution are designed in such a way as to facilitate cooperation without restricting individual freedom while promoting the positive sides of competition (e.g., higher productivity, increased effort) at the same time.

2.4.6 Modularity

Modularity is a technological feature of software projects and has two purposes. Modularity reduces the time and effort individual developers have to spend on coordinating their activities, and allows developers to work in a decentralized way. Modular systems are more robust and respond faster to a changing environment. Since there are only weak interdependencies between components only one (or a few) components have to be changed to adapt to a changing environment.

The idea of modularity was introduced by Simon (1962). For purposes of illustration he uses the metaphor of the two watchmakers, Tempus and Hora (p. 470). Both watchmakers assembled high-quality watches by combining thousand pieces. Tempus and Hora were called frequently by customers ordering watches, resulting in frequent interruptions of their work. Tempus assembled the pieces in such a way that whenever he got interrupted, he had to put the partly-finished watch down and it immediately fell into pieces. Hora, however, produced the same watches in a different way. He produced stable components of ten pieces each which he later combined into larger components until the watch was finished. So when Hora was interrupted by a call and put down his work to pick up the phone, he only lost the component he was working on at the moment. Since he lost only part of his work Hora prospered while Tempus became poorer and poorer.

As the metaphor of the two watchmakers illustrates, it can be useful to divide a large project into smaller components. In open source projects where there are not just one but many thousands of developers working on the same project modularity becomes even more important. In fact, it is a key principle of modular programming that a program is broken down into smaller components. The individual components are largely independent and can easily be recombined. They are what Simon called *stable intermediate components*.

The division of a system into stable intermediate components or subsystems (of a software project into modules) is particularly useful for nearly decomposable systems. In nearly decomposable systems the interactions between the individual components are weak, but not negligible (Simon, 1962). This implies that there are relatively few interdependencies between modules. Developers working on different modules have to spend only limited time coordinating their activities. Especially in open source projects this is important because individual developers self-select their tasks, each developer working on the part of the software that she is most interested in. Self-selection could become problematic if there were many interdependencies between modules. The modular architecture, however, reduces the need for coordination by reducing the interdependcies between modules. Each developer can work on the module she selected and coordination is only necessary when it comes to the interfaces which link the modules. Modularity decreases the costs of communication (Langlois, 2002). An implication that immediately follows is that modules can be produced independently from

one another allowing developers to work decentralized at different times and places.

Modularity is often used in conjunction with the idea of granularity. Granularity refers to the sizes of the project's modules (Benkler and Nissenbaum, 2006). Ideally, the project should be fine-grained. Smaller modules are better because they allow more developers to make smaller contributions. If a project is fine-grained the time and effort it takes to complete one module will be smaller. The cost of a single contribution is reduced. Also, the time that it takes to understand the new contribution is reduced and others are more likely to understand the source code of the contribution. In fact in the Linux community a patch was rejected because it was considered to be too large (Weber, 2004; Iannacci, 2005).

2.4.7 Organizational Boundaries and Licenses

An open source community can be viewed as an organization for producing software. While in commercial organizations the boundaries are clear-cut, in open source they are somehow fluid. It is not clear who counts as a member of an open source community and who does not. The boundary of the community has to be defined somehow. Credit files and websites are two ways to delineate the boundary. Websites are also used to represent the community externally. They describe the functions of the software and the goal of the project. But contrary to most other organizations (e.g., firms or clubs) there is no mechansim that limits the size of the community.

With the emergence of open source licenses open source software developed a more rigid organizational structure. As we saw above in the conflict between Berkeley and AT&T, open source software can be appropriated. There always exists the risk that a developer claims the copyright for a piece of source code that is part of an open source application. The developer can then claim the copyright and this piece of source code has to be removed (as Berkeley did it) or the users of the open source application have to pay licensing fees. To avoid the risk of source code being appropriated and withdrawn from the public domain licenses and foundations have been created. Ideally, licenses create a boundary and ensure that the software remains open source. The function of licenses is to avoid legal disputes over property rights (Lerner and Tirole, 2002, p.201). Richard Stallman's *Free Software Foundation* developed the GPL. The GPL grants the right to modify the source code if the developed software is made available under the same

terms, i.e., the source code of the modified software has to be made available (Lerner and Tirole, 2002). The requirement that all derivative works must be distributed under the GPL license is known as *viral clause*. The viral clause ensures that no software can be withdrawn from the public domain. While the GPL is very restrictive in requiring that the modified software is licensed under the same terms, the Open Source Definition is more flexible. Developed in 1997 by the Open Software Initiative it does not require that the modified software is licensed under the same terms (Lerner and Tirole, 2002). This means that modifications can be sold while the unmodified software remains nonproprietary.[42]

While the GPL and Open Source License are confined to the development of software, there have been attempts to create counterparts in the realm of culture. The Creative Commons initiative has developed a set of licenses which allow others to display and distribute their work for noncommercial purposes (usually information and knowledge in the form of pictures, writings, videos etc.) if credit is give to the creator (Benkler, 2006, p.255).[43]

The open source licenses give a more rigid framework to open source by ensuring that derived products will stay in the public domain. Besides the development of licenses there are also open source foundations, often related to a specific license or software, acting as representatives for the product.

2.5 Upshot of Chapter 2

Due to the technological changes associated with the IT revolution, explained in section 2.1, there was a steep increase in social production, characterized in section 2.2. Social production existed for quite some time in its various incarnations like user-led innovation, user-generated content, open source software (section 2.3). With the IT revolution social production has been boosted and now it is a successful and still growing phenomenon. Section 2.4 described the organization of social production, explaining how a large number of individual contributions are aggregated into large, meaningful projects while at the same time keeping the costs of organization low. The institutions which are used for collective choice, coordination, deliberation, and conflict resolution further open communication and ensure a high de-

42 GPL and Open Source License are the two major open source licenses, although there are lots of other open source licenses. A full list can be found at http://www.opensource.org/licenses.

43 http://creativecommons.org/about/licenses/

gree of mental proximity. More importantly, by facilitating monitoring of individual behavior and exchange of social approval, these institutions not only coordinate individual contributions but also help to overcome the problem of underprovision.

The function of this chapter was to provide a background on social production and fix some terminology. The rest of this thesis will focus on the problem of mobilizing effort in social production communities, i.e., on individuals' motivations. Since social production communities supply goods that are nonrival and nonexcludable, we choose a public good game to model the problem of mobilizing effort in social production communities.

Chapter 3

Voluntary Contributions to Public Goods

All forms of social production discussed in chapter 2 produce information and digital goods which are nonrival in consumption. Think of the instruction on how to improve your kiteboard. Once the instruction is available, it can be used by everyone without reducing its value for others. The same holds for an entry in the Wikipedia encyclopedia and open source software. Once the article has been published on Wikipedia, everyone can read it and benefit from its information, and once the software is available everyone can download and use it without limiting the availability of the software to others.

The information and digital goods produced by social production are nonrival and nonexcludable, hence they are *public goods* by definition. Closely associated with public goods is the *problem of underprovision*. The costs of providing the public good or contributing to it are private while the benefits are public. This externality leads to a divergence of individual and social benefits. Rational individuals have no incentive to contribute to the public good if the community is large. The dominant strategy is free-riding, i.e., not contributing to the public good while reaping the benefits of others' contributions. This is a social dilemma because if everyone follows the dominant strategy and free-rides the public good will not be supplied.

In this chapter we introduce game theory (section 3.1) and discuss dilemma problems from a game theoretic perspective (section 3.1). We review three different solutions to dilemma problems (section 3.3) and argue that social production is an example of a self-organizing community, i.e., a community which sets up and enforces soial institutions of cooperation by itself. In section 3.4 we discuss empirical studies concerning contributors to social production and their motives. Finally, we present use value, intrinsic motivation, and social preferences as three explanations for contributions to social production (section 3.5). These three explanations are important but incom-

plete. Hence, social approval has to be taken into account, as we will argue in the next chapter.

3.1 Game Theory

Game theory studies multiperson interactions with *strategic interdependencies*. The existence of strategic interdependencies implies that a player's payoff not only depends on her own actions but also on the actions of other players.[44] We are concerned with non-cooperative game theory, i.e., the branch of game theory where no binding contracts can be made before the game is played. We will consider only pure strategies and games of complete information, i.e., games in which each player knows the payoffs and strategies available to other players. We assume that players act instrumentally rational by maximizing a well-behaved utility function. The information about the structure of the game (strategies and payoffs) and player's rationality is assumed to be common knowledge. A proposition $\mathcal{P}$ is common knowledge among a group of players if all players know $\mathcal{P}$, all players know that they know $\mathcal{P}$, all players know that they all know that they all know $\mathcal{P}$, ... , *ad infinitum*.

A game $\mathcal{G}$ can be represented in extensive form as a game tree or in normal form as a triplet $\mathcal{G} = \{I, A, U\}$. In the normal form representation $I = \{1, 2, ..., n\}$ denotes the set of players, A is the set of action profiles, and U denotes the set of payoff functions. Each player i has a finite set of actions, $a_i \in A_i$. The set of action profiles is given by $A = \times_i A_i$, $a \in A$. Payoff functions are collected in the set $U = \{u_i\}_{i=0}^{n}$ and payoffs are assigned by continuous functions from the set of action profiles to the n-dimensional Euclidian space, $U : A \rightarrow \mathbb{R}^n$.

For purposes of illustration consider the nonrepeated prisoner's dilemma game played by Row and Column. The extensive and normal form representations are depicted in figures 3.1 and 3.2. In figure 3.1 the dotted line indicates that both nodes belong to the same information set, meaning that Column has the same information available at both nodes since she did not observe Row's move. We interpret this as both players making their moves simultaneously. The set of players is I = {Row,Column}. Since the game is symmetric the *action profiles* for both players are identical,

44 For a more detailed introduction to game theory the reader is referred to Holler and Illing (2009), chapter 7 in Mas-Colell et al. (1995) or Gibbons (1997); a critical introduction is presented in Hargreaves Heap and Varoufakis (2004).

$A_{Row} = A_{Column} = \{\text{Cooperate,Defect}\}$. The *set of action profiles* is the Cartesian product of the individual action profiles, $A = \{\text{Cooperate,Defect}\}^2$. Payoffs are given by

$$(u_{Row}, u_{Column}) = \begin{cases} (R,R) & \text{if } a_{Row} = a_{Column} = \text{Cooperate} \\ (P,P) & \text{if } a_{Row} = a_{Column} = \text{Defect} \\ (S,T) & \text{if } a_{Row} = \text{Cooperate and } a_{Column} = \text{Defect} \\ (T,S) & \text{if } a_{Row} = \text{Defect and } a_{Column} = \text{Cooperate} \end{cases}$$

A central notion in game theory is a *strategy*. A strategy is defined as a plan telling the player which action to choose in every possible circumstance of the game. It is a plan for all contingencies. In the nonrepeated prisoner's dilemma each player has only one decision to make so a strategy consists of just one action, cooperate or defect. We denote player i's strategy by σ_i and summarize the strategies of all players in the *strategy profile* $\sigma = (\sigma_1, \sigma_2, ..., \sigma_n)$. The space of all possible strategies for player i is denoted by S_i. We will see later that in finitely and infinitely repeated games strategy spaces get very large and strategies can become quite complex.

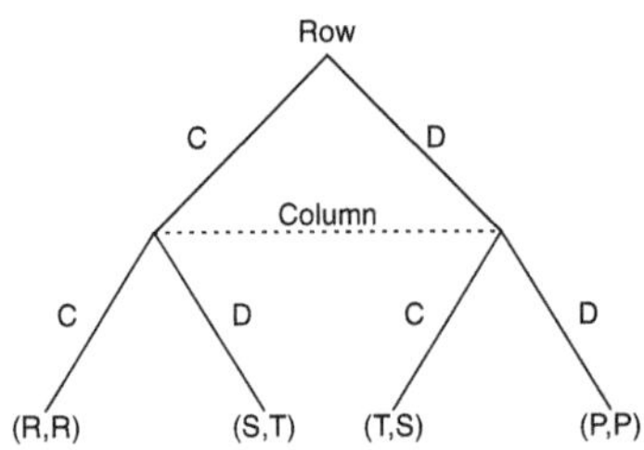

Figure 3.1: Extensive form representation of the prisoner's dilemma.

		Column C	Column D
Row	C	R,R	S,T
	D	T,S	P,P

Figure 3.2: The standard PD game; T = temptation to defect, P = punishment for mutual defection, R = reward for mutual cooperation, S = sucker's payoff; $T > R > P > S$.

Having defined the structure of the game and the notion of strategies, the next thing we need is a *solution concept.* A solution concept prescribes a strategy for all players. The most prominent solution concept is the *Nash equilibrium.* Economically, a Nash equilibrium describes a situation in which no player can gain by uniformly deviating from her strategy and hence has no incentive to deviate. Formally, a Nash equilibrium is a strategy profile $\sigma^* = (\sigma_1^*, \sigma_2^*, ..., \sigma_n^*)$ such that

$$u_i(\sigma_i^*, \sigma_{-i}^*) \geq u_i(\sigma_i, \sigma_{-i}^*) \quad \forall \quad \sigma_i \in S_i \tag{3.1}$$

The Nash equilibrium can also be described as the intersection of *best-response functions.* In a two-player game a best-response function maps the other player's actions into the player's own actions. It asks: *Given the other player's strategy what strategy will maximize my payoff?* In the prisoner's dilemma the best-response function tells the Row player to defect if Column cooperates because $T > R$, and to defect if Column defects because $P > S$. Since the game is symmetrical the same reasoning holds for Column. Hence in the Nash equilibrium both players will defect. In the prisoner's dilemma the Nash equilibrium is unique but in general this has not to be the case.[45]

3.2 Dilemma Problems

Having introduced the basic concepts of game theory we now take a step back and look at the problems that we will investigate. Public good games, prisoner's dilemmas and common-pool-resource games are well-known examples of so-called dilemma problems. In dilemma problems rational in-

45 To be precise, a Nash equilibrium is an equilibrium in strategies and believes. In the prisoner's dilemma each player beliefs that the other player defects because defection always yields a higher payoff than cooperation. In coordination games the relation between strategies and beliefs becomes more clear. Suppose we have a symmetric two-player game. Each player can choose either action A or B. If both players coordinate their actions and choose the same actions each player gets a payoff of one. Otherwise they will get nothing. Further, suppose that player 1 beliefs that player 2 will play A, so it is reasonable for player 1 to also choose A. Now there are two possibilities. Either player 1's beliefs are correct; both players choose A and will receive a payoff of 1, resulting in a Nash equilibrium. Or player 1's beliefs are false, which is the case if player 2 chooses B. Because of her false beliefs player 1 has chosen action A, so both players receive a payoff of zero. This is not a Nash-equilibrium because either player 1 could switch to action B, or player 2 can switch to action A, both changes resulting in a Pareto-improvement for both players. In the first case player 1 recognizes that her beliefs were wrong, changes her beliefs and switches to action B because player 1 now beliefs that player 2 will play B. A similar reasoning applies to player 2.

dividuals will, by definition, not arrive at the socially optimal outcome. In public good games the public good will be undersupplied, in the prisoner's dilemma the players will defect, and in common pool resource games the resource will be overused.

The payoff structure in dilemma games exhibits externalities which are not taken into account by individual players making their decisions. The widely discussed prisoner's dilemma is a two-player public good game. Many results from the prisoner's dilemma also hold for public good games (n-player prisoner's dilemmas). Common pool resource games have a similar structure than public good games. In contrast to a public good, a common pool resource is rival in consumption, and common pool resource games face the problem of overuse because there are negative externalities in consumption. While in public good problems the dilemma concerns the supply of the public good before the good can be used, in common pool resource games the dilemma concerns the use a resource after it is supplied. Impure public goods, i.e., public goods that have a negative externality in consumption, are an intermediate case. A local park, for example, is an impure public good because everyone is free to take a walk in the park, but if it gets too crowded, the enjoyment of the walk in the park decreases. Since our focus is on the provision of pure public goods, what follows will be centered around prisoner's dilemma and public good games.

3.2.1 The Prisoner's Dilemma

The prisoner's dilemma is a two-player game which already was introduced above (figures 3.1 and 3.2). It is assumed that $T > R > P > S$ and $2R > T + S$. There are two players facing monetary payoffs as stated in figure 3.2. The first number in each cell is the payoff for Row, the second the payoff for Column. Both players only care about their own monetary payoffs.[46] Each player arrives at her best outcome if she defects while the other player cooperates. And if the other player would defect, the best response is to defect too. No matter what action my opponent chooses, defection will yield a higher payoff than cooperation. Defection dominates cooperation. Payoffs are symmetrical, hence both players engage in the same reasoning and will defect. Mutual defection is a suboptimal outcome because both players could have gained a payoff of R if they had coordinated their actions of mutual cooperation.

46 This assumption will be changed in section 3.5.3 where we consider social preferences.

3.2.2 Public Good Games

Assume that there is a group of n players. Each player has an endowment of e_i which can be used for private consumption or can be contributed to a public good. Denote each player's contribution to the public good by c_i, where $0 \leq c_i \leq e_i$. All players make their decisions simultaneously. The payoff for each player i in the group is given by equation 3.2 where $0 < \nu < 1 < n\nu$.

$$\pi_i = e_i - c_i + \nu \sum_{j=1}^{n} c_j \tag{3.2}$$

The *marginal per capita return* (MPCR) from a contribution to the public good is smaller than the marginal per capita return to private consumption, $\nu < 1$. It is individually rational to allocate all resources to private consumption and to contribute nothing to the public good. Free-riding is the dominant strategy and we will have $c_i = 0$ for all players. In this unique Nash equilibrium each player earns a payoff of e_i. To see that the Nash equilibrium is not Pareto-optimal consider the situation in which all players contribute all their resouces to the public good, $c_i = e_i$. The total amount of the public good is ne_i which yields utility νne_i for each player. Since $\nu n > 1$ each player would be better off.[47]

In public good experiments we do not observe free-riding, as predicted by theory, but we observe that subjects contribute a significant fraction of their endowment. Subjects contribute about half of their endowment at the beginning of the game, but over time contributions decline. Also, we observe that higher contributions in experiments with a higher marginal per capita return (MPCR). We will come back to public good experiments in relation to our experiment in section 6.1.1. For excellent surveys of the experimental economics literature on linear public good games the reader is referred to Croson (2007) and Holt and Laury (2008).

3.3 Three Solutions to Dilemma Problems

The prisoner's dilemma illustrates a situation of strategic interdependence. The payoff for Row is not determined by Row's strategy but is dependent on

47 For the purposes of our thesis it is sufficient to consider only linear public good games. The conditions for the efficent provision of public goods go back to Samuelson (1954), a detailed treatment can be found in Mas-Colell et al. (1995).

Column's strategy. In order to arrive at the optimal outcome the players have to coordinate their actions. Coordination can be achieved in a centralized or decentralized way. In order to arrive at the optimal outcome players have to coordinate their actions on both playing C, foregoing a possible short-run gain. This section discusses three solutions (central authority, markets, self-organizing communities) that are prominent in the literature (see e.g., Bowles, 2004).

3.3.1 A Central Authority

Thomas Hobbes' Leviathan (1651) is the most famous example for centralized control. In the *state of nature* there is a war of all against all, corresponding to mutual defection. A social contract establishes a strong central authority and subordinates all people. The state as a central authority has the exclusive right to punish defectors, hence the payoffs are altered and the dilemma structure is changed because the payoff to defection is reduced.

If a public good is supplied by the state an efficent provison of the public good can be achieved. Two problems associated with this solution concern (i) information and (ii) individual freedom. For an efficient provision of a public good by the state it has to be assumed that the state knows the quality and quantity of the public good desired by its citizens (i.e., hte state has to know the true preferences). As information is distributed in society it is often costly or even impossible for the central authority to collect all relevant information. As a result of having only incomplete information the central authority will not be able to determine and implement the socially optimal outcome (Mas-Colell et al., 1995, p. 356). Secondly, if the central authority uses its legal power it constrains people's individual freedom which is problematic from a moral point of view. Since in social production communities no central authority exists, we do not discuss this point any further.

3.3.2 Internalize External Effects by Redefining Property Rights

Two decentralized mechanisms solving the free-rider problem and achieving an efficient provision of the public good are markets and self-organizing communities. In general, a public good will not be supplied by the market if its price equals its marginal cost. However, by making a public good excludable the public good can be transformed into a private good and consequently will be supplied by the market. This solution is only possible if

exclusion by property rights is effective so that external effects can be internalized (Coase, 1960).

Through the definition of property rights knowledge can be made excludable and producers can appropriate the rent by charging a price above marginal cost. The public good will be supplied by private companies interacting in the regulated market because they are able to cover their costs. Through trade secrets, patents, and copyrights knowledge can be protected and the producers of knowledge can enjoy the fruits of their innovative activity over a limited period of time. Innovators now receive profits which derive from the commercial value of knowledge. The system of patents provides incentives for private companies to engage in innovative activity and produce a gain in dynamic efficiency. This gain, however, implies that there are losses in static efficiency, resulting from the underutilization of knowledge. Due to the patent, knowledge can be sold at a positive price, i.e., the price is above marginal cost. Gains from dynamic efficiency and losses from static inefficiency can be balanced by varying the duration of the patent (Stiglitz, 1999). A longer duration implies that innovators will receive higher profits at the cost of having an inefficient allocation of knowledge for a longer period of time. In addition to the loss in static efficiency due to the underutilization of knowledge there are two other negative external effect of intellectual property rights. (1) Intellectual property rights can give rise to patent races in which private companies compete in research and development. Since property right will only be granted to the winner of this competition the duplication of effort is a social inefficiency. (2) If information, culture and knowledge are the inputs for the production of more information, culture and knowledge, stronger property rights makes the acquisition of inputs more expensive and will, ceteris paribus, slow down the speed of innovation or production of new information (see also p. 13 in Arrow, 1959). This was already emphasized in section 2.1.1 discussing the recombinant nature of information and digital goods. Since in social production communities no attempts are made to define property rights and to exclude anyone from using the publicly available product, we do not discuss the internalization of external effects any further.

3.3.3 Self-Organizing Communities

In many cases public goods are supplied by self-organizing communities. Social production is but one example for the voluntary provision of public

goods by self-organizing communities. The term self-organizing community goes back to Elinor Ostrom and her work on common pool resources (Ostrom, 1990).[48] In various field studies she observed that self-organizing communities have institutions that prescribe certain types of behavior. Ostrom defines institutions as "the set of working rules that are used to determine who is eligible to make decisions in some arena, what actions are allowed or constrained, what aggregation rules will be used, what procedures must be followed, what information must or must not be provided, and what payoffs will be assigned to individuals dependent on their actions" (Ostrom, 1990, p.51). The presence of institutionally prescribed behavior, however, is not sufficient. Institutions have to be enforced by rewarding behavior in accordance with the institution and/or punishing deviation. But in contrast to the centralized solution, in self-organizing communities there is no external agent who monitors behavior and punishes anti-social behavior. As Ostrom puts it: "The immediate issue is that a self-organized group must solve the commitment problem without an external enforcer. They have to motivate themselves (or their agents) to monitor activities and be willing to impose sanctions to keep conformance high" (Ostrom, 1990, p.44). The enforcement of the institution is associated with private costs and creates a public benefit, hence it has itself dilemma structure. Self-organizing communities are somehow able to solve this second-order dilemma. They use their experience to craft enforceable institutions. Often all community members are involved in crafting the institutional rules, and most times they unanimously agree on a rule (Ostrom, 1990, p.65). This is very similar to communication in social production communities with a high degree of mental proximity (Sacchetti and Sugden, 2009). Key features of robust institutions are low costs of monitoring and private benefits allocated to those who monitor (Ostrom, 1990, p.94-96). Institutional rules are defined in such a way as to resolve the dilemma structure by changing the incentives in the second-order dilemma. Consequently, the second-order dilemma is resolved and the community is able to enforce the institution.

48 Ostrom mainly focuses on the dilemma problem associated with common pool resources. In contrast to common pool resources, (pure) public goods exhibit no crowding out effects. Public goods are nonrival in consumption hence the problem of overuse disappears but and we can concentrate on the problem of underprovision. Most forms of social production are public good problems which are solved by self-organizing communities.

3.4 Empirical Studies of Contributors and Their Motives

In the previous section we have argued that social production communities are examples of self-organizing communities. In this section we take a closer look at the communities and ask: *Who contributes and why?* To answer this question we present empirical studies on contributors' characteristics and their motives.

A fraction of contributors to open source software are software developers working for private companies. Those developers receive monetary compensation although they contribute to a public good. The companies benefit from the availability of high-quality open source software since they sell complementary services. For the companies it is rational to contribute to the public good. According to Lerner et al. (2006) private companies are more likely to contribute to large open-source projects. Using a panel dataset tracking about one hundred open-source projects for about two years they estimate that cooperate contributions are 22 percent in the smallest quartile and 44 percent in the largest quartile. We omit any discussion of private companies' motivations and confine our analysis to the motivations of individual contributors who receive no direct monetary compensation.

Bitzer and Geishecker (2010) analyze survey data from German IT employees, i.e., their sample consists of both contributors and non-contributors. According to their findings young, male individuals who are university dropouts or unemployed are more likely to contribute while education and degree seems to have no effect on individuals' willingness to contribute. It could be that university dropouts are more likely to contribute because of a lack of job-satisfaction, but it could also be that contributing to open source software prevents them from obtaining a degree. Also, the number of work hours is negatively correlated with the probability to contribute, indicating that most contributions are made during leisure time. The aim of Bitzer and Geishecker's study was to identify the characteristics of employees who contribute to OSS but they state that "regardless of how we describe typical OSS contributors based on observable characteristics, it is also important to note the limitation of our model. With a pseudo-R^2 of only around 16 percent, the most important determinants of voluntary OSS contributions remain unidentified since factors relating to the intrinsic motivations of individuals to voluntary contribute to OSS, such as fun or peer respect, are unobserved" (Bitzer and Geishecker, 2010, p.169). The study by Bitzer and Geishecker points to the limitations of empirical survey studies.

Another empirical study on individual contributions to social production is a study by Franke and Shah (2003) on user-led innovation. Franke and Shah conducted qualitative interviews and questionaire studies with lead-users from four sporting communities. Within the communities no individual received direct monetary compensation. In fact, monetary rewards as incentives were explicitely rejected. Asked for the reasons for giving assistance to others in the community respondents reported the following reasons, listed in descending order of importance: "(1) It is my opinion that in a community, one should assist others; (2) It is fun to create something jointly; (3) In my community there is the norm that members should assist each other free of charge; (4) If I assist others today, I will receive assistance in the future; (5) I enjoy giving others advice as an expert; (6) I wanted to use the product itself; (7) It was nice to receive recognition; (8) I was paid well for my assistance" (Franke and Shah, 2003, p.170).

Similar results are obtained from Hertel et al. (2003) who conducted an internet-based questionaire study with 141 Linux kernel contributors. They summarize their results as follows: "The main motivational factors were (a) a more general identification factor as a Linux user, (b) a more specific identification factor as a Linux developer or with a Linux subsystem, (c) pragmatic motives related to the improvement of one's own software and career advantages, (d) norm-oriented motives related to reactions of relevant others (family, friends, colleagues), (e) social and political motives related to supporting independent software and networking within the Linux community, (f) hedonistic motives such as pure enjoyment of programming, (g) and motivational obstacles related to time losses due to Linux-related activities." (Hertel et al., 2003, p.1174)

We take the just-mentioned studies as representative since other empirical studies about contributors' motivations (e.g., Lerner and Tirole, 2002, and Bitzer et al., 2007) arrive at similar results. Based on the empirical studies we can infer several facts.

First, we observe that *use value* is an important selective incentive for users (see 6 and c). Second, *intrinsic motivation* is another incentive inducing contributions to the public good (5 and f). Third, the importance of team identity, established through identification with the community and the joy of creating something collaboratively is emphasized (2, a, b and d). Fourth, political motives (giving rise to a certain ideology, like Stallman's position described in sections 2.3.3.a and 3.5.3.b) are mentioned (e). The last two points, team identity and ideology, are explanations for *altruistic behavior*. We discuss al-

truism, together with *reciprocity*, which is identified as another motive (1, 3, 4 and d), in section 3.5.3 on *social preferences*. Lastly, there are recognition (7) and career advantages (c), which discuss in detail in the next chapter on social approval. Note that social approval is not explicitely mentioned in both studies. However, as Lerner et al. (2006) observe, giving credit is crucial: "Open-source projects are scrupulous about keeping track of contributors, which reflect the fact that giving credit to authors is essential in the open-source movement" (p. 116). Eric Raymond, one of the key figures in the open source movement, confirms the importance of social approval and argues that the role of social approval is underestimated (Raymond, 2001). Many contributors resist the ego explanation and show a strong reluctance to admit that their behavior is motivated by a desire for social approval. The culture "distrusts and despises egotism and ego-based motivations" (p. 14) and teaches that ego-satisfaction is a bad. "Only sublimated and disguised forms like 'peer repute', 'self-esteem', 'professionalism' or 'pride of accomplishment' are generally acceptable" (Raymond, 2001, p.14). The importance of social approval is reaffirmed by William Quiviger, head of the European Mozilla Community, stating that open communication and social approval are the key determinants of successful open source communities (Tißler, 2009). Although some useful information can be obtained from the survey studies, these studies have to be treated with caution because there are strong reasons to believe that social approval is underestimated.

3.5 Why Contribute?

In a public good game free-riding is the dominant strategy for rational individuals. The only way to solve this dilemma is by changing the payoffs which can be done by changing players' utility functions or by introducing selective incentives (or a combination of both). One obvious candidate is use value as a selective incentive. If the benefit from use value outweighs the cost of contributing, rational individuals will contribute. We discuss use value in section 3.5.1. Changing players utility function is done by introducing intrinsic motivation or social preferences. By considering intrinsic motivation we argue that players derive a private benefit from the activity of contributing. Intrinsic motivation will be discussed in section 3.5.2. By considering social preferences utility functions are changed since players take into account the payoffs of others. The most important social preferences for our analysis

are altruism and reciprocity. A preference for altruism can be the result of team identity so that players take into account the team's payoff in addition to their own payoff. Pure altruism, however, cannot explain the voluntary provision of public goods in large groups, as we explain below.

Reciprocity is the second social preference which we discuss. The basic idea of reciprocity is to respond to other's behavior likewise. In social dilemma games reciprocity means that cooperative behavior will be rewarded while free-riding will be punished. In social production communities two forms of reciprocal behavior can be distinguished. The first form of reciprocity is a contribution to the public good as a response to other people's contributions, known also as conditional cooperation (Fischbacher et al., 2001; Frey and Meier, 2004). The second form of reciprocity is the exchange of non-monetary rewards, often in the form of social approval, which is directed at a particular contributor. We argue that this second form of reciprocity (in which social approval is given to a contributor and increases the contributor's private benefit) is more effective for inducing higher contributions because (i) the cost of giving social approval is relatively low compared to the cost of a contribution, and (ii) the benefit from social approval is a private benefit for a contributor, instead of a public benefit.

3.5.1 Use Value

Ideas for new products or new products themselves originate either from a single individual or from a small group of individuals, as we have seen in chapter 2. These individuals are users of the products which they invented or customized, suggesting that use value is a potential explanation for contributions to social production communities.

Use value is often the driving force for starting a new project (Bitzer et al., 2007). In user-led innovation this is the case if an existing product is customized. Products available on the market do not fulfill the users' personal needs. For a specific task no product might be available, or the products that are available are defective or inappropriate for this specific task (Faulkner and Runde, 2009). Information about users' personal needs is sticky and cannot easily be acquired by private companies, leading to a persistent information asymmetry (see section 2.2.2). The stickiness of information and the resulting information asymmetry implies that users cannot hire somebody else to supply the product. By customizing an existing product users innovate and supply information about their personal needs. The new infor-

mation supplied by the user-community is a public good since it is nonrival and nonexcludable. In principle, the information can be digitized and made available as a digital good (e.g., providing the information on the internet like DIY instructions).

The role of users as innovators, generating new ideas which producers can incorporate has been discussed in section 2.2.1. For goods with high marginal costs (non-digital goods) it is often the case that users supply new information about their needs which is used by firms who incorporate the information and manufacture the product. If the product itself, and not just the information about users' needs and ideas, is a digital good, this is different because the complete production process resides within the social production community. The prime example is open source software. Open source communities supply both the ideas about users' needs and the product itself. This is possible because software in particular, and digital goods in general, are infinitely expandable. In both cases, however, the initial decision is triggered by the expectation that use value can be derived from the innovation.

Users who are dissatisfied with existing products innovate. They derive a benefit from the innovation because the innovation is customized to their personal needs. In fact, users have heterogeneous needs suggesting that there is much room for customization and innovation (von Hippel, 2005, Chapter 3). Empirical evidence for use value as the driving force behind innovation is found in Lerner and Tirole (2002) who discuss several cases in which use value was the driving force behind innovation in open source. The development of the Apache server software was initiated by Brian Behlendorf because he was frustrated with the software that he was using (a Unix-based software written at the National Center for Supercomputer Applications) and there was no alternative available on the market. In a similar way, the absence of viable alternative solutions stimulated the development of Perl and Sendmail. Perl, developed by Larry Wall, is a programming language that software developers use for tasks related to system administration. The Sendmail applicaton allows networks with different communication protocols to communicate. It was developed by Eric Allman while facing the imcompatibility of two computer networks at Berkeley. Further evidence for use value being a plausible explanation for the emergence of open source projects is found in Raymond (2001) mentioning different mail-clients that were developed as solution to an existing problem. In describing his experience with open source projects Raymond generalizes the importance of use value in his principles 1, "Every good work of software starts by scratching

a developer's personal itch.", and 18 "To solve an interesting problem, start by finding a problem that is interesting to you" (p. 49).

Although the preceeding examples illustrate that use value drives user-innovation in many cases, there are exceptions to the rule. The Linux kernel is such an exception because it was started by Linus Torvalds mostly out of intellectual curiosity (Lerner and Tirole, 2002). In fact, Torvalds biography is called *Just for Fun* (Torvalds and Diamond, 2001), indicating that fun was one of the main reason to start Linux.

Although use value is an important motive for starting a project, there are two puzzles. The first puzzle concerns the relation between use value and free revealing. As we will see, this puzzle can be solved. The second puzzle shows that there is a large number of contributions which cannot be concealed with an explanation based on use value because these contributions (e.g., documentation) have only small effects on use value.

First, it could be argued that use value cannot explain free-revealing. Users who innovate could sell the innovation instead of giving it away for free. At a first sight, an explanation based on use value cannot explain why innovators refrain from using property rights to protect the innovation and reap the benefits. However, protection through property rights is expensive and not very effective, as Harhoff et al. (2003) point out (see also section 2.2.4). Because of high costs and ineffectiveness free revealing becomes more attractive. High costs and ineffectiveness of copyright protection can explain why innovations are not protected, but it cannot explain why social production communities actively spread their innovations by advertising them on newsgroups and the like. This suggests that there are additional benefits associated with free revealing. Free revealing results in higher rates of adoption, increasing the speed of diffusion and attracts more contributors. If we accept the argument that free revaling increases use value through inducing further innovations, use value can explain free revealing. This argument, however, does not imply that use value is the only incentive.

Second, use value cannot explain why members of open source communities care for their projects after the initial problem is solved. Use value cannot explain why members of social production communities engage in tasks that are of relatively limited immediate use, like administration and documentation. Use value cannot explain why users who did not initiate the project give assistance to others. Franke and Shah (2003) empirically investigate why members of sporting communities contribute to the community's innovation process by giving assistance. The use value explanation "I wanted

to use the product myself" ranked only sixth (p. 170). More important than personal benefits, like use value, recognition and pay, were community benefits, like the fun of creating something together and adhering to the norms of the community.

We see that use value can explain why user-led innovation and open source software are there in the first place. Use value is crucial at the beginning of a project and is an important motivation for a subgroup of contributors, namely founders or initiators. Use value, however, cannot explain why communities are successful over long periods of time and why members of the community devote their efforts to tasks like administration and documentation.[49]

3.5.2 Intrinsic Motivation

It is often claimed that intrinsic motivation is key to understanding the success of open source communities (Raymond, 2001; Benkler, 2006; Benkler and Nissenbaum, 2006; Hertel et al., 2003; Osterloh et al., 2001; Bitzer et al., 2007). The authors argue that contributors derive intrinsic motivation from contributing to an open source project. Support for this claim comes from empirical studies (Hertel et al., 2003; Franke and Shah, 2003) revealing that there is such a thing as the "pure enjoyment of programming". People are said to be intrinsically motivated if they derive enjoyment from carrying out an activity instead of deriving enjoyment from the outcome ot the activity. Altough intrinsic motivation is important it is only necessary but not sufficient. As we will explain later in this chapter, only intrinsic motivation together with social approval can provide a convincing account for the success of open source communities because social approval explains why intrinsic motivation is high. Before that, we will explain the core idea underlying the concept of intrinsic motivation.[50]

Let us assume a situation in which extrinsic incentives are absent. If an individual engages in intrinsically motivated activities there is no apparent

49 Of course there are projects which are never complete (e.g., the use value of Wikipedia can always be increased by adding a new article), but generally use value will cease to be important over time. Especially in open source software there are contributions which solve a problem that has already been solved, but the new contribution solves the problem more efficiently or more elegantly. Contributions which carry only small, incremental use value, cannot be explained by use value because the cost of the contribution exceeds use value, hence there have to be other incentives.

50 An in-depth introduction to intrinsic motivation can be found in Edward Deci's seminal contributions (Deci, 1975; Deci and Ryan, 1985).

reward except the activity itself. The engagement in the activity is an end rather than means to an end. The reward comes from within the individual if she engages in an intrinsically motivated activity.

An activity is perceived as intrinsically rewarding if it satisfies the individual's psychological needs and desires. According to psychological research (especially cognitive evaluation theory and self-attribution theory, see chapter 2 in Deci, 1975, and the references therein, and Fehr and Falk, 2002) humans have a tendency towards self-determination, mastery, and development. Feelings of self-determination, mastery, and development result from being in control of one's fate, i.e., being able to effectively act on one's environment. Autonomy and competence are key. If the individual chooses her challenge herself, and if she successfully reaches her self-selected goal, feelings of self-determination, mastery, and development are induced. These feelings are intrinsic rewards and increase intrinsic motivation.[51]

In order to obtain intrinsic rewards individuals will seek out activities that are challenging. If the activity is too easy, engaging in it will be boring and provide no stimulation. If the activity is too hard, engaging in it will not result in feelings of competence and mastery. Hence, intrinsic motivation "leads people to situations which provide challenges which make optimal use of their abilities" (Deci, 1975, p.57). Here we implicitely assume that success is strongly correlated with own effort so that mastery of the challenge can be attributed to the individual's effort and individuals can take pride in their own work.

Intrinsic motivation is affected by external stimuli. External stimuli can be the controlling influence of your supervisor looking over your shoulder, a wage payment or a fine, or any non-monetary reward or punishment that comes from someone else. If an external stimulus is introduced, motivation can either increase or decrease. The overall effect on motivation is referred to as Crowding-In and Crowding-Out. For a detailed discussion of Crowding theory the interested reader is referred to Deci and Ryan (1985), Frey and Jegen (2001) and Bénabou and Tirole (2003).[52]

Crowding-Out and Crowding-In can be explained by cognitive evaluation theory or self-attribution theory. According to *cognitive evaluation theory* intrinsic motivation decreases because the individual's needs for self-

51 Interestingly, an idea similar to intrinsic motivation can be found in Veblen's writings where he refers to the *instinct of workmanship* and *idle curiosity* (1994/1899).

52 A related aspect, which we do not discuss here, is the effect of self-confidence and self-esteem on intrinsic motivation (Bénabou and Tirole, 2000, 2002).

determination, competence and autonomy are reduced if rewards like money are perceived as controlling. *Self-perception theory* takes a different route by arguing that individuals search for reasons why they perform a task. If monetary incentives are present there is self-attribution to extrisic motivation since money is salient (see section 4 in Fehr and Falk, 2002).[53]

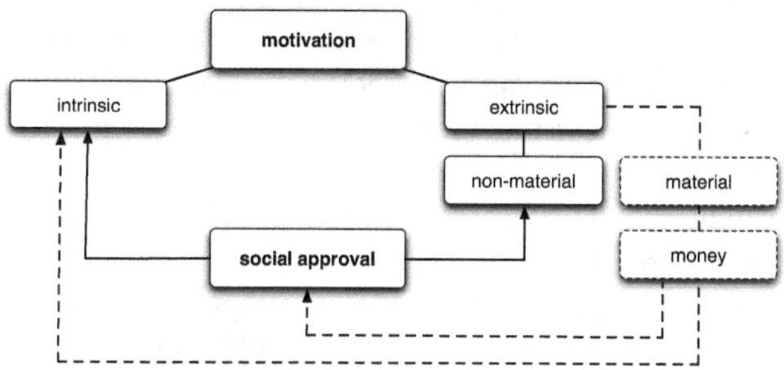

Figure 3.3: Interdependencies between social approval, money, and motivation; adapted from Frey (2010, p.12); dashed lines because monetary rewards are absent in social production.

The interdependencies between social approval, money and motivation are illustrated in figure 3.3. Motivation is differentiated into intrinsic and extrinsic motivation. Intrinsic and extrinsic motivation are affected by material and non-material incentives. Money and social approval are examples of material and nonmaterial incentives which we use for purposes of illustration. Money increases extrinsic motivation through its nature as an extrinsic reward, but also affects intrinsic motivation. In general, the effect of material rewards on intrinsic motivation depends on how the rewards are perceived. Consider the example of a wage-increase. The employee's extrinsic motivation will increase. If the wage-increase is perceived as an expression of the employer's regard for the employee's abilities intrinsic motivation will also increase. But if the wage-increase is perceived as reducing autonomy and self-determination, intrinsic motivation will be reduced. The overall effect on motivation depends on the effect of the material reward (the wage-increase) on intrinsic and extrinsic motivation. Crowding-Out refers to a situation in which the negative effect on intrinsic motivation exceeds the positive effect on extrinsic motivation, resulting in a decrease in overall

53 For a specific example in which both Crowding-Out and Crowding-In can occur the reader is refered to Menges and Traub (2009) who investigate the willingness to donate to the public good "green electricity".

motivation. Crowding-In refers to a situation in which the overall effect on motivation is positive.

Of interest to us is the link between social approval and money. By receiving social approval individuals can signal their quality to others (e.g., workers signaling their ability to potential employers) which might result in higher incomes in the future. We will examine signaling in more detail in section 4.1.2.

Monetary compensation or controlling influences decrease feelings of self-determination and consequentially reduce intrinsic motivation. Overall motivation decreases although monetary compensation has been increased. Since the vast majority of participants in social production do not receive monetary compensation we will neglect the influence from money on motivation (the dashed lines in figure 3.3). Much more important for us is the interaction between social approval and motivation. Social approval is a positive feedback resulting in a sense of belonging and recognition on the receiver's side and will increase, or crowd-in, intrinsic motivation.

In social production monetary incentives are absent, allowing us to focus on intrinsic motivation and the effects of non-material incentives on intrinsic motivation. There is no formal hierarchy, not much controlling influences, and a high degree of mental proximity suggesting that the individual's desires for self-determination and competence are likely to be fulfilled. As a result, individuals' intrinsic motivation will be high. Also, there are many opportunities for communication and to express social approval. This positive feedback will further increase intrinsic motivation (Deci, 1975, p. 144). The empirical results mentioned above (Franke and Shah, 2003, and Hertel et al., 2003) reveal that individuals derive a sense of pride from contributing, suggesting that the enjoyment of the activity is high.

A particular intrinsic reward satisfying individual's need for competence and self-determination is the reward from learning. Learning is the improvement of the individual's skills and enlargement of her capacity as a result of her engagement in a particular activity. Learning belongs to intrinsic motivation since it is a reward that is independent from the activity's outcome. The reward is process-oriented rather than outcome-oriented. Learning increases competence and the capacity to deal effectively with your environment (Deci, 1975). By writing a contribution to the Linux kernel, for example, I learn the programming language, regardless of the quality of my contribution. However, contributors do not work in isolation and contributions attract social approval from other members of the community. This makes it

hard to separate the motivation derived from learning from the motivation derived from social approval.

Summarizing this section we can say that intrinsic motivation is high in social production since social production is organized in such a way that contributing satisfies the individual's desire for self-determination, mastery, and development. Intrinsic motivation is likely to be high because of the absence of any controlling influences, self-selection of tasks, and the large number of ways in which social approval can be exchanged, which crowds-in motivation.

3.5.3 Social Preferences

Experimental findings reveal that in market-style interactions subjects behave competitive only caring about their own payoff (for example Roth and Erev, 1995). In more personal settings, however, subjects do not behave as predicted by rational self-interest (for example Blinder and Choi, 1990, and Falk et al., 2003). How can these two opposing findings be reconciled? Theories of social preferences (Rabin, 1993; Fehr and Schmidt, 1999; Bolton and Ockenfels, 2000; Charness and Rabin, 2002) reconcile these findings by assuming that there are some individuals that care not only about their own payoff but also about other players' payoffs. Not necessarily all but some individuals have altruistic preferences, or preferences for fairness or equity. In addition, individuals are motivated by reciprocity, meaning that they treat others who behave fair in a nice way while punishing those who behave unfair. Depending on the situation there are more or less individuals with social preferences. In a competitive market or auction, for example, most individuals will only care about their own payoff and not about other players' payoffs. In this section we discuss altruism and reciprocity, two forms of social preferences which are particularly relevant in social production communities. First we introduce altruism, distinguish between pure and impure altruism, and discuss altruism in social production; then we introduce a general model for social preferences, taken from Charness and Rabin (2002), and discuss the role of reciprocity in social production.

3.5.3.a Altruism

Contributions to a public good can be considered to be based on altruism. Altruistic behavior has always been a fundamental puzzle to biologists and

economists since it is not clear how altruistic behavior can survive in a competitive environment (Trivers, 1971; West et al., 2006). A solution has been proposed by William D. Hamilton's theory of kin selection (Hamilton, 1964a,b). By helping a relative an individual increases the chances that the relative will survive and her genes will be passed on to the next generation. Behavior that is altruistic from the viewpoint of the individual is actually selfish from the viewpoint of the gene. In this way, altruistic behavior among relatives can be explained. In biological settings the theory of kin selection is plausible, for concrete examples see West et al. (2006, p.482).

Consider a player who contributes to a public good. The player behaves altruistically if her behavior increases everyones payoff. If she contributes ten dollars to the public good, she behaves altruistically because she bears the cost in that her personal consumption is lowered by ten dollars, and a benefit is transferred to everyone since the supply of the public good is increased. Altruistic behavior tells us nothing about the underlying motives but it is often assumed that altruism among humans is associated with one's positive concern for others based on love, team identity, ethical and moral beliefs. Altruism is said to be paternalistic if an individual's utility depends on the goods and services that others consume (not the utility that others derive from their consumption). Altruism is said to be nonpaternalistic if an individual's utility depends not only on her own utility but also on others' utility. Formally, nonpaternalistic altruism results from interdependent utility functions. For example, consider my contribution to AllRecipes.com. My contribution is based on paternalistic altruism if I contributed because I think that everyone would be better off if everyone would use my recipe. But if I contributed because I think that my recipe helps others to get well-fed, my contribution is based on nonpaternalistic altruism.[54]

Regardless of the underlying motives, a contribution to a public good is said to be *pure altruism* if the contribution results from demand for the public good (i.e., if individuals contribute because the benefit from the public good outweighs the cost of contributing). A contribution to a public good is said to be *impure altruism* if the contribution not only increases the supply of the public good but also results in a private benefit for the contributor.[55]

54 This work goes back to Becker (1974) discussing altruism in the context of the family. Another area building upon altruism are intergenerational models (see Arrow (1973) for paternalistic altruism and Ray (1987) for nonpaternalistic altruism in an intergenerational context).

55 For the sake of completeness: If an individual contributes to a public good and is motivated only by the warm glow her contribution is said to be *purely egoistic*.

In models of impure altruism a component capturing a player's private gain from behaving altruistically is added. This is illustrated in the following two models of impure altruism.

Warm Glows (Andreoni, 1990): In Andreoni's model of impure altruism (1990) contributing to a public good results in a private benefit, called *the warm glow of giving*. Utility increases in the player's own contribution.

$$u_i = u_i(x_i, PG, c_i) \tag{3.3}$$

In equation 3.3, $x_i = e_i - c_i$ is private consumption, e_i denotes the endowment, ν is the marginal per capita return, $PG = \nu \sum_{i=1}^{n} c_i$ is the public good, and c_i is the individual's contribution. It is assumed that the utility function is concave. The utility function differs from the traditional utility function because a player's contribution enters twice. First, a player's contribution enters as a contribution to the public good, generating utility for all players. Second, a player's contribution enters as a private benefit that is derived from the act of giving or the feeling resulting from this act. Taking endowment and others' contributions as given we can maximize equation 3.3 and derive a donation function. The donation function reveals that players contribute for both egoistic and altruistic reasons. Under certain conditions a unique Nash-equilibrium can be derived (Andreoni, 1990, p.467). Contributions will be higher than without the warm glow of giving but will still be below the social optimum.

Moral Self-Image (Brekke et al., 2003): In Andreoni (1990) contributions to the public good are higher because there is an additional reward called the warm glow. The warm glow is a reward that comes from the individual herself, i.e., the reward is an intrinsic motivation. Andreoni does not model the source of the warm glow, he simply assumes that people experience warm glows. Brekke et al. (2003) model the source of the warm glow and thereby explain the presence of intrinsic motivation. In the model by Brekke et al. individuals have an identity or self-image. A warm glow or intrinsic motivation is then the utility that a player experiences when behaving in accordance with her self-image. The player's actual choice is the result of a tradeoff between the benefit from conforming to her own ideal behavior and the cost of acting in conformance with her ideal behavior. Formally, each individual i maximizes her utility subject to a time constraint.

$$\max_{L_i} u(x_i, L_i, PG, I_i) \quad \text{subject to} \quad c_i + L_i = \bar{L}$$

Inidviduals contribute time to the public good, where $\bar{L}$ denotes the maximum amount of time available, c_i denotes the contribution (measured in units of time) and L_i denotes leisure time. PG refers to the amount of the public good that is supplied, x_i is private consumption, and I_i is individual i's self-image. Labor supply and income are exogenously fixed and the utility function is increasing and strictly quasi-concave. The individual's self image suffers when the actual contribution, c_i, and the morally ideal contribution, c_i^* diverge, which is captured by the following function (where ξ is a positive constant).

$$I_i = -\xi(c_i - c_i^*)^2$$

Before deciding how much time to contribute to the public good individual i computes her morally ideal contribution by maximizing a social welfare function (the unweighted sum of all players' utilities) subject to the production function of the public good and subject to the assumption that all players contribute the same amount of time to the public good at the social optimum ($c_i^* = c_j^* \, \forall \, i,j \, \in \{1,2,...,n\}$).

In defining a measure of the individual's self-image as a morally responsible person caring about her self-image Brekke et al. go one step further than Andreoni (1990). However, the model by Brekke et al. also predicts underprovision because the marginal benefit of an additional contribution approaches zero as contributions become closer to the morally optimal behavior.

3.5.3.b Pure Altruism and Social Production

Much of the early literature on the motives of open source participants explains contributions by altruism (see Lerner and Tirole, 2002; Wichmann, 2002; van Wendel de Joode, 2005). The question that runs through the rest of this section is the following: Do contributors have altruistic preferences? If yes, how important are altruistic preferences compared to competing explanations for the private provision of public goods in social production communities. Altruistic behavior can result from a set of moral and ideology, from team identity, and patternalism, as already mentioned above. In the following we describe morals and ideology, and team identity in relation to social production before we point out two shortcomings.

Morals & Ideology: If we accept an explanation based on altruism, we would argue that developers write open source software because they care

about others' well-being. Why should this be the case? First, there is an argument along the lines of Richard Stallman, founder of the Free Software Foundation (FSF). The FSF's emphasis is on the individual's freedom to copy and re-use the software. The FSF claims that software that is not free, according to the FSF guidelines and the Copyleft License (see chapter 2), restricts individual's freedom and thus is bad for moral reasons. According to the principles of the FSF developers should make their software freely available because otherwise they would restrict others' freedom. Stallman's original manifesto[56] certainly is indicative of the altruism explanation. He compares sharing code to helping your neighbor putting out a fire (Weber, 2004). Stallman's argument explains the existence of altruism by a shared moral code prescribing that software should be free. A small number of open source developers might be ideologically motivated. Along the lines of Stallman they believe that proprietary software is unsocial, unethical, and that software should be free, but it is implausible that the majority of contributors is motivated by ideology.

Team Identity: A second explanation for the existence of altruistic preferences is team identity. Identification as a member of a particular social production community was shown to be an important factor in the empirical studies mentioned at the beginning of this chapter. In discussing the problem of shirking which arises in team production Alchian and Demsetz (1972) emphasize team identity. They define team identity as all members of a team pursuing a common interest. Establishing team identity can be thought of as a change in the utility function. Team identity is high (low) if team members put a high (low) weight on the common interest. With team identity being high contributions to the public good will be higher. In game theoretic terms, we could say that the utility to contributing has increased. This could be the case because the creation of team identity affected the parameters for social preferences in the player's utility function.

The importance of team identity becomes obvious by looking at team sports, but in private businesses it is harder to establish a team identity. "The difficulty, of course, is to create economically that team spirit and loyalty. It can be preached with an aura of moral code of conduct – a morality with literally the same basis as the ten commandments – to restrict our conduct toward what we would choose if we bore our full costs" (Alchian and Demsetz, 1972, p. 791). The theoretical results reached by Alchian and Demsetz

56 Richard Stallman's "Philosophy of the GNU Project", available at http://www.gnu.org/philosophy/philosophy.html.

are in line with the empirical results obtained by Eckel and Grossman (2005). They investigate the relation between team identity and free-riding by conducting public good experiments framed as team production. Team identity is established in different ways, and the effect of team identity is larger if established not by simple assigments to teams but by getting team members engaged in collaborative activities. "Our results suggest that just being identified with a team is, alone, insufficient to overcome self-interest. We do find, however, that actions designed to enhance team identification contribute to higher levels of team cooperation. Working together on an unrelated and unpaid project prior to the team production task significantly enhanced the subjects' cooperative tendencies relative to their self-interest" (pp. 384-385). As the quotes from Alchian and Demsetz and Eckel and Grossman illustrate, team identity is established not by words but by deeds.

Team identity can also be the result of a common cultural background of the team's members. Individuals with similar or identical cultural backgrounds have common attitudes, values, and norms, creating group cohesion (Katzenbach and Smith, 1994; Eckel and Grossman, 2005). Typical examples of altruism deriving from a common background are kinship structures, citizens of the same country, and even individuals with similar names (Oates and Wilson, 2002). In open source communities it is likely that contributors share at least some of their interests. All members of the community are users of the same software, and all contributors have at least some background in software development, suggesting that members of open source communities share a common background. Another, but related determinant of team identity is a set of clearly defined rules and commitments (surveyed in chapter 2), defining each member's role and responsibility.

In user-led innovation team identity arises from a common interest and is furthered by personal meetings. In user-generated content and open source, web-based interaction is substituted for personal interaction. Since face-to-face interactions are rare one could suspect that it is almost impossible to establish a team identity, but as the literature on virtual teams (i.e., a temporary team whose members are geographically dispersed, culturally diverse, and use web-based communication) reveals, this is not the case. According to Jarvenpaa and Leidner (1999) team identity can be successfully established in virtual teams if the team's members engage in intense communication and exchange substantive feedback. Positive leadership, individual initiative, substantial and timely responses, and the communication of enthusiasm result in swift trust which supports team identity. Swift trust, in contrast

to trust which is established through face-to-face interactions and resides in interpersonal relations, is trust which is established on the basis of others' actions (Meyerson et al., 1996). Social production communities rely on the open exchange of information and others' actions can easily be observed. Positive leadership and intense communication is emphasized (Raymond, 2001; von Hippel, 2005), hence there are good reasons to believe that team identity is established despite the rareness of face-to-face interactions.[57]

Two Arguments Against Altruism: Taken for granted that a small number of software developers are more altruistic than others due to some kind of hacker-ethic or team identity, any explanation based on altruism is limited for the following two reasons. First, team identity is harder to establish in large groups. Even if a team identity is established in large groups, the impact of an individual contribution decreases with the size of the group, reducing the incentive to contribute. And second, an explanation based on altruism cannot explain the skewness of the size of social production communities (to be explained below).

Several successful open source projects involve a large number of participants. As Olson (1965) argues, large groups will fail to achieve an efficient provision of public goods. In a large group no individual has an incentive to contribute since the effect of her contribution will be relatively small. If one member contributes, her contribution might go unnoticed because it will have no significant impact on the value of the public good. Even if altruism can explain why you help your neighbor putting out a fire at her house, to use Stallman's analogy, altruism cannot explain why you should help a stranger at the other end of the world to put out a fire at her house (Weber, 2004, p.131).[58] A similar argument has been demonstrated by Andreoni (1988a) investigating the relationship between altruism and the private provision of public goods in large economies. Andreoni shows that as the size of the economy increases, free-riding becomes the dominant strategy. With increasing size of the economy the number of contributing individuals will de-

57 There exists a vast literature in different fields of research, emphasizing the positive relationship between social interactions and altruistic behavior. A theoretical model of the relationship between social interactions and altruistic behavior is found in Dur and Sol (2010). To the best of our knowledge, Andreoni and Rao (forthcoming) is the first experiment investigating the effect of social interaction on altruism. Further empirical support is found in the literature on psychology (Nielsen et al., 2000) and management (Price and Mueller, 1981; Mossholder et al., 2005), emphasizing the importance of social interactions for job satisfaction and team identity.

58 See Olson (1965, p.50) for individual contributions and collective goods and Brennan (1993) for an application to voting.

crease and the size of their contributions converges towards zero. Andreoni (1988a) suggests, along the lines of Olson (1965), that selective incentives like guilt, envy, sympathy or a preference for fairness must be used to explain the provision of public goods by large groups.

The size distribution of open source projects is skewed (van Wendel de Joode, 2005; Lerner et al., 2006). There is a very large number of relatively small projects and a small number of relatively large projects. The argument by Olson and Andreoni suggest that altruism cannot explain contributions in large communities, but can altruism explain contributions in small communities? This leads us to the second point. If altruism is the driving force behing the majority of contributions, we would expect to see more contributions to small projects because in large projects there is more anonymity, and it is less likely that contributors do know each other personally, indicating that the level of altruism is low. Consequently, small projects would grow faster than large projects and we would expect a size distribution of projects which is less skewed. Since this is not the case, most contributions must be made to large projects.[59]

Put differently: Team identity is important, as the empirical studies mentioned at the beginning of this chapter showed. Team identity and a common cultural background support the claim that members of social production communities have altruistic preferences. Altruism is more plausible in small communities but has problems explaining contributions to large projects. As we observe more contributors contributing to large communities (Lerner and Tirole, 2002; Lerner et al., 2006), the empirical observations are at odds with the predictions based on pure altruism.

3.5.3.c Impure Altruism and Social Production

In the preceeding section we argued that pure altruism is not a good explanation for the voluntary provision of public goods by social production communities. In this section we discuss impure altruism as an explanation, according to which individuals contribute for altruistic and egoistic reasons. Egoistic reasons are the so-called warm glows, defined as an increase in utility resulting from the act of giving in addition to the utility generated from the public good (Andreoni, 1989, 1990). Besides the just-mentioned definition Andreoni (1990) mentions guilt, and sympathy as examples of a warm

59 The growth process of open source projects can be described by preferential attachement models which go back to Yule (1925) and Simon (1955). In such models each project's growth is positively correlated with its size, generating skewed distributions.

glow. Brekke et al. (2003) are more precise by modeling a player who has a preference for her self-image. According to this logic, a warm glow increases the player's self-image. In social production communities, possible warm glows result from behavior in conformance with internalized norms, intrinsic motivation, feelings of self-regard and self-esteem. Since the importance of internalized norms and intrinsic motivation was identified in the empirical studies reviewed above (section 3.4), it is plausible that impure altruism explains part of the voluntary contributions in social production communities.

3.5.3.d Fairness, Reciprocity, and Inequality Aversion

Models of social preferences assume that players care not only about their own payoff but also care about differences in payoffs and social welfare. Adopting a model from Charness and Rabin (2002) we define a player's utility as the weighted sum of all players' payoffs (denoted by π). For two players A and B player B's utility is given by equation 3.4.

$$u_B(\pi_A, \pi_B) = (\rho_{SP} r_{SP} + \sigma_{SP} s_{SP} + \theta_{SP} q_{SP})\pi_A + (1 - \rho_{SP} r_{SP} - \sigma_{SP} s_{SP} - \theta_{SP} q_{SP})\pi_B \tag{3.4}$$

The value of the parameters r_{SP} and s_{SP} depend on player B's relative payoff with $r_{SP} = 1$ and $s_{SP} = 0$ if $\pi_B > \pi_A$ and $r_{SP} = 0$ and $s_{SP} = 1$ if $\pi_B < \pi_A$. The parameter q_{SP} depends on A's past behavior with $q_{SP} = -1$ if A misbehaved and $q_{SP} = 0$ otherwise. We can write the utility function in a more intuitive way.

$$u_B(\pi_A, \pi_B) = \begin{cases} (\rho_{SP} + \theta_{SP} q_{SP})\pi_A + (1 - \rho_{SP} - \theta_{SP} q_{SP})\pi_B & \text{if } \pi_B > \pi_A \\ (\sigma_{SP} + \theta_{SP} q_{SP})\pi_A + (1 - \sigma_{SP} - \theta_{SP} q_{SP})\pi_B & \text{if } \pi_B < \pi_A \end{cases} \tag{3.5}$$

The parameter θ_{SP} is included to take reciprocity into account, and the parameters ρ_{SP} and σ_{SP} capture "distributional preferences" which depend only on the outcome.[60] Charness and Rabin (2002, p.823-824) distinguish three cases depending on the parameters σ_{SP} and ρ_{SP}. For $\sigma_{SP} \geq \rho_{SP} \geq 0$ we have the case of *simple competitive preferences*. Player B likes her payoff to be high relative to A's payoff. For $\sigma_{SP} < 0 < \rho_{SP} < 1$ players have *difference*

60 There are no a priori restrictions on the parameters. In their paper Charness and Rabin (2002) use experimental data to estimate the three parameters θ_{SP}, ρ_{SP} and σ_{SP}. Depending on the underlying model of behavior different restrictions on the parameter values are employed in the estimation.

aversion. Players minimize the difference between payoffs aiming at payoffs that are equal. Similar models of difference aversion are Fehr and Schmidt (1999) and Bolton and Ockenfels (2000). The third case is players with *social welfare preferences* where $1 \geq \rho_{SP} \geq \sigma_{SP} > 0$. In this case B's utility increases in both players' payoffs and player B's weight on her own payoff is higher if her payoff is below player A's payoff.

Assuming that a positive fraction of individuals have social preferences voluntary contributions to a public good can be explained. Since fairness and inequality aversion are not mentioned in empirical and theoretical studies on open source but reciprocity is emphasized, the next section discusses reciprocity in relation to social production.

3.5.3.e Reciprocity in Social Production

Reciprocity is the behavioral phenomenon of responding to other's behavior likewise. Reciprocity is a contingent social preference. Depending on the behavior of a reference person a reciprocal individual values the reference person's payoff positively or negatively (Fehr and Falk, 2002). Behavior is said to be reciprocal if people react to (un)kind treatments likewise. In social dilemmas an individual reciprocates by rewarding prosocial behavior and punishing antisocial behavior. Here it is crucial how the opponent's behavior will be perceived. In the utility function introduced above (equation 3.5) the perceived kindness of the opponent is measured by the parameter q_{SP}. Empirical research reveals that the perceived kindness of a gift depends not only on the monetary value of the gift but on its nature (Kube et al., 2010). Nonmonetary gifts are considered to be more thoughtful and reflect regard more credibly.

Reciprocity means that something is given back to those, who deserve it without thinking about reputational concerns. Empirical evidence for reciprocity can be found in Fehr et al. (1997); Fehr and Falk (2002); Falk et al. (2008); Kube et al. (2010). Reciprocity is backward-looking behavior since the underlying motive is not an increase in expected payoff. Since "reciprocity is not driven by the expectation of future material benefits" (Fehr and Falk, 2002, p.689) explanations based on reciprocity are different from explanations based on signaling, which will be considered in section 4.1.2 below.

Reciprocity is a key element in studies that explain social production as gift exchange (Kollock, 1998; Raymond, 2001). Gift exchange differs from

market exchange. In a typical market goods are exchanged for money. Goods and money change hands simultaneously, and there is an explicit contract governing the exchange relation. In a typical gift exchange a gift is transferred from giver to receiver. The giver expects to get something in return, but there is no explicit agreement or contract. The typical example of gift exchange is a dinner invitation: If you invite me for dinner, you expect me to reciprocate in some way (I am indebted). The giver of the gift is not completely divorced from the gift because she can expect something in return, i.e., a reciprocal gesture. Timing and value of the reciprocal gesture is left to discretion but is regulated by social norms (Mauss, 1954; Offer, 1997). The gift creates an obligation to give something back and so it creates a bond of loyalty. Gift exchange is self-reinforcing and builds up a personal relation between giver and receiver. On the receiver's side the gift combines three elements: (i) the gain from receiving the gift itself (the dinner itself), (ii) the satisfaction stemming from the gift as a source of regard (the pleasure from being invited for dinner), (iii) the indebtedness to the giver (Offer, 1997).

How does the metaphor of gift exchange fit to social production, and more specifically to open source? In gift exchange relations prestige derives from what you can give away. In open source communities it is your contribution – a chunk of source code, a bug report or part of the documentation – that you give to the community. According to Ljungberg (2000) the parallel between open source and gift exchange is faulty because the gift is a digital good. Since digital goods are infinitely expandable and nonrival the gift remains in the posession of the giver. It is not clear why this should be a problem. Ljungberg claims that digital goods have no value as gift since they are infinitely expandable and nonrival, hence not scarce. Surely, this is not the case since the creation of the first copy (instantiation) involves high opportunity costs. It is only after the first copy of a particular piece of software is written that this piece of software becomes an infinite resource.

In a related criticism Ljungberg (2000) claims that the gift exchange analogy is misleading because (as Ljungberg claims) gift exchange is driven by personal relations while open source communities are groups of relatively anonymous individuals. Members of open source software could give something back to the community by contributing, but why should they give something back to an anonymous community? We think that Ljungberg's argument is wrong for the following two reasons. First, there exists a team identity among users of the same software, as discussed above. They iden-

tify themselves as Linux users or Apple users, for example.[61] The empirical studies cited at the beginning of this chapter emphasize the relevance of team identity. The low costs for using the internet facilitates communication and creates a team identity which can be substituted for face-to-face relations (Offer, 1997). Zeitlyn (2003) reaffirms this: "A gift includes an obligation to make a return presentation. This compulsion to return a gift has special force in a small social world. The public world of the net, especially that of the software engineer is a very small world no matter where they are physically based" (p. 1287).

Another perspective is gained if we do not consider the contribution in isolation but combine it with the social approval that individuals receive for their contributions. This is the second reason for why we expect reciprocal behavior. In open source communities there are various institutions which facilitate monitoring of individual behavior and the exchange of social approval. Contributors' names are attached to the source code, visible in credit and maintainers lists, or listed at the homepage of the particular project, making it is possible to identify individual contributions with individual contributors. Social approval can be expressed through emails, mailing lists, chat, discussion fora, and on homepages. This allows for reciprocal gestures directed not only at the community but directed at particular contributors. Social approval will be directed at individuals who made a contribution (and will be discussed in greater length in the next chapter). As a gift, social approval differs from contributions like source code in that social approval is not a public but a private good the benefit of which goes only to the receiver. The reciprocal exchange that is going on here consists of giving source code to the community, and some members of the community will reciprocate by expressing social approval (Bitzer et al., 2007).[62]

To recapitulate: Individuals behave reciprocally if they respond to other's behavior likewise. Reciprocal behavior is often explained as gift exchange. It is important how other's behavior, i.e., the value of the gift is perceived and interpreted. The monetary value of the gift is unimportant relative to the signal the gift conveys. In order to convey meaning, the gift exchange relation

61 Apple users, for example, often attach Apple-stickers (which come with every Apple product) to their cars.

62 This is similar to academia. Scholars contribute to the public good knowledge by writing papers. Of course your colleagues reciprocate by writing papers and providing information that you can use in further research, but more importantly you trade your papers for social approval (in the form of citations, invitations to seminars and conferences, scholarships, honorary degrees etc.) from colleagues (Ljungberg, 2000; Albert, 2008, 2011).

requires a shared frame of reference. The shared frame of reference can result from personal relations. In open source, however, individuals are rather anonymous but a common team identity is substituted for personal relations. Open source is inherently nonmonetary since both contributions and social approval can be interpreted as a non-monetary gift. Nonmonetary gifts are often perceived as more thoughtful, suggesting that in social production contributions are perceived as a generous and kind gesture which are reciprocated by social approval. Two ways of reciprocating can be distinguished. The first form is a gift to the community, for example a few lines of source code. The second form is social approval, which is a nonmonetary reward directed at indvidual contributors. The cost of giving a gift to the community is higher than the cost of expressing social approval. Also, expressing social approval is itself a reward that is given to selected individuals, as we will discuss in more detail in the next chapter.

3.6 Upshot of Chapter 3

In this chapter we showed that social production is the voluntary provision of public goods by self-organizing communities. After reviewing empirical studies on contributors and their motives we examined three particular motives – namely use value, intrinsic motivation, and social preferences – in more detail. Although it is crucial at the beginning of a project, use value cannot explain contributions which are of little or no use value. Intrinsic motivation is likely to be high and is reinforced through the exchange of social approval, i.e., the exchange of social approval crowds in intrinsic motivation (Deci, 1975; Frey and Jegen, 2001). Regarding social preferences we focused on altruism and reciprocity since other social preferences, like inequality aversion and fairness are neither identified in empirical studies on contributing behavior nor mentioned in the existing literature on social production. We distinguish between pure and impure altruism. Pure altruism can be explained by team identity, morals and ideology which can be identified in social production communities, but pure altruism cannot explain voluntary contributions, except in small communities. Impure altruism, however, can explain voluntary contributions through the existence of so-called warm glows, i.e., private benefits for the contributor. The second social preference which we discussed is reciprocity. Reciprocity has been criticized because (according to Ljungberg, 2000) it is implausible in large, anonymous

communities. In social production communities this criticism does not apply because contributors identify with the community and a team identity can be established. Hence we do not deny that reciprocity can explain voluntary contributions but point to reciprocity for explaining the exchange of social approval within social production communities.

Taken together, use value, intrinsic motivation, impure altruism, and reciprocity are explanations for the voluntary provision of public goods in social production communities. These explanations are not mutually exclusive and operate simultaneously. However, we argue that another incentive, social approval, has not yet received adequate attention, possibly because it is underreported in empirical studies due to norms of modesty. In social production communities the exchange of social approval is frequent and almost costless, and there are several reasons to believe that the strength of social approval (in particular the intrinsic value of social approval) is high. In order to emphasize the importance of social approval we will dicuss the role of social approval in the next chapter.

Chapter 4

Social Approval as a Reward

In this chapter we introduce social approval as a reward. We examine social approval in section 4.1 and distinguish between the intrinsic and extrinsic value of social approval. We discuss both the intrinsic and extrinsic value of social approval, but since our focus is on the intrinsic value we put more weight on this aspect. In section 4.2 we discuss rewards and punishments from a game theoretic perspective and point out that there is a second-order dilemma if giving rewards is costly. Although cooperation can be explained in infinitely repeated games, cooperation is only one out of many possible equilibria. Hence we introduce evolutionary game theory in section 4.4 and argue that evolutionary game theory is the appropriate method for modeling the exchange of social approval as well as emergence, stability, and enforcement of a social institution in a population of boundenly rational players.

4.1 Social Approval

Social approval is a nonmonetary reward. It is the expression of a favorable opinion. By giving social approval someone recognizes the worth of someone or something. Synonyms that are often used to describe the expression of social approval are regard, recognition, respect, appreciate, admire, and esteem.[63] Regard is the most neutral of these terms and refers to a favorable or unfavorable impression (e.g., to regard someone as a ruthless competitor). Recognition refers to acknowledgement and officical approval. Respect is used to emphasize the deferential aspect of regard. Appreciate, admire, and esteem are expressions of approval of various strengths. You can appreciate something if you understand it completely so that you are in a position to judge its value critically. You admire something if you appreciate its supe-

63 Here we follow the definitions found in the *New Oxford American Dictionary* and *Webster's New World Dictionary*.

riority. Esteem is generally used to imply admiration of the highest degree. Esteem is the strongest expression of social approval and, in contrast to all other ways of expressing social approval, it cannot be generated voluntarily. Throughout this thesis we will use the term social approval to refer to expressions of favorable opinion in general and we will use the term esteem to indicate the involuntary expression of social approval of the highest degree.[64]

Social approval is an integral part of human communication. It is omnipresent and is expressed through facial expressions (e.g., smile), gestures (e.g., applause), spoken and written messages, gifts and symbolic awards. All behavior, as long as it is observed by others, will attract social approval. Throughout this section we use the terms *giver* and *receiver* to denote individuals who give and receive social approval. We refer to the receiver's behavior as her *performance*; and we use the term *audience* for referring to the group of individuals observing the performance. Note that social approval is different from the warm glow of giving. While both result in a private benefits for the contributor, the warm glow comes from (within) the contributor herself whereas social approval comes from the giver. Individuals will experience warm glows also if there is no audience or if contributions and identities are not revealed.[65]

Social approval is given for two intertwined things: (i) for the *consequences* of the performance, and (ii) for the *meaning or identity* that the performance reveals. The first aspect is purely consequentialist. Someone is being appreciated, admired, or esteemed for her skills in acting, sports, politics, education, etc. Social approval is a subjective measure of how well someone is able to perform or accomplish a particular activity. The second aspect is concerned with expressive rationality. Social approval is assigned not based on consequences but on motives and dispositions (Brennan and Pettit, 2004). What is evaluated are not the consequences but the meaning or identity that the action reveals about the actor, where meaning and identity depend on cultural

64 Besides social approval there is self-respect, self-regard and self-esteem (a non-material reward from with the individual). Feelings of self-respect, self-regard and self-esteem constitute a psychological reward stemming from behavior that conforms with one's values or internalized norms (for public good games, see Andreoni's warm glow and empirical evidence in Kahneman and Knetsch, 1992 and Freeman, 1997). In this section we will neglect self-respect, self-regard and self-esteem and focus on social approval, i.e., non-monetary rewards from others.

65 One possibility to define the warm glow as the exchange of social approval would be to define a Freudian super-ego who monitors and evaluates the ego's performance. The super-ego would be audience and giver at the same time, and the ego would be the receiver.

background and on how the audience interprets the action. By acting in a specific way the individual expresses something about herself, hence this aspect is also called expressive rationality (Elster, 1983; Hargreaves Heap, 1989, 2001).

The receiver values social approval for intrinsic and extrinsic reasons (figure 4.1). There are extrinsic reasons for valuing social approval if there are delayed effects, i.e., if receiving social approval today leads to additional benefits tomorrow. The extrinsic effect is known as reputation and signaling. The distinction between intrinsic and extrinsic value of social approval can also be found in social pychology. Although social psychologists do not deny that people are motivated by social approval per se, they prefer a functional interpretation of people's need for social approval. According to a functionalist interpretation social approval increases an individual's relational value which eventually translates into group leadership (Hogg and Vaughan, 2008; Fiske et al., eds, 2010).[66] We discuss the extrinsic effect in more detail in section 4.1.2 (and in section 6.1 in relation to the design of our experiment) and discuss the intrinsic effect of social approval in the following section.

4.1.1 The Intrinsic Value of Social Approval

The intrinsic effect of receiving social approval can be distinguished into (i) emotional effects, (ii) expressive effects, and (iii) status effects, as shown in figure 4.1. Consider these seriatim.

(i) People care what others think about them, and they care even more if

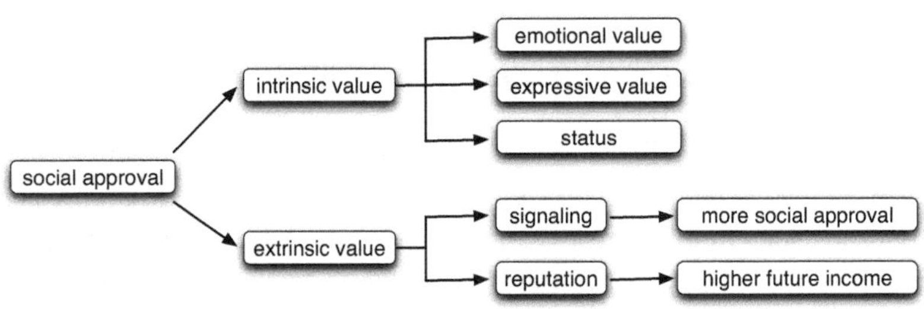

Figure 4.1: Social approval and its effects on motivation.

66 Also, social psychology investigates differences in the need for social approval (for example Satow, 1975, and Deutsch and Lamberti, 1986), and attempts to measure the desire for social approval (for example Crowne and Marlowe, 1960).

others express their opinions through facial expressions, gestures, and verbal feedback. The expression of opinion, and also the anticipation of it, creates a nonmonetary payoff since individuals feel emotions like shame and pride when considering others' opinions of them (Brennan and Pettit, 2000; Ellingsen and Johannesson, 2008).

(ii) Social approval means showing an evaluative attitude in response to the receiver's performance. By undertaking the performance the receiver reveals one or more of her character traits. Social approval satisfies the innate human desires for meaning and distinction since it allows them to choose and express their identities (Akerlof and Kranton, 2000, 2005). By choosing an identity, or conforming to behavior as prescribed by a social category, people create a sense of themselves. In the process of establishing one's identity social approval is feedback that reinforces a person's identity. By choosing my behavior I am able to create my identity. With respect to identity, social approval is feedback telling me that I have successfully created my identity, or telling me about how others perceive my identity.[67]

With respect to the expressive value of consumption, economists and anthropologists have studied consumption patterns in different cultural groups and have focused on the meaning of different patterns of consumption (Veblen, 1994 (1899); Douglas and Isherwood, 1978; Schor and Holt, 2000). A hybrid car brings me from A to B (its function) but it also expresses my concern about the environment, for example. In choosing consumption patterns people take into account both extrinsic and expressive value. Besides consumption, a second – and for our analysis more important area – is the expressive value associated with gift exchange. Contributing to a public good represents a gift since a benefit is voluntarily conferred to others. Giving a gift has expressive value and creates identities, like being a generous person or a skilled developer.

(iii) Social approval has a comparative or positional effect, often referred to as status. If social approval is visible, measurable and comparable across individuals social approval gives rise to a hierarchy. This is equivalent to saying that the preference for social approval is a social preference. People do not only value social approval per se but care about receiving more social approval than others. For example, they care about receiving more than the average, or not being at the last position (Frank, 1985). The status effect of

67 Choosing one's identity is easy in the internet, similar to artists or actors choosing pseudonyms. Choosing a pseudonym can also be an insurance strategy by reducing the risk of ridicule (see Brennan and Pettit, 2004).

social approval, however, is not always present, or present but weakened. If social approval is expressed in private, I do not know how much social approval you have received and hence I cannot compare myself to you. And even if social approval is exchanged publicly it might not be comparable since different ways of expressing social approval cannot be compared. The status effect of social approval is only salient if social approval is exchanged publicly and if the different ways of expressing social approval are comparable.

4.1.1.a The Strength of Social Approval

Having identified emotional, expressive, and status effects as being responsible for the intrinsic value of social approval, we turn to the conditions affecting the strength of social approval. To be effective, social approval has to satisfy the *sincerity and exchange constraints* (Brennan and Pettit, 2000). These constraints being satisfied, the strength of social approval depends on observability, the size and quality of the audience, the relation between giver and receiver, and the receiver's perception.

If there is a straightforward exchange under offer, the sincerity of social approval will be in question. For example, if I would openly pay you ten euros for appreciating my qualities as a soccer player, no-one would believe your judgement. Even if others did not know about me paying you, I would certainly not believe that your judgement is sincere and it would not be a source of social approval. For the judgement to be sincere it must be the case that the true motive for giving social approval is hidden. Suppose Alice and Bob are equally good at playing soccer. It might be the case that I appreciate Alice's qualities instead of Bob's because I expect that it is more likely that Alice will reciprocate. This exchange would satisfy the sincerity constraint since the true motive for giving social approval is hidden. Brennan and Pettit (2000) even argue that the true motive might not just be hidden from observers but that the true motive might also be hidden for the giver, i.e., the concern for reciprocity operates unconsciously.

The exchange constraint refers to the fact that esteem represents a justified judgement that cannot be generated voluntarily but is generated in a reflex, involuntary fashion. For example, I cannot voluntarily decide whether the meal you have prepared tastes delicious. What I can do, however, is to pay close attention to how you prepared the meal. Paying attention is something that I can decide to do voluntarily and is called an esteem service. By paying

attention to how you have prepared the meal I might find that you decorated the table in a particular way that pleases me and I will express this. Esteem services can be provided voluntarily and give rise to the involuntary expression of social approval and esteem. It follows that social approval cannot be exchanged like conventional goods or money. Since it represents a justified judgement, it cannot be transfered from one person to another (Brennan and Pettit, 2000; Ellingsen and Johannesson, 2007).

The strength of social approval as a reward will depend on the *observability* of my performance. Observability increases with the size of the audience, the likelihood of being observed, and the quality of the audience (Brennan and Pettit, 2004). If I expect that more people will see my performance, either because there are more people, or because there is the same number of people but it is more likely that they will look at me, I will expect to attract more social approval from the audience, and the approval incentive will be stronger. The strength of social approval also depends on the quality of the giver. To be valued, the expression of social approval has to be a *qualified judgement*. Someone giving social approval must be in a position to evaluate my performance. For example, I can only give valuable social approval for your ballet-performance if I have at least some knowledge about ballet.

Next there is the *relation between giver and receiver* on which the strength of social approval depends. Social approval is stronger if given by a close friend or relative. If social distance between giver and receiver is low, the receiver is more likely to value the judgement. In constrast, a stranger expressing social approval will induce a minor increase in utility (Gächter and Fehr, 1999).

Closely associated with the relation between giver and receiver is the *perception* of social approval. The effectiveness of social approval is not determined by the giver's judgement but depends on the receiver's perception of the expression of social approval and her perception of the giver. In his work on awards, Frey argues that the motivational salience of awards depends mainly on the signaling value, not on the monetary value, of the award (Frey, 2006, 2007; Frey and Neckermann, 2008; Frey, 2010). His findings suggest that an award that has no monetary value can nonetheless increase motivation if the award is perceived as a sign of social approval or esteem. These findings are complemented by Ellingsen and Johannesson (2007) emphasizing that social approval, a sign of respect expressed by an employer, depends on the employer's character. "One key determinant of whether employer actions are interpreted as showing respect or disrespect is the worker's perception of the character of their employers" (p. 142).

The exchange of social approval creates a *bond of loyalty* between giver and receiver and thus changes the social structure (Titmuss, 1970; Offer, 1997). By social structure we refer to the relations between individuals, like social distance, for example. The change in social distance can be explained by reciprocity. Social approval is a gift because it is transferred voluntarily and confers a benefit to the receiver. If having a preference for reciprocity, the receiver will reciprocate by behaving in such a way that increases the giver's payoff. Efficiency wages can be explained analogously. By paying a wage above the market-clearing wage the firm transfers a gift to the employee and establishes a bond of loyalty. Employees reciprocate by working harder, thus increasing the firm's productivity (Akerlof, 1982; Fehr and Falk, 2002). As a result of the firm's gesture (paying a higher wage) employees are induced to take the firm's preferences into account when choosing effort. But as has been recently shown in a field experiment nonmonetary gifts are more salient than higher wages. They signal the employee's kindness more effectively and the increase in employees' effort levels is significantly higher (Kube et al., 2010). According to Kube et al. the prevalence of reciprocal reactions is determined not by the monetary value but by the nature of the gift. A non-monetary gift is more thoughtful and personal, and more credibly reflects social approval.

4.1.1.b Social Approval in Social Production

Now we turn to the relation between social approval and social production. The main argument is that social production is organized in such a way as to ensure that the intrinsic effect of social approval is high.

To begin with, we give a few paradigmatic examples of (i) how information about contributors and contributions is provided, (ii) how the exchange of social approval is used to maintain a high quality of contributions, and (iii) how contributors can express their identities in social production communities. (i) The credit files mentioned in section 2.4.4 are but one example for how information about contributors and their contributions is provided. Making information about contributors and their efforts publicly available is a necessary precondition for the expression of social approval. (ii) One particular way of expressing social approval is by evaluating the quality of a contribution. The two most frequent possibilities to evalute the quality of a contribution are rating systems and comments, both being used at Amazon's book reviews and AllRecipes.com. At Amazon, individuals write

book reviews which are displayed together with the book, thus providing information for potential buyers. Although everybody is allowed to write a review the quality of reviews is relatively high. One mechanism responsible for the high quality is a decentralized rating system where users can give a vote indicating whether the review was helpful or not. Another possibility, associated with higher opportunity costs, is the possibility to write a comment. In a similar way users can rate recipes and write comments at AllRecipes.com. In this system of quality control the quality standards are set by users who evaluate contributions through the exchange of social approval. Hence the exchange of social approval is necessary in order to ensure quality and in order to motivate effort. (iii) Another way for contributors to attract social approval and to express their identity is the possibility for contributors to provide information about themselves at so-called user pages or profiles. In section 2.3.2 we already mention that contributors at AllRecipes.com can create a profile listing cooking interests, hometown etc., but more importantly, profiles allow contributors to represent their achievements. For example, Wikipedia contributor "woohookitty" describes her interests and proudest achievements on her user page[68] and lists her awards on a specific awards page.[69] "Woohookitty" engages in disambiguation (resolving conflicts which arise because a word or phrase is ambiguous) and has received several barnstars from other users, expressing appreciation and acknowledgement.[70] Although it would be possible to provide many other examples we stop at this point because we believe that these examples are sufficient to illustrate that the exchange of social approval is ubiquitous (the existence of many ways to express social approval), important (to ensure quality), and almost costless (low opportunity cost). Next, we turn to theoretical studies about social approval in social production communities.

The empirical studies reviewed before (section 3.4) show that social approval did not rank among the most important motives for contributing. Numerous theoretical studies, however, emphasized the importance of expressing talent to peers and attracting social approval. For evidence from user-led innovation see chapter 9 in von Hippel (2005), for evidence from open source see Raymond (2001); Ljungberg (2000); Lerner et al. (2006); Leadbeater (2009). The discrepancy between contributors' stated motivations and

68 http://en.wikipedia.org/wiki/User:Woohookitty
69 http://en.wikipedia.org/wiki/User:Woohookitty/Awards
70 In many internet communities barnstars are given for hard work. Barnstars are a symbol for a shared work experience and can be traced back to the American tradition of barn raising in which all members of the community came together to erect a barn.

theoretical arguments can be explained by contributors' modesty and is most clearly emphasized by Raymond (2001). Raymond argues that developers show a strong reluctance to admit that their behavior is motivated by the desire to attract social approval. The open source community "distrusts and despises egotism and ego-based motivations" and "[o]nly sublimated and disguised forms like 'peer repute', 'self-esteem', 'professionalism' or 'pride of accomplishment' are generally acceptable" (Raymond, 2001, p.14). Further support for the importance of social approval comes from one of the unwritten rules of open source: "Surrepitiously filing someone's name off a project is, in cultural context, one of the ultimate crimes. Doing this steals the victim's gift to be presented as the thief's own"(Raymond, 2001, p.13). These quotes point to the importance of social approval and suggests that the importance of social approval is likely to be underestimated in empirical studies. The underestimation of social approval in emprical studies is not a phenomenon that is confined to open source or social production. In many cultures it is the case that there is a norm of modesty, prescribing not to seek social approval too openly. As Elster (1983) states: "nothing is so unimpressive as behaviour designed to impress" (p. 66). Empirical support for the existence of the norm of modesty and its variations across cultures can be found in Huberman et al. (2004). They argue that in some cultures, especially in Sweden and Finland, status is pursued only in small circles rather than publicly because of the norm of "Jante", prescribing to keep a low profile and not to act superior.

Support for the importance of social approval can also be derived by examining the exchange constraint and the sincerity constraint in relation to open source. As mentioned above, the exchange of esteem is constrained because esteem is a judgement that cannot be generated voluntarily. So-called esteem services like paying attention and expressing your opinion can be supplied voluntarily, and esteem services will ensure the appearance of esteem (Brennan and Pettit, 2000). In open source esteem services are crucial and there are various institutions ensuring the presence of esteem services. To ensure that my contribution will be compatible with the rest of the project, I have to pay close attention to existing contributions. Maybe I have to ask other contributors for feedback and help, or I have to discuss my contribution with them. As mentioned above, the exchange of esteem services is also necessary to avoid low-quality contributions. As a result of esteem services, which are inevitable, social approval and esteem will be generated.

According to the sincerity constraint the exchange of social approval must be hidden, i.e., the true motive for giving social approval cannot be expressed openly. In open source interactions, which are largely anonymous, the sincerity constraint is likely to be fulfilled. The norms for conflict resultion (section 2.4.5) presribing that only the quality of the contribution but not the competence of contributors should be judged, making it unlikely that expressions of social approval or disapproval are motivated by personal reasons (Raymond, 2001).

In open source it is the norm that the quality of the code should speak for itself, and elegance of source code is emphasized (see section 2.4.5). In order to judge the quality of the code accurately there should be no noise. Noise could come in if the discussion moves away from quality and elegance of the source code towards attacks on the author and her competence or ego-driven posturing (Raymond, 2001). What is of primary interest to the open source community is the source code. There are norms prescribing that discussions concerning the author rather than the code should be avoided since members of the community are mostly anonymous hence not in a position to judge other members. Also, trashing putatively defective work should be avoided. Taken together, these norms imply that discrimination is reduced to a minimum since the contributor's age, sex, gender, religion, nationality and ethnicity are unknown to the audience (if the contributor does not reveal it, see also Sennett, 2008).

The members of the audience, consisting of users, active users, developers and the core (see section 2.4.1) are more or less involved in the project. They use the particular open source software and can provide feedback from an user's point-of-view, or they are developers who can provide feedback regarding the quality of the source code. Together, they form a close-knit group of users and developers. The different open source communities provide specific and segmented audiences since each member is associated with a specific community in which she is user or developer. Each member of a particular community is engaged in the project and is in a good position to give judgement since she has the knowledge and information to make an accurat judgement. For the community's developers the provision of esteem services is even necessary in order to assure quality and compatibility of individual contributions. Since most developers of the community are skilled developers their judgement is valuable. The exchange of social approval takes place among peers, i.e., among individuals who share a similar background with respect to abilities, interests, and education. Although there are insti-

tutions that ensure that open source software can be modified by anyone and in any direction (the open source licenses described in chapter 1, section 2.4.7), only some contributions are incorporated into the next official version of the program. The users who downloaded and use the latest official version of the program do not directly transfer a reward to developers, but the fact to have worked on a program that is used by millions of users (and eventually replaces all alternative programs) is a source of social approval and esteem. In this somehow paradoxical situation, users, who are free riders in the production of the public good open source software, do help solving the second-order dilemma by indirectly assigning rewards to contributors.

Our main claim is that the instrinsic value of social approval is important in order to explain voluntary contributions in social production. To recapitulate we list the reasons for why this is the case:

- There exist various channels through which social approval can be expressed at low cost.

- In order to ensure quality of and compatibility between contributions members have to provide esteem services by paying attention to others' contributions.

- Intense and open communication ensures that monitoring of individual contributions is possible and that social approval is visible to a large audience.

- Members of social production communities share a similar background, hence they are in the position to give a qualified judgement.

- The focus is on the quality of the contribution and discrimination is reduced to a minimum, hence judgements are accurate.

- Social approval is a sincere judgement since the giver has nothing to gain from giving social approval.

- Due to the large size of the community the community's average judgement is likely to be more accurate than any individual judgement.

- Since the focus is on the quality of the contribution it is possible to seek social approval not too openly.

4.1.2 The Extrinsic Value of Social Approval

This section discusses the extrinsic value of social approval, i.e., the value of social approval as a means to an end. We discuss signaling and reputation. Although there is evidence for signaling as an incentive for voluntary contributions in social production communities, its importance is limited because the signaling explanation only applies to a fraction of contributions. Reputation is closer to the intrinsic value of social approval in that a good reputation helps to attract more social approval.

4.1.2.a Signaling

According to the signaling explanation, skilled developers want to signal their talent to potential employees.[71] Thereby they hope to improve their chances of getting a well-paid job by gaining reputation which eventually can be monetized through employment by a commercial software company. Economic theory (Spence, 1973; Milgrom and Roberts, 1992) predicts that incentives for signaling will be stronger if performance is more visible to the relevant audience and if the impact of effort on performance is higher, i.e., if performance is a good proxy for effort. Due to the open character of open source projects (the source code which is needed to assess the developer's quality is visibly for everyone) and the strong identification of each contributor with her contribution the quality of the contribution is a good proxy for effort. And indeed, there are several individuals (prominent in the open source world) who are now employed in commercial software companies (see table 2 in Lerner and Tirole (2002) for concrete examples). The individuals listed by Lerner and Tirole are software developers who were highly visible in their communities since they made a large number of contributions and acted as project leaders. The vast majority of contributors, however, make only one, or a very few, contributions. It is unlikely that these contributors' main motive is job market signaling. If signaling would be their main motive, they should contribute more often. Since this is not the case several authors concluded that signaling is only a minor motive applicable to a small fraction of all contributors (Raymond, 2001; Osterloh et al., 2001; Bitzer et al., 2007).

71 Since our focus is on the intrinsic value of social approval we do not present any formal models of signaling. Such models, however, can be found in Spence (1973), Holmström (1999), or chapter 5 in Milgrom and Roberts (1992) for an introduction.

The importance of signaling is further weakened by Weber (2004, p.143) arguing that there are only very few people who read the source code. Most people just use the software and read the source code only if the program does not work. And last but not least, an emprical study about the Linux community found that only 4,633 out of 129,109 contributions represent source code (Dempsey et al., 1999). The majority of contributions consists of comments, documentation and bug reports, contributions that contain less (if any) information about the contributor's talent. Summarizing the available evidence on signaling we conclude that signaling is of only minor importance because (i) it cannot explain the skewness of the contributions, i.e., why most individuals make only very few contributions, (ii) most source code is not read, and (iii) most contributions are not source code and hence are not a good proxy for the contributor's effort or quality.

4.1.2.b Reputation

Reputation is similar to signaling. By contributing to social production contributors can build up a reputation. Reputation is the opinion of other members of the community towards a particular individual and is based on the individual's past behavior. Individuals gain reputation by behaving in a certain way, while this behavior is observed by others and communicated to others. Reputation is a signal about the individual's qualities. By effectively using this signal, the individual can increase her future payoff. This can happen, for example, by signaling competence and power which translates into a higher future income (Huberman et al., 2004). This is exactly what we discussed at the beginning of this section, where signaling refers to the buildup of a reputation which increases career prospects, but reputation is more general than signaling. While signaling refers to the buildup of a reputation for the improvement of career prospects, the effect of reputation is not confined to the labor market. In social production communities there is a close relation between reputation and social approval. Reputation leads to social approval being more salient by extending time frame and audience (Brennan and Pettit, 2004). If A tells B about C's valueable contribution, the extend of C's reputation is increased in time (from the date the contribution was made to today) and audience (although B has not looked at the contribution she hears about it). C is now known to make valueable contributions, and even people who did not look at C's contributions know about C's quality in making contributions. As a result, C will receive more social approval because

C's new contributions will be judged based on both the quality of the new contribution and C's reputation (i.e., the signal about the quality of C's past contributions). Although a good reputation might have value in itself, it has mostly extrinsic value because it increases the amount of social approval to be received in the future (Ljungberg, 2000). This implies that the presence of reputation does not decrease but increase the importance of social approval.

4.2 Rewards and Punishments

As seen in the previous chapter, social preferences transform the utilities that are attached to each outcome of the game by changing the utility function. Since players maximize utility, not payoffs, cooperation can be explained. Another solution to dilemma problems is to keep the assumption that players only care about the payoffs of the game (i.e., utility = payoff) and directly change the payoffs by introducing rewards and punishments.[72] A reward can be given to cooperators, or defectors can be punished. A combination of rewards and punishments is also possible. The underlying idea is to change the payoffs by lowering the payoff to defectors or increasing the payoff to cooperators, as can be seen in figure 4.2. Subsidies and taxes are examples of rewards and punishments which come from a central authority, i.e., not from the players themselves. If the additional benefit from the reward to contributors or the reduced benefit from being punished outweights the costs of contributing to the public good the dilemma structure of the game is dissolved. In the prisoner's dilemma this is the case if $b \geq T - R$ where b is the benefit from the reward or the loss from punishment. The game is changed into a game where Nash equilibrium and social optimum coincide, and the dilemma structure is eliminated. As mentioned above, a solution through the imposition of rewards and punishments by a central authority relies on rather strong informational assumptions. The central authority has to know the players' payoffs in order to determine the optimal size of the rewards and punishments. In real world situations this rarely is the case.

Let us now turn to the more realistic case in which rewards and punishments will not be given by a central authority but by the players themselves.

72 Note that the endogeneous sanction mentioned in our definition of institutions (see chapter 1) is different from punishment. The endogenous sanction refers to the difference in payoffs between two hypothetical outcomes of the game (the outcome in which all players cooperate and the outcome in which all players defect) while punishment refers to a change in the payoff to defection (regardless of the outcome of the game).

	C	D
C	$R+b, R+b$	$S+b, T$
D	$T, S+b$	P, P

	C	D
C	R, R	$S, T-b$
D	$T-b, S$	$P-b, P-b$

Figure 4.2: The PD game with rewards (left) and with punishment (right).

This corresponds to the case in which members of social production communities give rewards to each other. In this case, rewards and punishments solve the dilemma only if they are costless to give. If it is costly to give rewards or punishments, a second-order dilemma is created. The second-order dilemma is shown in figure 4.3 where h is the cost of giving a reward and b refers to the benefit of receiving a reward.

Assume that players give rewards to cooperators. If all players give rewards to cooperators, they have an incentive to cooperate in the first stage of the game. The situation on which all players give rewards and contribute is a Nash equilibrium if giving rewards is costless ($h = 0$). But if giving a reward is costly there is no incentive for giving a reward in the second-stage of the game. Then, the Nash equilibrium is not to give rewards and not to contribute. Of course, there could be a third stage of the game in which rewards are given to those who gave a reward in the second stage of the game. But it should be clear by now that costly rewards (or punishments) do not resolve the dilemma structure. Instead, rewards and punishments shift the dilemma problem to the next stage of the game. The problem of *Who rewards those, who gave rewards in the stage before?*, or, *Who punishes those, who did not punish in the stage before?* always remains and we end up in an endless regress. Game theory predicts that no rewards or punishments will be given and we are back to the standard dilemma game where defection is the domi-

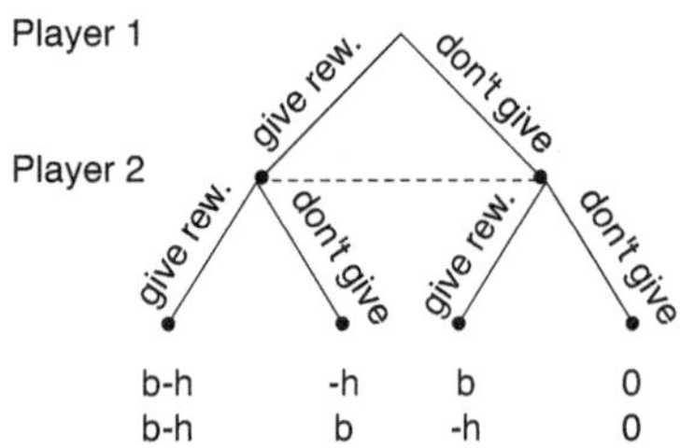

Figure 4.3: The second stage of a PD with rewards. A second-order dilemma.

nant strategy. The tentative conclusion is that costly rewards or punishments alone cannot solve the dilemma problem because they create a *second-order dilemma*.

It is interesting to note that this prediction is not confirmed in the experimental economics literature. In fact, there are various studies investigating the effect of costly rewards and punishments in public good games (Fehr and Gächter, 2000; Dickinson, 2001; Sefton et al., 2007) and common-pool-resource games (Ostrom et al., 1992). They find that rewards and sanctions are employed by the subjects although this is costly, inducing higher contributions to public goods. Over time, however, contributions converge towards the Nash-prediction.

4.2.1 Repeated Games

A repeated game is a game that is played multiple rounds. In repeated games players can use contingent actions. In the second round of a two-player game, for example, a player can make her decision on the basis of the observed moves from the first round. In the following we exclude social preferences and assume that players are motivated only by their own payoffs, i.e. $u = \pi$.

To discuss repeated games some additional definitions are necessary. Let us assume that players possess perfect recall, meaning that each player remembers all of her own and the other players' past moves. The set of all possible combinations of moves up to time t is called a history of the game and is defined as the Cartesian product of all past rounds' action profiles $\mathcal{H}^t = A^t$ (remember that A is an action profile for one round). Moreover it holds that $\mathcal{H}^{t+1} = \mathcal{H}^t \times A$ and per definition $\mathcal{H}^0 = A^0 = \{\emptyset\}$. A particular sequence of actions for all players up to point t is a possible history h^t. The history of the game contains all possible histories up to point t, $h^t \in \mathcal{H}^t$. In an infinitely repeated game the set of all possible histories is given by $\mathcal{H} = \bigcup_{t=0}^{\infty} \mathcal{H}^t$. Qualitatively, a history describes every event that is possible. Being rational and possessing perfect recall players think through all possible histories and compute their best responses. Players anticipate every eventuality and make a plan of how to react to it, if it occurs.[73] The player's plan for all contingencies is called a complete strategy. A complete strategy

73 In their *Theory of Games and Economic Behavior* John von Neumann and Oskar Morgenstern 1944 use the analogy of all players submitting their choices to an umpire who then determines the outcome of the game.

for player i is a mapping from the set of all possible histories into the set of actions $\sigma_i : \mathcal{H} \rightarrow A_i$.

Remember that players know the sequence of moves and the payoffs and that rationality is common knowledge. The complete strategy σ_i can be thought of as a list. Before the game is played each player computes a complete strategy. This is done as follows. In her mind the player walks through all nodes of the game tree. At any node where she has to make a decision she asks herself: *I know that the other players' want to maximize their payoffs. I know the particular history h^t, that is, I have information about all past moves that led me to this node in the tree. Given that information, how should I choose at this and all future nodes in order to maximize my payoff?* The answer to this question is player i's continuation strategy induced by h^t and is denoted by $\sigma_{i|h^t}$. It is the strategy that player i would choose if history h^t is realized. The complete strategy for player i is then the list of continuation strategies for all possible histories. As before, the strategy profile is defined as the set of all players' strategy profiles, $\sigma = (\sigma_1, \sigma_2, ...\sigma_n)$.

All players' decisions based on their complete strategies result in an outcome, or outcome path. The outcome in a game that is repeated exactly $\bar{t}$ rounds is a sequence of action profiles $a = (a^0, a^1, a^2, a^3, ...) \in A^{\bar{t}}$. For an infinitely repeated game the outcome path is an infinite sequence of action profiles $a = (a^0, a^1, a^2, a^3, ...) \in A^{\infty}$.

In a finite (infinite) game each outcome results in a finite (infinite) stream of payoffs for each player, $(\pi_i(a^0), \pi_i(a^1), ...)$ for all $i \in I$. It is common to assume a discount factor $\delta \leq 1$ and define the discounted payoff from the repeated game as

$$\Pi_i(\sigma) = \sum_{t=0}^{\bar{t}} \delta^t \pi_i(a^t)$$

where $T = \infty$ if the game is infinite.

4.2.1.a Finitely Repeated Games

For illustrative purposes let us consider a prisoner's dilemma which is played twice. The first round could be interpreted as the decision whether or not to contribute to the public good, and the second round could be interpreted to be the decision whether or not to give social approval. At the begining of the first round the history is given by $h^0 = \{\emptyset\}$ since no moves are made. Assume that player 1's strategy is Tit-For-Tat (TFT for short) and that player

2 will always defect, i.e., the strategy profile is $\sigma = (TFT, ALLD)$. Both TFT and ALLD are complete strategies since they define an action for all contingencies. ALLD simply defects no matter what the opponent plays, and TFT is a complete strategy which is contingent only on the opponent's last move. A TFT player starts with cooperation, cooperates if the opponent cooperated in the previous round and defects otherwise. The two players' continuation strategies at the beginning of the first round are $\sigma_{1|h^0} = C$ and $\sigma_{2|h^0} = D$. The realized history after round 1 is given by h^1.

$$h^1 = (C, D) \quad \in \quad \{(C,C),(D,C),(C,D),(D,D)\} = \mathcal{H}^1$$

For round two player 1's continuation strategy depends on her opponents last move and can be written as

$$\begin{aligned} \sigma_{1|h^1} &= C \quad \text{if} \quad h^1 \in \{(C,C),(D,C)\} \\ \sigma_{1|h^1} &= D \quad \text{if} \quad h^1 \in \{(D,D),(C,D)\} \end{aligned}$$

Player 2's continuation strategy is given by $\sigma_{2|h^1} = D$ for all possible histories $h^1 \in \mathcal{H}^1$. Player 2 defects no matter what happened in the past. Since the particular history that was realized in the first round was $h^1 = (C, D)$ both players will defect in the second round.[74] The realized history at the end of the second round is then given by $h^2 = \{(C,D),(D,D)\}$. Since the game ends after two rounds the reaized history h^2 will also be the outcome of the game $\{a^0, a^1\} = \{(C,D),(D,D)\}$. Taking δ_1 and δ_2 as discount rates the discounted payoffs associated with this outcome are

$$\Pi_1(\sigma) = S + \delta_1 P$$

and

$$\Pi_2(\sigma) = T + \delta_2 P$$

In a repeated game a Nash equilibrium is a strategy profile in which each player is best responding to the strategies of the other players. Formally, a strategy profile σ^* is a Nash equilibrium if for all players $i \in I$ and strategies $\sigma_i \in S_i$ we have

$$\Pi_i(\sigma_i^*, \sigma_{-i}^*) \geq \Pi_i(\sigma_i, \sigma_{-i}^*)$$

74 This is not a Nash equilibrium since player 1 could gain by defecting in the first round.

Intuitively this means that it is not possible for a player to get a higher payoff by making a different move in one round of the game, given that all other players keep their strategies constant.

In repeated games the Nash equilibrium is not always a good prediction of how the game will be played because it allows for uncredible threats. The concept of subgame-perfection is stronger than the Nash equilibrium concept. A subgame is a subset of the game consisting of a decision node and all succeeding nodes. A strategy profile σ is a *subgame-perfect Nash equilibrium* (SPNE) of the repeated game if for all histories $h^t \in \mathcal{H}$, $\sigma|_{h^t}$ is a Nash equilibrium of the subgame starting at this decision node. By requiring the strategy to be optimal at every subgame the SPNE rules out uncredible threats. As the Nash equilibrium concept, subgame-perfectness implies that there are no profitable one-shot deviations.

In finitely repated games we can find the SPNE by applying *backward induction* (Selten, 1975). Let us illustrate the idea of backward induction with a finitely repeated prisoner's dilemma. Starting at the last decision node we ask for the optimal strategy. In this case the last decision is the simultaneous decision of both players in the last round. In the last round, no-one would be better off if she would cooperate while the other player defects. Hence both players defecting is a Nash-equilibrium in the subgame. Now we move backwards to the next decision. The next decision is the players' decision in the second-to-last round of the game. Since common knowledge of rationality is assumed each player knows that the other player will play the Nash equilibrium in the last round. Each player asks herself about the optimal strategy in the second-to-last round of the game, given that both players will defect in the last round. Since the actions in the second-to-last round have no influence on the actions in the last round, both players choose to defect. Continuing backward induction yields the SPNE which in this example predicts that both players will defect in each round. In fact, in this case there is only one Nash-equilibrium, which is identical with the SPNE.

We saw above that costly rewards and punishments do not resolve the dilemma structure but rather shift it to another stage of the game. This can be modeled as a repeated prisoner's dilemma game. If the game is repated a finite period of times we can apply backward induction to arrive at a solution. The solution is the subgame perfect Nash-equilibrium, predicting that both players defect in each period of the game.

4.2.1.b Infinitely Repeated Games

We now move on to infinitely repeated games. Since there is no last round of the game we cannot apply backward induction. For illustrative purposes let us consider an infinitely repeated prisoner's dilemma. Assume that each player's strategy space is restricted to the two strategies TFT and always defect (ALLD). The following four outcomes and associated payoffs for player 1 are possible. Since the game is symmetric player 2's payoffs are the same, as can be seen in figure 4.4.

$$\Pi_1(TFT, TFT) = R + \delta R + \delta^2 R + ... = \frac{R}{1-\delta} \quad (4.1)$$

$$\Pi_1(TFT, ALLD) = S + \delta P + \delta^2 P + ... = S - P + \frac{P}{1-\delta} \quad (4.2)$$

$$\Pi_1(ALLD, TFT) = T + \delta P + \delta^2 P + ... = T - P + \frac{P}{1-\delta} \quad (4.3)$$

$$\Pi_1(ALLD, ALLD) = P + \delta P + \delta^2 P + ... = \frac{P}{1-\delta} \quad (4.4)$$

		Player 2	
		TFT	$ALLD$
Player 1	TFT	$\frac{R}{1-\delta}, \frac{R}{1-\delta}$	$S-P+\frac{P}{1-\delta}, T-P+\frac{P}{1-\delta}$
	$ALLD$	$T-P+\frac{P}{1-\delta}, S-P+\frac{P}{1-\delta}$	$\frac{P}{1-\delta}, \frac{P}{1-\delta}$

Figure 4.4: Payoff matrix for the two strategies TFT and ALLD in an infinitely repeated prisoner's dilemma.

Player 1 thinks about her optimal strategy. If player 2 plays ALLD, player 1's best response is to also play ALLD since $\Pi(ALLD, ALLD) > \Pi(TFT, ALLD)$. But if player 2 plays TFT, player 1's best response is TFT if $\Pi(TFT, TFT) > \Pi(ALLD, TFT)$ and ALLD else. If player 2 plays TFT, TFT is the best response if $\frac{T-R}{T-P} \leq \delta$ (see also Axelrod, 2006 (1984), and Elsner and Heinrich, 2009).

$$\frac{T-R}{T-P} \leq \delta \quad (4.5)$$

Assume that this is indeed the case and TFT is the best response to itself. The game in figure 4.4 is equivalent to a stag hunt game and there are two Nash equilibria, (TFT,TFT) and (ALLD,ALLD). Which one will be selected depends on the players' beliefs. Denote player 1's belief that player 2

will play TFT by $\tilde{p}$. Then, player 1's expected payoffs from playing TFT and ALLD are defined as follows.

$$E\Pi_1(TFT) = \tilde{p}\Pi_1(TFT, TFT) + (1 - \tilde{p})\Pi_1(TFT, ALLD) \quad (4.6)$$

$$E\Pi_1(ALLD) = \tilde{p}\Pi_1(ALLD, TFT) + (1 - \tilde{p})\Pi_1(ALLD, ALLD) \quad (4.7)$$

It can be shown that TFT yields the higher expected payoff if $\tilde{p} > \frac{P-S}{\frac{R-P}{1-\delta}+2P-S-T}$. We see that the strategy which player 1 will choose depends on her beliefs about her opponent. If inequality 4.5 holds and if both players' beliefs ($\tilde{p}$) are high enough, both players will choose TFT and hence cooperate forever, which is called the single-shot solution (Elsner and Heinrich, 2009; Elsner et al., forthcoming). Otherwise they will end up defecting forever.

Following Elsner and Heinrich (2009) we examine the critical factors for cooperation. First, let us look at equation 4.5. Cooperation is logically possible if this inequality holds which is more likely the lower the *opportunity costs of common cooperation* $(T - R)$ relative to the *opportunity costs of common defection* $(T - P)$. Also, the discount factor δ that players apply within the repeated game is of critical importance. The payoffs in figure 4.4 can be interpreted in two ways. First, they can be interpreted as the payoffs for a prisoner's dilemma which is repeated infinitely often. In this case δ is the players' discount factor. Second, the payoffs can be interpreted as the payoffs resulting from a prisoner's dilemma which is repeated indefinitely often. In this case δ can be decomposed as follows.

$$\delta = \frac{\hat{\delta}}{1+r} \quad (4.8)$$

In equation 4.8 the parameter r is the player's time preference, which is inversely related to cooperation. The more weight players put on consumption today as opposed to consumption tomorrow, the less likely is the emergence of cooperation. The parameter $\hat{\delta}$ is the *probability that the game continues* and is directly related to cooperation. The higher the probability that the repeated game continues, the more likely is the emergence of cooperation. This is referred to by Axelrod (1984) as the *shadow of the future*.[75]

75 The expected length of an interaction is also the starting point of 'horizonal theory', investigating the relation between the efficient use of resources and the planning horizon. A 'horizon effect' shifting the planning horizon further into the future thus increases the probability that resources are used efficiently, i.e., a Pareto-improvement can be achieved (Jennings, 2005, 2010).

The parameter p has two different interpretations, depending on the assumptions about how the game is played. First, in a two person setting p is a player's prior probability about the other player's strategy. Second, in a population perspective p is the expected probability to meet a TFT player. In both cases a high value of p is favorable for the emergence of cooperation. This line of research investigating the conditions for cooperation to be possible in the repeated prisoner's dilemma has a long tradition (Schotter, 1981; Kreps and Wilson, 1982; Kreps et al., 1982; Axelrod, 1984; Elsner, 2005; Elsner and Heinrich, forthcoming). By focusing on the parameters p, $\hat{\delta}$, and r cooperation can be achieved if players have appropriate beliefs, play the game a large number of times with the same opponent, and have a low time preference. In explaining cooperation in social production communities we do not pursue this line because members of social production communities can leave the community at any time, thus making it unlikely that the game is played a large number of times with the same opponent. Furthermore, there is no evidence that members of social production communities have a low time preference. In explaining cooperation in social production communities through social approval we take a different perspective and show how cooperation can be explained even if players do not play the game a large number of times with the same opponent and even if players do not have a low time preference.

4.3 Complex Strategy Spaces and Multiplicity of Nash Equilibria

Up to now we considered only two simple strategies, TFT and ALLD, but in (finitely and infinitely) repeated games a large number of strategies is possible in principle and the number of Nash equilibria gets very large. Axelrod's and Lindgren's simulations, which we discuss below, can be considered to be a response to the complexity of strategy spaces and the multiplicity of Nash equilibria.

The complexity of strategy spaces can be illustrated by looking at the size of a player's strategy space, i.e., the total number of strategies that one player could use. A player's strategy space grows double-exponentially in the number of repetitions of the game (Okada and Neyman, 2003). At each round t the history $\mathcal{H}^t$ represents the information available to each player at the beginning of the t-th round. Player i's strategy at the t-th round is a mapping

$\sigma_{i,t} : \mathcal{H}^t \rightarrow A_i$. Player i's strategy in the repeated game can then be represented as a sequence $\sigma_{i,1}, \sigma_{i,2}, \sigma_{i,3} \ldots, \sigma_{i,\bar{t}}$. We denote the set of all $\sigma_{i,t}$'s by $S_{i,t}$. The strategy space of player i is the Cartesian product $S_i = S_{i,1} \times S_{i,2} \times \cdots \times S_{i,\bar{t}}$. The total number of possible strategies for player i in a game which is repeated $\bar{t}$ times is given by equation 4.9 where $m_i = |A_i|$ denotes the number of actions available to player i and $\bar{m} = m_1 \times m_2$ (for a two-player game). A concrete example for the repeated two-player prisoner's dilemma is given in table 4.1.

$$|S_i| = |S_{i,1}| \times |S_{i,2}| \times \cdots \times |S_{i,\bar{t}}| = m_i^{\bar{m}^0} \times m_i^{\bar{m}^1} \times \cdots \times m_i^{\bar{m}^{\bar{t}-1}} = m_i^{\frac{\bar{m}^{\bar{t}}-1}{\bar{m}-1}} \tag{4.9}$$

t	$\|S_{i,t}\|$	$\|S_i\|$
1	2	2
2	16	32
3	65,536	more than 2 million
$\vdots$	$\vdots$	$\vdots$
T	$2^{4^{T-1}}$	$2^{\frac{4^T-1}{3}}$

Table 4.1: The size of a player's strategy in each stage (second column) and the size of the complete strategy space (last column). A player's strategy space grows double-exponentially with the number of repetitions (example for the two-player prisoner's dilemma, i.e., $m_i = 2$ and $m = 4$).

The size of a player's strategy space summarizes all possible ways in which the player could play the game. The double-exponential growth of a player's strategy space illustrates the huge computational burdon which is placed upon players. As the game is repeated, the strategy space grows and strategies become more complex, meaning that each player has to consider more and more possible ways to play the game. This makes it increasingly

difficult, for both the rational economic agent and the economist, to determine the optimal strategy.[76]

Although unrealistic assumptions about players are not a problem per se, they generate a problem if they reduce the predictive power of the theory. Hand in hand with the computational complexity resulting from the double-exponential growth of the strategy space there is the problem of multiplicity of Nash-equilibria in repeated games. Formally, all strategies that satisfy the minimax-criterion can be rationalized as Nash-equilibria. The minimax conditions state that each player will minimize her maximum possible loss. It is fulfilled if the strategy yields a payoff higher or equal to the minimax payoff $\underline{v}_i$, which is the worst outcome for player i given that player i behaves optimally.

$$\underline{v}_i = \min_{a_{-i} \in A_{-i}} \max_{a_i \in A_i} \Pi_i(a_i, a_{-i}) \tag{4.10}$$

This result is known as Folk theorem, stating that in repeated games every outcome that satisfies the minimax conditions is a feasible solution concept (Friedman, 1971; Rubinstein, 1979). The Folk theorem proves that a large number of outcomes are possible and tells us that cooperation is only one outcome which is logically possible.

In contrast to the finitely repeated prisoner's dilemma where defecting in every round is the only subgame-perfect Nash-equilibrium, in the infinitey repeated game cooperation is one out of many feasible outcomes. On the one hand, this is a positive result since it reveals that it is possible to achieve cooperation, but on the other hand, it is a negative result because cooperation is only one among many possible outcomes thus severely restricting the predictive power of the model.

An increase in predictive power can be achieved by arguing that strategies that yield a high payoff will be employed by the players. The focus shifts from the question *What strategy would a rational player choose?* (the SPNE) to *What strategy yields the highest payoff?* In order to find out the performance of

76 Complexity can be reduced by exogenously restricting the growth of the strategy space by means of finite automata and bounded recall (Kalai, 1990; Neyman and Okada, 2000). Both finite automata and bounded recall introduce limitations on the amount of information a player can process. An example would be a player who can remember only the last three repetitions of the game. By restricting players' memory it is implicitly argued that players are boundedly rational. This form of bounded rationality results from players' bounded memory, but players' decisions are still the outcome of a (bounded) cost-benefit calculus. This is different in Gigerenzer and Selten's definition of bounded rationality, according to which players rely on heuristics, to be described later in this chapter.

a large number of strategies Robert Axelrod conducted a computer tournament.

In his first tournament Axelrod (1984) conducted a two hundred round repeated prisoner's dilemma. He invited scholars from various disciplines to submit strategies. All strategies competed in a round-robin tournament, each strategy playing against each other strategy. In addition each strategy was matched with a copy of itself and the strategy RANDOM which cooperates and defects with equal probability. Each submitted strategy was a computer program that took the history of the game as input and computed the player's next move. Since the number of possible strategies grows double-exponentially with time, the strategy space can become quite large and strategies can become quite complex. For example, the strategy DOWNING uses the complete history of the game to estimate conditional probabilities of the opponent's next move and then chooses the action that maximizes the expected payoff. Despite being a sophisticated strategy (33 lines of code), DOWNING only came out at the tenth position. Surprisingly, one of the simplest strategies (only three lines of code), TFT submitted by Anatol Rapoport, won the tournament. We already know that TFT starts with cooperation and then copies the opponent's move each round.

After the success of his first tournament Axelrod made his results available and again invited scholars to submit strategies for a second tournament. His second tournament was pretty much like the first tournament, with two changes. First, while in the first tournament the prisoner's dilemma was played exactly two hundred rounds, the end game effect was eliminated in the second tournament where each round the game continued with probability 0.99654, so that the expected median length of a game is two hundred rounds (Axelrod, 2006, p. 42 and p. 217). Second, the results from the first tournament were known to scholars, allowing them to improve upon well-performing strategies from the first tournament. In total, 62 strategies were submitted, and again, TFT won the tournament.

What can we learn from Axelrod's tournaments? A major finding is that the performance of more sophisticated strategies is not necessarily better than the performance of simple strategies. Examining all strategies that were submitted Axelrod identified three properties of successful strategies. (i) Successful strategies are *nice*. Nice strategies are never the first to defect. They perform well with each other because a nice strategy cooperates as long as the opponent cooperates. (ii) Axelrod called the propensity to cooperate again although the opponent defected in the past *forgiveness*. TFT

is unforgiving in the first move after the opponent's defection but then TFT is totally forgiving. (iii) The third property of successful strategies is that they are *retaliatory*. Retaliatory strategies are incited by the opponent's defection and behave retaliatory by seeking revenge (for example by defecting the next round). TFT is nice, forgiving and retaliatory. In addition, TFT is a clear strategy which can easily by recognized.

Is TFT the best strategy? Unfortunately, the answer turns out to be no. There is no single best strategy independent of the strategy of the other player (Axelrod, 2006). In the following we will illustrate this by looking at another strategy called Win-Stay, Loose-Shift (WSLS) and at Lindgren's evolution-of-strategies approach.

After Axelrod's tournaments much attention was focused on TFT. Soon it was found that there are two weaknesses associated with TFT (Selten and Hammerstein, 1984; Nowak and Sigmund, 1993; Imhof et al., 2007). First, in a noisy environment TFT does not perform well because it cannot correct mistakes. Suppose that two TFT players are matched and one of them erroneously defects in the first round, giving rise to retaliatory defection. This small error carries through all rounds of the game, and, starting from the second round, both players will always defect. Second, TFT is not evolutionary stable since it can be replaced by ALLC (getting the same payoff) in the presence of random drift. The ALLC population can then be invaded by ALLD strategies. In Axelrod's tournaments the first weakness was not visible since the tournaments were played in an error-free environment and the second weakness was not visible since only two strategies were matched each round of the tournament.

As a reaction to the disadvantages of TFT Nowak and Sigmund (1993) and Imhof et al. (2007) came up with a strategy similar to TFT but without the two weaknesses. The strategy win-stay, loose-shift (WSLS) repeats the previous move if the payoff was above a predefined treshold and changes otherwise. More precisely, if the payoff is T or R, WSLS repeats the same move (win-stay) and otherwise it switches to the opposite move (loose-shift). While TFT is a good strategy for getting cooperation going, its weakness is that it can be replaced by random drift.[77] WSLS, in contrast, is not so good at starting cooperation since it is exploited every second round if matched with ALLD, but if the level of cooperation is high it is more stable than TFT since it is not replaced by ALLC in the presence of random drift. Put bluntly, the strat-

77 Random drift refers to the fact that, in the absence of evolutionary pressure, the frequency of one strategy can increase due to chance.

egy TFT is a catalyst for getting cooperation started but once there is a high level of cooperation WSLS outperforms TFT. We see that the performance of a strategy depends on the environment, i.e., the strategies TFT is matched with.

Lindgren and Nordahl (1994) model the evolution of strategies in an unbounded space of strategies, illustrating the fact that there is no single best strategy independent of the environment from a different perspective. Strategies are modeled similar to genomes as bitstrings (i.e., sequences of zeros and ones). New strategies are created by a process of point mutation, gene duplications and split mutations. A point mutation changes just one bit, a gene duplication produces a more sophisticated copy of a genome/strategy by extending it, and a split mutation creates a new strategy by breaking up an existing strategy and keeping one part of it. Mutation is an endogeneous mechanism constantly introducing new and more sophisticated strategies (i.e., strategies that use more of the information contained in the history $\mathcal{H}^t$ to compute the next move), thereby changing the environment. Lindgren and Nordahl find that for a limited period of time a strategy which is similar to TFT (nice, forgiving, retaliatory) and WSLS (error-correcting) is dominant, but no single strategy will stay dominant for long periods of time. As new strategies evolve the dominant strategy gets replaced by a newer strategy that will stay dominant until an even more sophisticated, but similar strategy takes over. Again, we see that the performance of a strategy depends on the environment.

4.4 Evolutionary Game Theory

Classical game theory models the interactions of a small number of rational players. It is inherently static since at the beginning of the game players compute their strategies which are executed throughout the game. Evolutionary game theory, in contrast, is dynamic. The underlying game is played repeatedly and, over time, the frequencies of the strategies change. There is a variety of strategies in a large population and in response to selectionary pressures fitter strategies (i.e., strategies which yield an above average payoff) replicate faster while strategies that perform poorly go extinct.[78]

An important difference between classical and evolutionary game theory concerns their solution concepts. In classical game theory the central solu-

78 For a short introduction to evolutionary game theory see chapter 8 in Holler and Illing (2009), for a detailed introduction see Weibull (1997).

tion concept is the Nash equilibrium which is selected by perfectly rational players. The solution concept which is employed in evolutionary game theory is the *evolutionary stable state* (ESS) which is a state of the population in which the frequency distribution of strategies remains constant. Moreover, it is required that the population state is robust to mutations, meaning that mutants, playing another strategy, cannot invade the population. In evolutionary game theory players do not select the ESS but arrive at it through the invisible hand of natural selection. Stratgies which achieve low payoffs are wiped out through selectionary pressure.

How does the change from classical game theory to evolutionary game theory relate to our conception of the players? In evolutionary game theory players do not make choices as to maximize their payoffs. Rather, players can be thought of to make their choices according to rules-of-thumb or heuristics which they acquire through a process of imitative learning and cultural evolution. Cultural evolution can be understood as change in beliefs where a player imitates another player's strategy or experiments with a new strategy. Such a conception of players is more realistic than the idea of instrumentally rational players being characterized by unlimited cognitive abilities and unlimited computational capacities. The players in evolutionary game theory are closer to boundedly rational players who satisfice (adjust their strategy in order to attain an aspiration level) rather than optimize (Simon, 1957; Newell and Simon, 1972).[79]

According to Newell and Simon (1972) players use heuristics which incorporate "a common body of beliefs acquired through participation in a common culture" (p. 753), meaning that players do not come up with their heuristics on their own but aquire their heuristics through interaction with others. Empirical studies in cognitive sciences provide support for the use of heuristics (Gigerenzer and Selten, eds, 2001). In studying how people actually make their decisions they find that people reduce the complexity of the decision problem to manageable levels by using *fast-and-frugal heuristics*, i.e., heuristics which are efficient, easy to implement, and require minimal cognitive abilities. A heuristic works for a class of problems which are structured similarly, but might fail if applied to other problems. Hence Gigerenzer and

79 A problem with satisficing concerns the question of how players choose their aspiration levels. Unfortunately, Simon remains silent on this question, but the reader is referred to Sauermann and Selten (1962) or Selten (1998) for the first mathematical statement of aspiration adaption theory, Siegel (1957) for an early experiment, March (1988) for an application to decision making under risk, and Easterlin (2001) for the relation between households' aspirations and income.

Selten suggest that people are equipped with an "adaptive toolbox" containing different domain specific heuristics. The "adaptive toolbox" provides a model for decision making in which people do engage in rational deliberation to the extent of which they are capable. However, for complex decision problems in large worlds characterized by strong uncertainty and low information the extent to which players can engage in rational deliberation is limited. For such situations the "adaptive toolbox" provides a more realistic and empirically supported model for decision making which is built on peoples' actual cognitive abilities.

Returning to evolutionary game theory, a standard assumption is random matching in a very large population of strategies, meaning that all pairwise interactions are equally likely. Employing the random matching assumption transforms the stochastic interactions at the micro level into deterministic equations at the macro level. Mathematically, the dynamics in the frequency distribution of strategies is modeled as a system of differential equations (Taylor and Jonker's replicator dynamics to be introduced below). A stable fixed point in the dynamical system is then interpreted as the long-run distribution of strategies which is an ESS. Strategy X is evolutionary stable if equation 4.11, known as the *first-order best reply conditions*, holds with strict inequality, or if equations 4.12, known as the *second-order best-reply conditions*, hold (Maynard Smith and Price, 1973; Maynard Smith, 1974). (The payoff of strategy X playing against strategy X is denoted by $\pi(X, X)$ and the payoff of strategy X playing against strategy Y is denoted by $\pi(X, Y)$.)

$$\pi(Y, X) \leq \pi(X, X) \quad \forall \quad y \tag{4.11}$$

$$\pi(Y, X) = \pi(X, X) \qquad \pi(Y, Y) < \pi(X, Y) \quad \forall \quad Y \neq X \tag{4.12}$$

Next, we illustrate evolutionary stability using the prisoner's dilemma. Each period players are drawn from the population and pairwise matched. Each pair of players plays the underlying game, which in our case is the prisoner's dilemma. Players have one of two strategies, either they are cooperators, or they are defectors. Let λ be the fraction of players being cooperators, hence $(1-\lambda)$ is the fraction of defectors. Let the probabilities of meeting a cooperator and meeting a defector be given by p_C and p_D, respectivly. The vector $x = \begin{bmatrix} \lambda \\ (1-\lambda) \end{bmatrix}$ defines the population state.

$$\pi(C,x) = p_C R + p_D S = \lambda R + (1-\lambda)S \tag{4.13}$$

$$\pi(D,x) = p_C T + p_D P = \lambda T + (1-\lambda)P \tag{4.14}$$

$$\pi(x,x) = p_C \pi(C,x) + p_D \pi(D,x) = \lambda \pi(C,x) + (1-\lambda)\pi(D,x) \tag{4.15}$$

Equations 4.13 to 4.15 define the expected payoffs to cooperators, defectors, and the average payoff, respectively. Due to the random matching assumption and the very large size of the population the probability for a player meeting a cooperator is equal to the frequency of cooperators in the population, $p_C = \lambda$, and the probability of meeting a defector is equal to the frequency of defectors in the population, $p_D = 1 - \lambda$. If we plot these equations (see figure 4.5) we see that the expected payoff to defectors (dashed line) always exceeds the expected payoff to cooperators (solid line). Defection is the dominant strategy. Consequently, one would expect λ to converge to zero as the game is played repeatedly. Over time, players learn that defection yields a higher payoff. Cooperators will change their strategy and will imitate defectors.

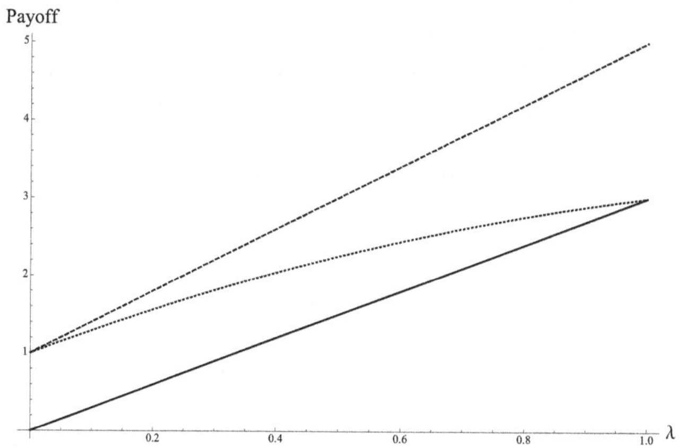

Figure 4.5: Payoff functions for $T = 5$, $R = 3$, $P = 1$ and $S = 0$; payoff to defectors is the dashed line, payoff to cooperators is the solid line, and average payoff is the dotted line.

The replicator dynamics (Taylor and Jonker, 1978) are given by equations 4.16 and 4.17, the former describing the evolution of cooperators' share, the latter the evolution of defectors' share.

$$\dot{\lambda} = [\pi(C,x) - \pi(x,x)]\,\lambda < 0 \tag{4.16}$$

$$(1 \dot{-} \lambda) = [\pi(D,x) - \pi(x,x)]\,(1-\lambda) > 0 \tag{4.17}$$

From the equations it is clear that the population share of cooperators (defectors) is always declining (increasing) for $\lambda \in (0,1)$. Solving for stationary states we get $\bar{\lambda} = 0$ (stable) and $\bar{\bar{\lambda}} = 1$ (unstable). Hence, over time we expect cooperators to die out. Defectors will be the only players that survive. We see that in the evolutionary stable state all players play the Nash equilibrium strategy. In fact, it can be shown that this will always be the case if the random matching assumption is used (Weibull, 1997, p.37).

Next, we consider how this relates to social production and the second-order dilemma. Social production communities successfully solve the public good dilemma. We consider social approval to be a main incentive motivating individuals to contribute to social production. This transforms the basic public good game into a public good game with rewards. If contributions are rewarded (through social approval) the payoffs of the game are changed. If the payoff to contributors is higher than the payoff to free-riders, free-riding is no longer the dominant strategy. If the reward comes from an third party (i.e., not from the players themselves) the dilemma is solved. If players themselves can give rewards, there is a caveat. Assuming that giving a reward is costly for the giver players have no incentive to give rewards. This is called a second-order dilemma, illustrated in equations 4.18 and 4.19. $\pi(X_1X_2)$ denotes the payoff from action X_1 in the first stage and action X_2 in the second stage of the game; C stands for contributing to the public good, R for giving a reward, N for not contributing or not giving a reward, and $h > 0$ are the costs of giving a reward.

$$\pi(CR) = \pi(CN) - h \tag{4.18}$$

$$\pi(NR) = \pi(NN) - h \tag{4.19}$$

We see immediatelly that (CN) strictly dominates (CR) and (NN) strictly dominates (NR).[80] Again, the result is a situation in which no rewards will be given and no contributions to the public good are made. The second-order dilemma can be solved through exclusion, and we will argue that this is the case in social production communities.

In chapter 5 we will build on this introduction to game theory. More precisely, we will consider an evolutionary model of a public good game with

80 Strategy A is said to dominate strategy B if the payoff to strategy A is not smaller than the payoff to strategy B, $\pi(A) \geq \pi(B)$. We speak of strict domination if the inequality between payoffs is a strict inequality, i.e., if $\pi(A) > \pi(B)$.

rewards played in a structured population, to be explained also in chapter 5. The reasons for choosing an evolutionary perspective are as follows. First, the players in evolutionary game theory are boundedly rational and follow fast-and-frugal heuristics. By modeling players this way we employ a theory of human behavior which we believe is more plausible and better supported by empirical evidence. Also, our choice of modeling players as boundedly rational alleviates the incredibly huge computational burdon which is placed onto rational players in repeated games. Second, as we learned from the Folk theorem, there are many outcomes which can be rationalized as a SPNE, and further refinement of the model is necessary to select one of the equilibria. Although evolutionary games can also have multiple equilibria, evolutionary game theory is a dynamic theory in the sense that it explicitely models how a population evolves towards equilibrium. The third reason for choosing evolutionary game theory over classical game theory is that the former explicitely models a population of players. Since social institutions exist in a population (even if not all members of the population follow the institution), we believe that evolutionary game theory is the appropriate method to model the exchange of social approval and emergence, stability, and enforcement of a social institution.

4.5 Upshot of Chapter 4

In this chapter we started with a detailed discussion of social approval as an incentive. We distinguished between the intrinsic and extrinsic value of social approval. Then, we focused in the intrinsic value of social approval and examined the exchange of social approval in a game theoretic model. We saw that the introduction of rewards gives rise to a second-order dilemma, and that game theoretic models cannot explain cooperation unless the game is played an infinite (or finite but unknown) number of times. The appropriate solution concept for repeated games is the subgame-perfect Nash equilibrium (SPNE) but in finitely repeated games the SPNE is uniform defection. If the game is transformed into an infinitely repeated game (or a finitely repeated game with unknown endpoint) cooperation becomes logically possible. The Folk theorem, however, tells us that cooperation is only one out of many possible outcomes since all strategies that fulfill the minimax-requirement are feasible outcomes (see Appendix A, Chapter 12 in Mas-Colell et al., 1995).

In his tournaments Axelrod investigated several strategies and identified the traits of successful strategies: nice, forgiving and retaliatory. Moreover, his tournaments together with Lindgren and Nordahl's results revealed that there is no single best strategy independent of the environment the game is played in.

The multiplicity of Nash equilibria in repeated games as well as the importance of the environment suggest that evolutionary game theory is the appropriate tool for modeling recurring decision situations among a large number of individuals.

As the game is played repeatedly the strategy space grows double-exponentially and cooperation is only one out of many possible equilibria, restricting the predictive power of the model. At the same time, the large strategy space makes it necessary to assume players with extremely strong cognitive and computational capacities. This is in sharp contrast with models in evolutionary game theory. Evolutionary game theory models a population of strategies which replicate under selectionary pressure. The individual strategy's payoff is dependent on the environment and an equilibrium is a situation in which no single individual has an incentive to change her strategy in the particular environment. We saw that in the evolutionary game theory model the evolutionary stable strategy coincides with the Nash equilibrium strategy of the underlying game. More general, ESS are a subset of Nash equilibria. This result relies on one particluar assumption about the environment in which the game is played. The random matching assumption basically assumes that the game is played in an unstructured population where all pairwise interactions are equally likely.

In chapter 5 we will drop the random matching assumption and present a model where individuals can select with whom to interact. By explicitely modeling structure and allowing structure to change our model is able to explain assortative matching and exclusion, as indicated in section 5.1 above. We explicitely model the structure of the population as a directed network that changes over time. By allowing individuals to select their opponents individuals can choose with whom to interact. The model that we will discuss in chapter 5 is a public good game with rewards. By assumption, no-one can be excluded from the benefit of the public good. As individuals learn with whom to interact defectors will be excluded from receiving rewards (retaliatory behavior) while cooperators will be rewarded (nice behavior). Using a dynamic network to model the changing structure our model is able to

explain exclusion which solves the second-order dilemma and hence can explain contributions to the public good.

Chapter 5

Emergence, Stability, and Enforcement of Institutions

In section 4.1 we elaborated on social approval as a selective incentive and argued that social approval is of fundamental importance in social production communities. This chapter presents a stylized model of a public good game with rewards. We will interpret the rewards as social approval, although in principal the rewards can also be interpreted to be material gifts. The game is played by a large number of players arranged on a dynamic network. The network allows us to explicitely model interpersonal relations, or more specifically, one attribute of interpersonal relations, namely social distance. In contrast to standard models in evolutionary game theory, which rely on random matching, matching is determined by social distance. Moreoever, the dynamic structure of the network allows us to model the process in which social distance changes over time. We assume that giving rewards changes the social distance between players. Since a reward represents a gift which is given voluntarily we think this is a plausible assumption.

Using this chapter's model we investigate the conditions for emergence and stability. By emergence we refer a situation in which, starting from a population of selfish players, a situation in which a critical mass of players behave as prescribed by the institution, comes into being. The size of this critical mass has to be such that an almost efficient provision of the public good can be achieved.[81] By stability we refer to a situation in which the behavior that emerged does not break down but is sustained over long periods of time. Our model shows that emergence and stability are possible and in-

81 Taken for granted that the formulation "an almost efficient provision of the public good" is somewhat vague, we think that it is warranted because due to the particular setup of the model (in section 5.5) an efficient provision will almost never be reached. Players mutate and randomly try out another strategy, hence the population will be at the Pareto-optimum in which all players contribute only for very short periods of time.

vestigates the conditions under which this is the case. Moreover, the model shows that social approval is exchanged reciprocally.

On a more abstract level our model shows that a social institution, prescribing a certain behavior, can emerge from a population of selfish players and can be sustained over a long period of time. The social institution that we are concerned with prescribes giving rewards to contributors. But, as we will see, this is not enough. The social institution also has to be enforced, which happens through exclusion. Since network and strategies change, players learn with whom to interact and how to act. Due to the dynamic nature of the network free-riders will be excluded and only contributors who give rewards will also receive rewards. The model shows that in order to successfully provide a public good a community needs (i) an institutions prescribing to give rewards to contributors and (ii) a mechanism for enforcement of the institution. We find that a social institution, prescribing prosocial behavior and thus solving the second-order dilemma, can emerge from a population of selfish players. This is due to the dynamic structure of the network, making it possible to exclude defectors from the benefits of the institution. Surprisingly, only a small fraction of players have to enforce the institution in order to achieve a stable and efficient provision of the public good.

5.1 Structure & Exclusion

Rewards and punishments do not solve the dilemma problem but shift it to the next stage of the game. This holds true in the classical game theory model discussed in section 4.2.1 and the evolutionary game theory model discussed in section 4.4 since the ESS from the evolutionary model is identical to the Nash equilibrium. In general, ESS are a subset of Nash equilibria. This, however, changes if we introduce structure.

What do we mean by structure? Standard models from evolutionary game theory employ the random matching assumption. All pairwise interactions are equally likely. Together with the assumption that the game is played in a very large population this allows to transform the stochastic interactions at the micro level into deterministic dynamics at the macro level. Models with random matching assume an unstructured population. However, people interact more often with others who are close to them or refuse to interact with strangers. By structure we impose certain restrictions on the matching probabilities between players. Structure is often (but not necessarily) mod-

eled as a neighborhood structure or network reflecting geographical or social distance. In a one-dimensional lattice, for example, it is often assumed that players only interact with direct neighbors (Eshel et al., 1998). In structured populations a player's payoff not only depends on her strategy but also on her position in the network. A TFT player having two TFT neighbors will get a higher payoff compared to a TFT player having two ALLD neighbors.

The structure can be static, keeping the matching probabilities constant, or dynamic, allowing for matching probabilities to change over time. A change in structure can be thought of as an individual moving to a different neighborhood or staying in the same neighborhood but choosing other players to interact with. If players can somehow recognize each other, TFT players might choose only to interact with other TFT players while refusing to interact with ALLD players. In this case, partner-selection would change the structure in such a way that ALLD players would be excluded from the benefits of exploiting a TFT player. Exclusion requires that players have the capacity to monitor others' behavior, to memorize it and to recognize other players. Cooperation can thrive in a structured population if a TFT interacts only with other TFTs and will never receive the sucker's payoff. Modeling structure allows for exclusion, which is an efficient mechanism for the enforcement of institutions, as we will see below.

5.2 Public Good Games and Networks

The literature on evolutionary games often employs the random matching assumption. Players are drawn from a very large, strictly speaking infinite, population and all pairwise interactions are equally likely (e.g., DeSilva et al., 2010). While both assumptions, infinite population and random matching, are appropriate in biological settings like large populations of bacteria, the assumptions are at odds with most interactions of human beings (Alexander, 2007). Using a local-interaction model allows us to work with small, finite populations and to add social structure to the model. Since the 1990s the role of social structure has been recognized and local interaction models have received much attention, for example Nowak and May (1993); Eshel et al. (1998); Stark and Behrens (2010). Local interaction models are more realistic since they allow us to model small populations and constrained interactions. An interaction is constrained if "the probability that any two agents (selected at random from the population) will interact is not constant across

the population" (Alexander, 2007, p.35). Although the realism of assumptions is debatable, adding structure to evolutionary models is desirable since structure makes a difference for the predictive power of the model (for concrete examples see Durrett and Levin, 1994).

In most local interaction models the underlying game is played on a simple network such as a ring or a two-dimensional lattice but in general all kinds of networks are possible. In most models the structure is fixed and only strategies evolve but recently there has been some work on modeling games played on dynamic networks (Skyrms and Pemantle, 2000; Hanaki et al., 2007; Jun and Sethi, 2009; Vignolo, 2010). In these models both the individuals' strategies and the structure of the underlying network is allowed to change. Strategies and structure can change at different speeds and models with fixed strategies or fixed structure can be seen as limiting cases.

The structure of local-interaction models breaks the assumption of random matching and the dynamic nature of the network structure allows cooperation to emerge by enabling players to select their partners. Under certain conditions this will lead to a setting where free-riders are excluded from enjoying the benefits of the public good and the public good will be provided by a close-knit group of players behaving prosocially (Spiekermann, 2008). Hence exclusion via dynamic networks can promote prosocial behavior in dilemma situations.

5.2.1 Models of Network Formation

Hand in hand with the growing interest in local-interaction models economists became increasingly interested in models of network formation.[82] Networks are modeled using terminology from graph theory. Relations between several players are modeled as a graph where vertices (or nodes) correspond to players and edges (or links) correspond to relations between the players. The simplest form of a network is a non-directed graph with unweighted edges, i.e., either two players are connected or not. Links are said to be reciprocal and represent mutual consent in the sense that both players' consent is needed to establish and maintain the link. This is different in directed networks where connections are not necessarily reciprocal. In a directed network player A might be linked to player B although player B is not linked

82 We take Aumann and Myerson (1988) as the starting point for formal models of network formation in economics. This paragraph is based on Jackson and Wolinsky (1996); Bala and Goyal (2000); Jackson and Watts (2002); Demange and Wooders, eds (2005); Jackson (2005, 2008).

to player A. For example, a network of coauthors is sensibly modeled as an undirected graph (both authors need to agree) but a network of links between websites is sensibly modeled as a directed graph.

A central idea in the literature on networks is that networks generate value (Granovetter, 1973). This can be thought of as a player receiving information from her (direct and indirect) links to other players. Opposed to the benefits are the costs since it is assumed that establishing or maintaining a link is costly. The decision to form or sever a link is then made according to a rational cost-benefit calculus. The focus is on players' myopic decisions, which might be appropriate in small networks where players know each other and the benefits and costs are common knowledge.

An early model of network formation is presented in Myerson (1991), where n players are engaged in a noncooperative game. Each player's strategy space is the set of all other players. Each player chooses with whom to establish a link. After all players made their decisions choices are revealed and links are established between two players if there is mutual consent (i.e a link is established between A and B if A selected B and B selected A). A problem which arises is the multiplicity of Nash equilibria, so there is the need for refinements such as Jackson and Wolinsky's concept of pairwise stability (Jackson and Wolinsky, 1996). Pairwise stability refers to a state of the network where (i) no player has an incentive to sever an existing link and (ii) all links from which two players would benefit are part of the network. Another approach to cope with the multiplicity of Nash equilibria is to introduce random perturbations (Jackson and Watts, 2002). By introducing perturbations Jackson and Watts analyze which network structures are more stable and hence more likely than others.

In most models the the dynamics consist of making or breaking links as the result of players' strategic decisions. Following Skyrms and Pemantle (2000) we take a different route and model the network as probabilities of interaction which evolve according to learning dynamics. By explicitely modeling the learning dynamics we can explain prosocial behavior as the result of jointly learned, habitualized behavior coming from recurrent interactions (Elsner and Heinrich, 2009; Elsner, 2010). The model of a dynamic social network as proposed in this chapter differs from the models of network formation presented above in two important aspects.

First, most strategic models of network formation consider only binary links, i.e., either a link is present or not. This omits the fact that links can be of various intensities. In contrast to the models reviewed above, in our

model links are weighted, representing the fact that social distance between players is not a binary variable.

Second, while in the models presented above links are established or severed as the result of players' strategic decisions, in our model the changes in network structure are not the result of strategic decisions. In our model there is a large number of players and a change in the network corresponds to a change in social distance between two players. There is no immediate benefit associated with a change in social distance. The change in expected payoff resulting from a change in social distance is unknown and cannot be determined in advance because rewards are given probabilistically. By choosing reinforcement learning to model the change in social distance makes our model more plausible and more appropriate for the use in an evolutionary game theory model where players are characterized by bounded rationality, limited cognitive abilities and limited computational capacity.

5.2.2 Reinforcement Learning

For economists, the most familiar way of modeling an individual player's learning process is belief-based learing.[83] The individual player is assumed to have an internal model of how the world works and beliefs about unknown parameters. New observations enter the player's state of mind as new pieces of information. The new information is integrated into the player's beliefs which then govern behavior. Bayesian updating is the most familiar form of belief-based learning.

Reinforcement learning differs from belief-based learning in that reinforcement learning does not require players to be capable of high-level processing. Reinforcement learning influences future choices, but, in contrast to belief-based learning, no rationality must be assumed. Instead, reinforcement learing is compatible with boundedly rational players and environments characterized by low information. It can also be the case that reinforcement learning operates unconsciously.

The basic idea of reinforcement learning is the following: The player's choice among a finite set of alternatives (of size l) is governed by a probability vector $(p_1, \ldots, p_l)$ whose elements evolve according to the reinforcement dynamics described below. A payoff is associated with each alternative. The payoff of the chosen behavior together with some parameters (e.g., speed of learing) determine the evolution of the probability vector.

83 For a detailed survey on modeling economic learning see Brenner (2006).

A generic model for the evolution of the probability vector was introduced in Luce (1959). In Luce's framework the payoff for an action chosen might modify its propensity multiplicatively, additively, or in some combination. Luce assumed that there is a vector of propensities $(w_1, \ldots, w_l)$ which evolves according to

$$w_i(t+1) = \beta_i w_i(t) + \gamma_i \tag{5.1}$$

where β_i and γ_i are functions of the payoff for action i. Using a linear response rule probabilities are obtained by normalizing propensities.[84]

$$p_i = \frac{w_i}{\sum_{j=1}^{l} w_j} \quad \forall \quad i \in \{1, ..., l\} \tag{5.2}$$

Herrnstein (1970), and more recently Roth and Erev (1995), tested the linear response model and obtained what is called the *Matching Law,* stating that the probability of choosing an action is proportional to the accumulated payoff. Formally this implies that $\beta_i = 1$ and γ_i equals the payoff if action i is chosen and zero otherwise.

We use reinforcement learning to model the change in social distance as players exchange rewards. Giving rewards changes the social distance from receiver to giver and creates an obligation. By lowering social distance the likelihood that the receiver will reciprocate increases. The receiver's decision to reciprocate at some point in the future is not necessarily a conscious decision, especially if the size of the reward is low. Our focus is on social approval as a reward since social approval is an important motivation in social production communities, as we have seen in chapter 4.

5.2.3 Stochastic Dynamic Networks

Skyrms and Pemantle (2000) and Bonacich and Liggett (2003) apply reinforcement learning to network formation. They model the network structure as a weighted and directed graph which is represented by the adjacency matrix **W**. Since the network is directed, the matrix will, in general, not be symmetric. Skyrms and Pemantle (2000) assign weights to all links. Each entry of the matrix **W** is the weight of the link with $w_{i,j} = 0$ if there is no link.

84 If payoffs are negative the linear response rule can become problematic and one often adopts the logistic response rule, $p_i = \frac{exp(\kappa w_i)}{\sum_j exp(\kappa w_j)}$ where κ is a learning parameter.

It is assumed that $w_{i,i} = 0$ for all i. Each row $(w_{i,1}, w_{i,2}, \dots, w_{i,n})$ measures the closeness of all other players to player i.[85]

$$\mathbf{W} = \begin{bmatrix} w_{1,1} & w_{1,2} & \cdots & w_{1,n} \\ w_{2,1} & \ddots & \ddots & w_{2,n} \\ \vdots & \ddots & \ddots & \cdots \\ w_{n,1} & \cdots & \cdots & w_{n,n} \end{bmatrix} \tag{5.3}$$

Initially a complete graph is assumed and the weights of all links are set to a constant ($w_{i,j} = \bar{w}$ for all $i \neq j$). The initial situation corresponds to random matching in the sense that all pairwise interactions are equiprobable. Then, weights evolve depending on the outcome of the game.

In the simplest model an underlying two-person game is played in a finite population of players. Players have fixed strategies and partner selection is modeled through reinforcement learning. Probabilities of interaction are obtained from the weights according to equation 5.2. Players do not interact with themselves, i.e., $p_{i,i} = 0$ for all $i \in \{1, ..., n\}$. Probabilities are collected in a matrix $\mathbf{P}$ representing the state of the network (equation 5.4). Figure 5.1 illustrates the social network and associates probabilities of interaction for $n = 5$.

$$\mathbf{P} = \begin{bmatrix} 0 & p_{1,2} & \cdots & p_{1,n} \\ p_{2,1} & \ddots & \ddots & p_{2,n} \\ \vdots & \ddots & \ddots & \cdots \\ p_{n,1} & \cdots & \cdots & 0 \end{bmatrix} \tag{5.4}$$

Each period all players are matched and play a game. The choice of partners is governed by equation 5.2, i.e., players will interact more often with players who are close to them. After each round of the game weights evolve according to the learning dynamics (equation 5.5).

$$w_{i,j}(t+1) = dw_{i,j}(t) + \pi(i,j;t) \tag{5.5}$$

85 The weights are inversely related to social distance. Higher values for $w_{i,j}$ indicate that the social distance between i and j is lower. One possible metric for social distance between players i and j is given by $(1 - p_{i,j}) \in [0, 1]$. The limiting case $p_{i,j} = 0$ then implies that player i has no link to player j, i.e., the social distance between them is at its maximum $p_{i,j} = 1$.

The parameter $d \in [0, 1]$ is a discount factor giving less weights to payoffs accumulated in the past, and $\pi(i, j; t)$ is the payoff for player i playing against player j at time t. Interactions which resulted in higher payoff are more likely to be repeated. Empirical evidence for the idea that the development of social distance depends on the outcome of past interactions can be derived from van Dijk et al. (2002) and van Winden et al. (2008). They conduct an experiment which consists of three parts. First, they test subjects' social value orientation, defined as the preferences for allocations of payoffs between the subject and an arbitrary other individual (pre-test). In the second part a public good game is played repeatedly against the same opponent (partner matching). Finally, a post-test measures the orientation towards the opponent. The difference between the pre-test and the post-test is then interpreted as a measure for the strength of social ties. Van Dijk et al. use the socio-psychological concept of a social tie as representing an individual's sentiments regarding a specific other, hence their use of social ties is imilar to our use of social distance. Van Dijk et al. find a positive correlation between the strength of social ties and subject's success in the public good game, where own earnings (in the two-player public good game) or others' contributions (in the four-player public good game) are taken as proxy for success. The results form the experiment support the hypothesis that the de-

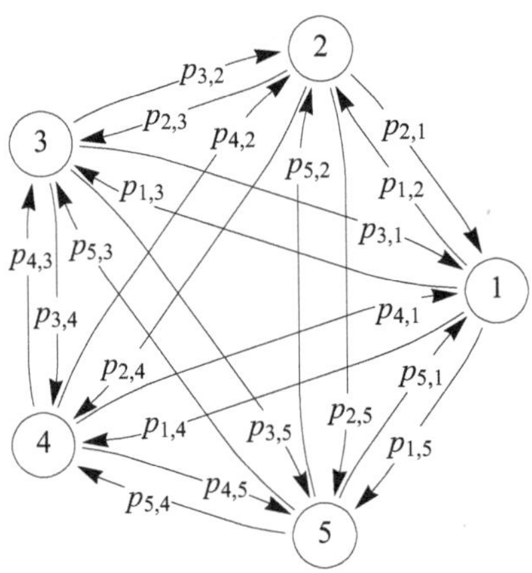

Figure 5.1: Social network and matching probabilities $p_{i,j}$ for $n = 5$.

velopment of ties depends on the success of interaction and thus provides support for the use of reinforcement learning in our model.

In our model we apply the idea of modeling a dynamic network to a public good game with rewards. The model shows that in a population of selfish players a social institution can emerge, leading to the efficient provision of the public good. Players learn to behave according to the institutionally prescribed behavior and sustain the institution by contributing to the public good and giving rewards to contributors. Deviation from the rule will be punished through exclusion from future rewards.

5.3 Social Approval as a Reward

Rand et al. (2009) argue that punishment generates a social loss and can give rise to acts of revenge, thus having negative effects on interpersonal relations. Rewards, however, do not generate a social loss and do affect interpersonal relations positively. Conducting public good games which were repeated over fifty periods Rand et al. (2009) show that the use of punishment declines over time while the use of rewards remains high, resulting in higher contributions to the public good. Building on their results we will consider rewards as gifts in the form of social approval.

In our model a reward can be given to contributors to the public good. We assume that the cost for the giver is lower than the benefit for the receiver, $h < b$. A gift is a reward that satisfies this inequality. Although almost anything can be a gift we will concentrate on gifts in the form of social approval. Such gifts are characterized by low costs for the giver but high benefits for the receiver.

5.4 A Public Good Game with Rewards

This section presents the basic structure of the game (section 5.4.1) before showing some results under random matching (section 5.4.2) and assortative matching (section 5.4.3). We find that under the random matching assumption the public good will not be supplied. Substituting assortative matching for random matching changes the dynamics of the model and the provision of the public good becomes possible. The underlying structure of the population is not explained but simply assumed. In section 5.5 we merge the model of a stochastic dynamic network and the public good game. Using

this model we show how a certain structure of the population can emerge and the public good will be provided.

5.4.1 The Structure of the Game

Public goods are associated with two distinct problems: overuse and underprovision. Assuming nonrivalry in consumption (a reasonable assumption for information and digital goods) the problem of overuse disappears and we can focus on the problem of underprovision. A social dilemma arises because individual and social benefits do not coincide. Since nobody can be excluded from the use of the public good once it is supplied, nobody has an incentive to contribute to the public good. One way of solving the dilemma is the giving of rewards. If rewards are given conditional on contributions, contributing becomes the dominant strategy.[86]

Assume that a group of n players, $\mathbf{N} = \{1, 2, \ldots, n\}$, is playing a public good game. After each round of contributions there exists an opportunity to give rewards. The game is played repeatedly and each repetition is referred to as a round of the game. Each round consists of two stages. In every stage all of the n players simultaneously make two decisions.

- **Contribution stage:** Each player decides whether to contribute to the public good or not. Let $c \geq 1$ be the cost of contributing to the public good. The public good is nonrival in consumption, hence the benefit of the public good goes to all players while costs are private. Assume that the quality of contributions is homogeneous and that $c_i = 1$ if player i contributed and 0 else, i.e. contributing is a binary decision. We will refer to the vector $\mathbf{c} = (c_1, c_2, \ldots, c_n)$ as the *contribution profile.*

- **Reward stage:** After the contribution stage players observe each others' moves, i.e., the contribution profile $\mathbf{c}$ is common knowledge. Each player is matched with a randomly chosen player (opponent) and has the opportunity to assign a reward to her opponent. Receiving a reward results in an additional payoff of b for the receiver at cost h for the giver. We assume the additional payoff from receiving the reward is higher than the cost of giving the reward, $h \leq b$.

For simplicity we assume that the public good has a linear production

86 Without an additional incentive for contributors defectors will enjoy the same public goods as contributors while only the latter will bear the costs. Consequently, contributors will be driven to extinction through selective pressure.

function and the value of the public good is given by the sum of contributions ($\nu = 1$).

$$PG(\mathbf{c}) = \nu \sum_{i=1}^{n} c_i = \sum_{i=1}^{n} c_i \tag{5.6}$$

In evolutionary game theory, a strategy's payoff is equivalent with the strategy's fitness or reproductive value. Analogous to Darwin's notion of the *survival of the fittest* it is assumed that fitter strategies replicate faster. This implies that payoffs are not necessarily monetary payoffs but that the payoffs are comparable between players. The payoff c then represents the loss in fitness from contributing to the public good, PG represents the gain in fitness from using the public good, b represents the gain in fitness from receiving a reward, and h represents the loss in fitness from giving a reward. Of course, the additivity of the payoff function is a simplification and is made for mathematical tractability.

A *strategy* is a blueprint specifying behavior for all contingencies (see chapter 3). In the public good game with rewards there are three choices. Let A_1 be the player's choice in the first stage and let $A_2|C$ and $A_2|N$ denote the choices in the second stage conditional on the opponent's behavior in the first stage. Since each player can condition her own action in the reward stage on her own and her opponent's action in the contribution stage, each player's strategy space consists of 32 strategies ($|S_i| = 2^5 = 32$, see table 4.1).

We assume that rewards are given only to contributors and that only contributors give rewards, which allows us to consider only a subset of the strategy space. We represent a player's strategy as an ordered pair $(A_1, A_2|C)$, defining the player's actions in each stage of the game. A_1 is the player's action in the contribution stage, and $A_2|C$ is the player's action in the reward stage if her opponent has contributed.[87] Then, the strategy space is the set containing all three pure strategies, $S_i = \{(CR), (CN), (NN)\}$ where C, R, N correspond to a contribution is given, a reward is given, and no contribution or no reward is given, respectively.

To facilitate further discussion of our model we introduce some terminology. *Enforcers* play strategy (CR) and behave prosocially in every respect. They contribute to the public good and enforce the institution by giving rewards. Players with strategy (CN) contribute to the public good but do not give rewards. We call players with strategy (CN) *Contributors*. Note that

87 Per assumption, $A_2|N = N$ for all players.

both *Contributors* and *Enforcers* contribute to the public good. The last strategy is (NN) which neither contributes nor gives rewards. Call players with this strategy *Free-Riders*. Correspondingly, there are three pure population states in which all players use the same strategy, called *Enforcement State, Contribution State*, and *Free-Rider State*.

Using open source as a public good to illustrate our naming convention we could say that a contribution to the public good consists of writing source code, and giving a reward consists of giving social approval. An individual writing source code and giving credit would be an *Enforcer*, an individual writing only source code but not giving credit would be a *Contributor*, and an individual who neither writes source code nor gives credit would be a *Free-Rider*.

Table 5.1 summarizes the labeling of the three strategies. The first two columns represent the strategy and its name. The third column gives the frequency of each strategy in the population. We will refer to the vector $s = (s_1, s_2, s_3)$ as the *state of the population*. The last column gives the name of the pure population state in which all players employ the same strategy.

Strategy	Name	%	Pure State
(CR)	Enforcer	s_1	Enforcement State
(CN)	Contributor	s_2	Contribution State
(NN)	Free-Rider	s_3	Free-Rider State

Table 5.1: Strategies and population states for the public good game with rewards.

5.4.2 Random Matching

Suppose that there is a very large population consisting of n players. The population is unstructured, i.e., there is no defined topology and there is uniform random matching. The probability that player i plays against player $j \neq i$ is given by $\frac{1}{n}$. We summarize all payoffs in the matrix $\mathbf{X}$.

$$\mathbf{X} = \begin{bmatrix} PG - c + b - h & PG - c - h & PG - c \\ PG - c + b & PG - c & PG - c \\ PG & PG & PG \end{bmatrix} \tag{5.7}$$

The payoff for a player using strategy i against a player using strategy j is given by the (i, j)-th entry of the matrix $\mathbf{X}$. Expected payoffs of all three strategies are given by the rows of $\mathbf{X}$ and spelled out in equations 5.8 to 5.10 where $PG = PG((s_1 + s_2)n)$.

$$E[\pi(CR)] = PG - c + s_1(b - h) - s_2 h \tag{5.8}$$
$$E[\pi(CN)] = PG - c + s_1 b \tag{5.9}$$
$$E[\pi(NN)] = PG \tag{5.10}$$

Reproduction takes place continuously over time. Assume that strategies evolve according to the well-known replicator dynamics (Taylor and Jonker, 1978), meaning that strategies with above (below) average payoff increase (decrease) in frequency.

$$\dot{s}_1 = s_1 [E[\pi(CR)] - \bar{\pi}] \tag{5.11}$$
$$\dot{s}_2 = s_2 [E[\pi(CN)] - \bar{\pi}] \tag{5.12}$$
$$\dot{s}_3 = s_3 [E[\pi(NN)] - \bar{\pi}] \tag{5.13}$$

$$\bar{\pi} = \sum s_j(\mathbf{X}s)_j = s_1 E[\pi(CR)] + s_2 E[\pi(CN)] + s_3 E[\pi(NN)] \tag{5.14}$$

The three differential equations 5.11 to 5.13 describe the evolution of the population state. $\bar{\pi}$ denotes the average payoff. The dynamics are visualized in figure 5.2. Each point in the simplex corresponds to a specific population state and the arrows indicate the dynamics. The vertices correspond to the *Enforcement State* (100 percent (CR)-players), the *Contribution State* (100 percent (CN)-players) and the *Free-Rider State* (100 percent (NN)-players), respectively.

As we can see from the expected payoffs, *Enforcers* (CR) are strictly dominated, $E[\pi(CN)] > E[\pi(CR)]$. This means that *Enforcers* will die out eventually. The two remaining strategies are *Contributors* (CN), and *Free-Riders* (NN). Since (NN) strictly dominates (CN) free-riding is the unique Nash equilibrium. The dynamics of the population state, visualized in figure 5.2,

confirm that the population will end up at the pure state with 100% *Free-Riders*.[88]

In section 4.2 we saw that the unique Nash equilibrium in the public good game with rewards is not to contribute and not to give rewards. With random matching the unique Nash equilibrium is also the evolutionary stable strategy (ESS). This can be proven by looking at the best reply functions. Strategy (NN) is the only strategy which is best reply to itself, hence it is an ESS.[89]

$$\pi(x, NN) \leq \pi(NN, NN) \quad \forall \quad x \in S_i \quad \text{with strict equality only if } x = NN \tag{5.15}$$

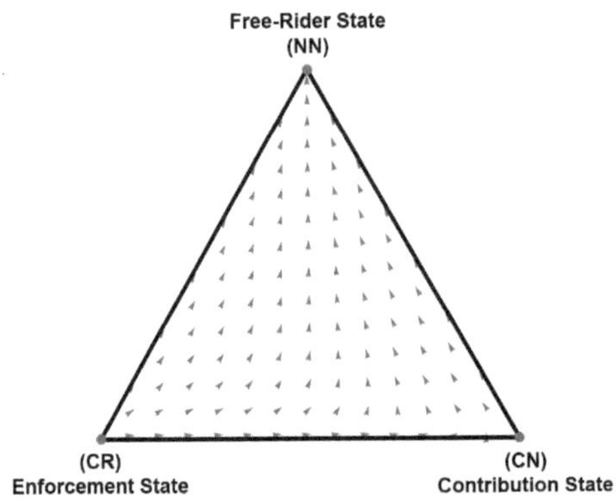

Figure 5.2: Simplex diagram showing the dynamics of the population state ($c = 1.0$, $h = 0.1$, $b = 1.3$). A population state on the line joining the lower left and lower right corner of the simplex correspond to an efficient provision of the public could.

Giving a reward is costly and *Enforcers* will always be dominated by *Con-*

88 The simplex diagram graphically depicts the frequencies of the three strategies. The simplex represents the state space of the population, i.e., each point in the simplex corresponds to a population state and the vertices correspond to the three pure population states. The vectors, derived from equations 5.11 to 5.13 and 5.8 to 5.10, illustrate the dynamics of the population state.

89 Introducing the strategy (NR) would make no difference since it is weakly dominated by (NN). Strategy (NR) yields a lower payoff than (NN) if $s_1 + s_2 > 0$ and the same payoff only if $s_1 = s_2 = 0$. A Nash equilibrium would then be any mixture of (NN) and (NR) players who would earn the same payoff. There are no contributions to the public good and no rewards are given. The behavior of both strategies is exactly alike. They are behaviorally indistinguishable and the only difference is based on a counterfactual, i.e., if another player had contributed (NR) would give a reward.

tributors, as well as *Contributors* will be dominated by *Free-Riders*. No rewards will be given and we are back to the public good game without rewards in which the dominant strategy is to free-ride. This result holds for any size of the reward. Rewards cannot solve the first-order dilemma because they introduce a second-order dilemma. If the second-order dilemma would be solved, i.e., if all players would give rewards, the first-order dilemma would be solved if the benefit of rewards is high enough ($(b - h) \geq c$).

In a similar model Sigmund et al. (2001) show that rewards or punishments fail to bring about prosocial behavior. Sigmund et al. then introduce reputation which means that players have information about the opponent's strategy before the game is played and can choose their own strategy accordingly. They show that reputation and punishment can solve the public good problem, but reputation and rewards produce complex and unpredictable behavior. Our model differs from Sigmund et al. (2001) because we do not consider reputation; instead we substitute contrained interactions for random matching.

5.4.3 Assortative Matching

With random matching *Contributors* will exploit *Enforcers*. *Enforcers* will change their strategy to (CN) first and then to (NN) represented by a counterclockwise movement in the simplex from the lower left corner to the upper corner. The public good will not be supplied.

The outcome of the game changes if the probability of exploitation is reduced by assortative matching which introduces a correlation between strategy and matching probabilities (Skyrms, 1996). Assume that players have some kind of sensory detection and are somehow able to recognize each other's strategy. For the moment let us assume that each player prefers to interact with players of the same strategy. Let the probability that a player with strategy x will interact with another player with strategy x be given by $p(s_x|s_x)$. The probability that a player with strategy x meets a player with strategy y in the second stage is given by $p(s_y|s_x)$.

$$p(s_x|s_x) = s_x + e(1 - s_x)$$

$$p(s_y|s_x) = s_y - es_y \quad \forall \quad y \neq x$$

Assortative matching changes the second stage of the game. The parameter e measures the strength of assortative matching with $e = 0$ for

random matching (uncorrelated encounters) and $e = 1$ for perfect correlation between strategies and matching probabilities. With random matching all players contributing to the public good (*Contributors* and *Enforcers*) have the same chance of receiving a reward since they have the same probability of meeting an *Enforcer* who gives a reward, $p(s_1|s_1) = p(s_1|s_2) = s_1$. With assortative matching the probability that two *Enforcers* meet is larger, $p(s_1|s_1) > s_1 > p(s_1|s_2)$, so *Enforces* will, on average, receive more rewards. Expected payoffs are now given by equations 5.16 to 5.18.

$$E[\pi(CR)] = PG - c + \underbrace{p(s_1|s_1)(b-h)}_{\text{increasing with } e} - \underbrace{p(s_2|s_1)h}_{\text{decreasing with } e} \qquad (5.16)$$

$$E[\pi(CN)] = PG - c + \underbrace{p(s_1|s_2)b}_{\text{decreasing with } e} \qquad (5.17)$$

$$E[\pi(NN)] = PG \qquad (5.18)$$

The expected payoff for free-riding, $E[\pi(NN)]$, remains unchanged since *Free-Riders* neither give nor receive rewards. For *Contributors*, (CN), the expected payoff decreases because they are less likely to meet an *Enforcer* from whom they will receive a reward. For *Enforcers*, (CR), assortative matching increases the expected payoff since they will meet more players of their own strategy who will give rewards to them.[90]

Assortative matching changes the population dynamics, as can be seen in figure 5.3 showing the dynamics for different values of e. With random matching the Nash equilibrium prediction and the evolutionary stable strategy coincide. This is not the case if we assume assortative matching. There is another stable state of the population in which all players contribute and give rewards. This is the *Enforcement State* corresponding to the lower left corner in the simplex.[91] If we compare Figures 5.3(a) and 5.3(b) we see that by increasing e the size of the basin of attraction for the *Enforcement State* increases. This means that if we start from random initial conditions the population is more likely to end up at the *Enforcement State* in which all players follow the

90 Also with assortative matching, introducing the strategy (NR) would make no difference since it is weakly dominated by strategy (NN). Strategy (NR)'s maximum payoff is PG which is achieved if $e = 1$ or if $0 \leq e < 1$ and $s_1 = s_2 = 0$, else strategy (NR) receives a payoff lower than PG. Strategy (NR)'s payoff is always PG, hence it is always greater or equal than strategy (NR)'s payoff.

91 There is also an additional unstable equilibrium lying on the line joining the lower left and the upper corner.

institutionally prescribed behavior (contribute and enforce the institution by giving rewards to contributors) and the public good will be supplied.

But how exactly is assortative matching supposed to arise? In this section we just assumed that players preferably interact with others of same strategy. For players who give rewards assortative matching is perfectly rational, but for all other players it is not. Every player is better off if she interacts with an *Enforcer* and can exploit her. The next section presents a model of the public good game with rewards played on a dynamic network. Starting from random matching the network evolves, leading to constrained interaction where *Enforcers* interact with each other (assortative matching).

5.5 Coevolution of Strategy and Structure

Stochastic dynamic networks have been introduced above (section 5.2.3). In this section we apply a model of a stochastic dynamic network to the public good game presented in section 5.4.1. First, we fix players' strategies and look at the structure of the network. Then, we allow for coevolution of structure and strategy and look at the long-run fractions of *Enforcers, Contributors* and *Free-Riders*.

Let us assume that the public good game with rewards is played on a

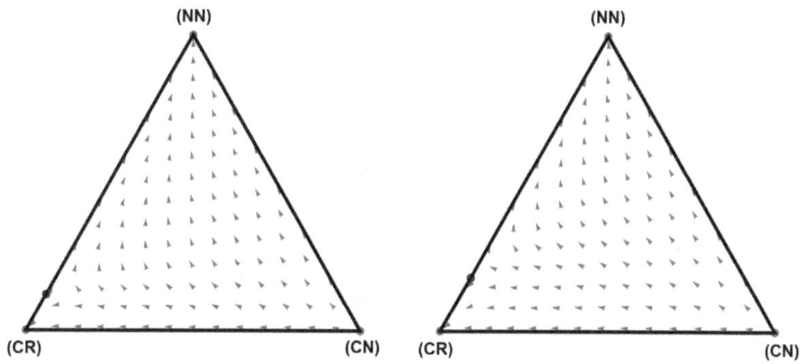

(a) (b)

Figure 5.3: Simplex diagram showing the dynamics of the population state with (a) weak assortative matching, $e = 0.25$, and (b) strong assortative matching, $e = 0.5$ ($c = 1.0$, $h = 0.1$, $b = 1.3$). The dynamics are derived from equations 5.11 to 5.13 and 5.16 to 5.18.

dynamic network. In the first stage players decide whether to contribute to the public good or not. The first stage has no direct influence on social structure. In the second stage players can give rewards to contributors. In the reward stage we allow each player to give m rewards at most. Equations 5.16 to 5.18 define the payoffs for $m = 1$, for the general case, $m \geq 1$, payoffs are given by equations 5.19 to 5.21.

$$E[\pi(CR)] = PG - c + p(s_1|s_1)m(b-h) - p(s_2|s_1)mh \quad (5.19)$$
$$E[\pi(CN)] = PG - c + p(s_1|s_2)mb \quad (5.20)$$
$$E[\pi(NN)] = PG \quad (5.21)$$

Giving rewards changes the social structure by decreasing the social distance between receiver and giver. Denote the set of all contributors containing all *Enforcers* and *Contributors* by **Q**. Each *Enforcer* i selects m other players at most (fewer than m players if there are fewer than m players contributing to the public good). The probability that a particular contributor j is selected by player i is proportional to the strength of the link $w_{i,j}$. This reflects the intuition that players are more likely to give rewards to contributors who are close to them. Denote the set of all players selected by player i as $\mathbf{Q}_i \subseteq \mathbf{Q}$. Player i now gives a reward to each player she has selected (all players in $\mathbf{Q}_i$). We assume that each *Enforcer* gives either zero or one reward (but not two or more rewards) to each contributor.

At the end of the reward stage new propensities of interaction are computed by equation 5.22, and probabilities are obtained according to equation 5.23.

$$w_{j,i}(t+1) = \begin{cases} dw_{j,i}(t) + b & \text{if player } i \text{ gave a reward to agent } j \\ dw_{j,i}(t) & \text{else} \end{cases} \quad (5.22)$$

$$p_{j,i} = \frac{w_{j,i}}{\sum_{s=1}^{n} w_{j,s}} \quad (5.23)$$

The reward creates a bond of loyalty by decreasing the social distance between giver and receiver. This is analogous to the social exchange of gifts (van Dijk et al., 2002; Brennan and Pettit, 2000; Holländer, 1990). Like a gift, a reward is given voluntarily, imposes costs on the giver and confers a benefit

on the receiver. The receiver will generally react with gratitude or sympathy. Thus it is not unreasonable that social distance decreases.

At this point it should be clear that the structure of the network is of crucial importance. Both *Enforcers* and *Contributors* are in the set Q and receive rewards. The distribution of rewards between *Enforcers* and *Contributors* depends on the structure of the network and determines the payoffs which in turn determine the population dynamics.

5.5.1 Fixed Strategies

Let us first look at the extreme case in which strategies are fixed and only the network changes. Let there be n players playing the public good game on a dynamic network. The three strategies (*Enforcers, Contributors, Free-Riders*) are randomly distributed and do not change. Players keep their initial strategy but the social structure evolves according to equation 5.22.

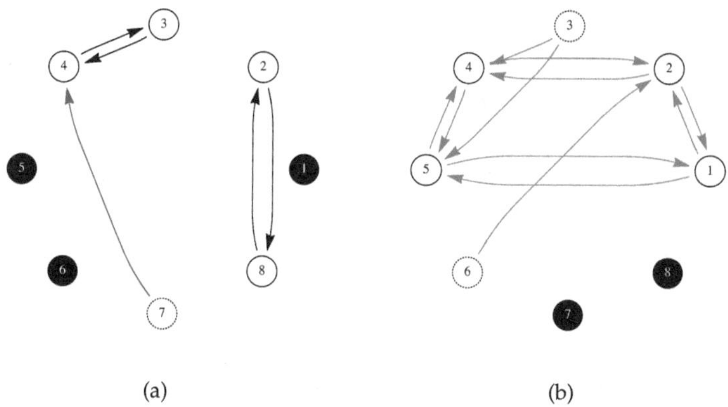

Figure 5.4: A reciprocal network. No updating of strategies, $m = 1, b = 1.3$ (left) and $m = 2$, $b = 0.7$ (right); other parameters are $d = 0.5$ and $h = 0.1$ (left and right). (CR) players (white, solid border) have reciprocal links, (CN) players (white, dotted border) have only outgoing links, and (NN) players (black) get isolated. Darker links correspond to higher probabilities of interaction (black if $p_{i,j} = 1$, white if $p_{i,j} = 0$).

Figure 5.4 shows the structure of the network after 1,000 periods and illustrates how players who do not behave as prescribed by the institution are excluded from the benefits produced by the institution. Figure 5.4(a) depicts a public good game where players could give give $m = 1$ reward. We see

that *Enforcers* form dyads and reciprocally give rewards to each other. Social distances are symmetric indicating the absence of hierachical relations. *Contributors* have only outgoing links, like player 6 in figure 5.4(b). At the beginning of the game player 2 gave several rewards to player 6, and these rewards strengthened the link from player 6 to player 2. This relatively strong link from player 6 to 2 means that if player 6 would change her strategy and become an *Enforcer*, she would be more likely to give a reward to player 2 than to any other player. The absence of incoming links reflects the fact that they do not receive rewards. The last group consists of *Free-Riders* who neither contribute nor give rewards. Since they do not give or receive any rewards they are isolated.

Figure 5.4(b) shows the structure of the network after 1,000 periods when players are allowed to give $m = 2$ rewards. While before *Enforcers* formed dyads, now they form triads. Within the triads social distances are symmetric indicating reciprocity. Equations 5.24 and 5.25 depicts the corresponding **P**-matrices. The rows not always some up to exactly 1.0 because the values are rounded.

$$\mathbf{P} = \begin{bmatrix} 0.000 & 0.143 & 0.143 & 0.143 & 0.143 & 0.143 & 0.143 & 0.143 \\ 0.000 & 0.000 & 0.000 & 0.000 & 0.000 & 0.000 & 0.000 & 1.000 \\ 0.000 & 0.000 & 0.000 & 1.000 & 0.000 & 0.000 & 0.000 & 0.000 \\ 0.000 & 0.000 & 1.000 & 0.000 & 0.000 & 0.000 & 0.000 & 0.000 \\ 0.143 & 0.143 & 0.143 & 0.143 & 0.000 & 0.143 & 0.143 & 0.143 \\ 0.143 & 0.143 & 0.143 & 0.143 & 0.143 & 0.000 & 0.143 & 0.143 \\ 0.005 & 0.005 & 0.005 & 0.857 & 0.005 & 0.005 & 0.000 & 0.117 \\ 0.000 & 1.000 & 0.000 & 0.000 & 0.000 & 0.000 & 0.000 & 0.000 \end{bmatrix} \tag{5.24}$$

$$\mathbf{P} = \begin{bmatrix} 0.000 & 0.500 & 0.000 & 0.000 & 0.500 & 0.000 & 0.000 & 0.000 \\ 0.500 & 0.000 & 0.000 & 0.500 & 0.000 & 0.000 & 0.000 & 0.000 \\ 0.108 & 0.035 & 0.000 & 0.328 & 0.425 & 0.035 & 0.035 & 0.035 \\ 0.000 & 0.500 & 0.000 & 0.000 & 0.500 & 0.000 & 0.000 & 0.000 \\ 0.500 & 0.000 & 0.000 & 0.500 & 0.000 & 0.000 & 0.000 & 0.000 \\ 0.118 & 0.601 & 0.049 & 0.049 & 0.084 & 0.000 & 0.049 & 0.049 \\ 0.143 & 0.143 & 0.143 & 0.143 & 0.143 & 0.143 & 0.000 & 0.143 \\ 0.143 & 0.143 & 0.143 & 0.143 & 0.143 & 0.143 & 0.143 & 0.000 \end{bmatrix} \tag{5.25}$$

Generally, it holds that without updating of strategies all *Enforcers* form a reciprocal network. *Enforcers* exchange rewards with each other in a reciprocal way and all other players are excluded from receiving rewards. This is

made more precise in the following two results, which hold if players do not change their strategies.[92]

Result 1 (Exclusion): If rewards are given based on contributions and social distance, rewards will be allocated to *Enforcers*, and both *Contributors* and Free-Riders will be excluded from rewards. In the long-run the probability that *Contributors* and *Free-Riders* will receive rewards converges to zero. This result holds independently of the parameters b, d and m. Changing the parameters only changes the time in which we arrive at the result.

Proof (Sketch): Assume that all weights $w_{i,j}(0) = 1$, $d = 1$, and $m = 1$. We partition the set of all players into three distinct sets according to their strategies, $\mathbf{S}_{CR}$, $\mathbf{S}_{CN}$ and $\mathbf{S}_{NN}$. Obviously, $\mathbf{S}_{CR} \bigcap \mathbf{S}_{CN} \bigcap \mathbf{S}_{NN} = \emptyset$. According to equation 5.22 a connection $w_{i,j}$ is reinforced if and only if j transfers a reward to i, hence a connection is reinforced if and only if $j \in \mathbf{S}_{CR}$. Since (CN)-players never return a reward no connections between (CR) and (CN) players are reinforced. Formally, $w_{i,j}(t) = 1$ for all t, $i \in \mathbf{S}_{CR}$ and $j \in \mathbf{S}_{CN} \bigcap \mathbf{S}_{NN}$. Interactions between (CR)-players, however, are reinforced and the weights $w_{i,j}(t)$ go to infinity if $i, j \in \mathbf{S}_{CR}$. We now see (from equation 5.23) that social distances between (CR)-players decrease ($p_{i,j}$ increase if $i, j \in \mathbf{S}_{CR}$) and the social distances from (CR)-players to non-(CR)-players increase ($p_{i,j}$ decreases if $i \in \mathbf{S}_{CR}$ and $j \in \mathbf{S}_{CN} \bigcap \mathbf{S}_{NN}$). This means that non only (NN)-players (who do not receive rewards per assumption) but also (CN)-players are excluded from rewards. Formally, $\lim_{t \to \infty} p_{i,j}(t) = 0$ for $i \in \mathbf{S}_{CR}$ and $j \in \mathbf{S}_{NN} \bigcap \mathbf{S}_{CN}$. Q.E.D.

Result 2 (Reciprocity): If rewards are given based on contributions and social distance, rewards will be exchanged reciprocally between *Enforcers*. For $m = 1$ this is illustrated in figure 5.4 showing the network containing all types of players, and in figure 5.5 showing the network containing only *Enforcers*. The corresponding **P**-matrices are shown in equation 5.26. If the number of players is even, players will form dyads. In case the number of *Enforcers* is odd there will be dyads and one star consisting of three players. In each period the player at the center of the star

92 Considering the mathematics of the dynamic network, the matrix **P** is a discrete-time Markov chain whose state space is the set of all $n \times n$ matrices whose rows sum up to one and with zeros on the main diagonal. To derive our results we are concerned with the asymptotic behavior of **P** as time tends to infinity. For a detailed analysis the interested reader is referred to Bonacich and Liggett (2003).

receives rewards from both other players and gives a reward to each of the two other players with probability 0.5. (For a proof see Bonacich and Liggett, 2003).

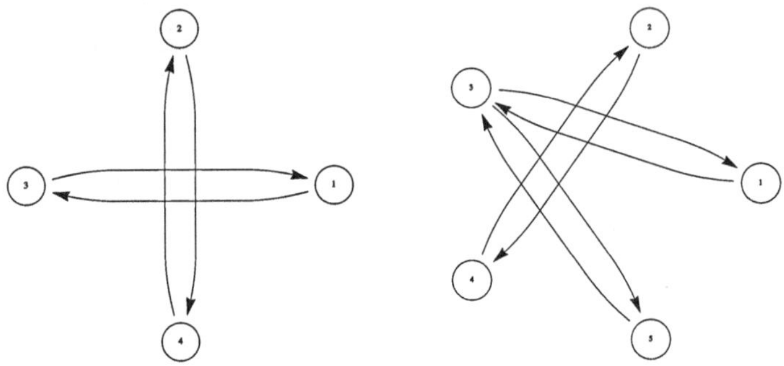

Figure 5.5: The reciprocal exchange of rewards. Here we look only at the network of (CR)-players where the number of players is even (left) and odd (right). Darker links correspond to higher probabilities of interaction (black if $p = 1$, white if $p = 0$).

$$\mathbf{P} = \begin{bmatrix} 0 & 0 & 1 & 0 \\ 0 & 0 & 0 & 1 \\ 1 & 0 & 0 & 0 \\ 0 & 1 & 0 & 0 \end{bmatrix} \qquad \mathbf{P} = \begin{bmatrix} 0 & 0 & 1 & 0 & 0 \\ 0 & 0 & 0 & 1 & 0 \\ 0.5 & 0 & 0 & 0 & 0.5 \\ 0 & 1 & 0 & 0 & 0 \\ 0 & 0 & 1 & 0 & 0 \end{bmatrix} \tag{5.26}$$

5.5.2 Strategy Updating

Now we consider the same model as above but in addition we allow players to change their strategy. At the end of each round each player wakes up with probability α and reconsiders her strategy. She looks at the player who has earned the highest payoff this round and imitates her strategy. With a small probability, η, players mutate and adopt a randomly choosen strategy. Since strategies and network coevolve, an equilibrium must be an equilibrium in strategies and in the structure of the network.

First, consider what happens if mutation is turned off, $\eta = 0$. Table 5.2 gives the number of simulations that converged to the *Enforcement State*, the *Contributing State* and the *Free-Rider State*. For each value of α, 100 simulations were run for 500 periods. Since all columns sum up to 100, we know that all simulations converged to one of the three pure states. At the pure states all players employ the same strategy and the network stays the same. If all players are *Enforcers* the network will be reciprocal, as described in section 5.5.1. By looking at the first row (table 5.2) we find that convergence to the *Enforcement State* becomes less likely if players change their strategies more often (higher α). From rows two and three we see that, if players change their strategies more often, the population converges to the *Contributing State* more often than to the *Free-Rider State*. This follows from the fact that for high values of α *Contributors* receive the highest payoff. If *Enforcers* are present, they will give rewards to *Contributors*. Since *Contributors* have the highest payoff, they will be imitated by all others and the population converges to the *Contributing State*. Of course this happens only if the network has evolved in such a way that *Contributors* are not exluded from the benefits of rewards. Otherwise, the population will converge to the *Enforcement* or *Free-Rider State*.

α	0.05	0.06	0.07	0.08	0.09	0.10	0.11	0.12	0.12	0.13	0.14
Enforcement State	99	95	86	70	67	61	43	36	25	14	10
Contribution State	0	2	5	19	21	20	36	41	53	57	63
Free-Rider State	1	3	9	11	12	19	21	23	22	29	27

Table 5.2: No mutation. Number of simulations (out of 100) that converged to the prosocial, dissembling and antisocial state. Parameters: $n = 100$, $d = 0.9$, $c = 1.0$, $m = 1$, $b = 1.3$, $h = 0.1$, $t = 500$.

Now we introduce a small probability of mutation ($\eta = 1\%$). Since there is persistent randomness if the probability of mutation is positive, any outcome can occur in principle. The question now changes from *What outcomes can arise?* to *What outcomes are more likely than others?*[93] In the presence of mutation it is still possible that the population converges to one of the states

93 For evolutionary games with persistent randomness the appropriate solution concept is not the evolutionary stable strategy but the stochasically stable equilibrium (Foster and Young, 1990) or the long run equilibrium (Kandori et al., 1993). These two (almost identical) concepts have been developed for games in which random matching is assumed to hold. Since we are not aware of any adaptions of these concepts to games in which the matching probabilities change, we do not use these concepts.

where all players have the same strategy, but the population will not stay there for long. All three pure states (i.e., states in which all players have the same strategy) are unstable since they can be invaded by a small number of mutating players.

If every player is an *Enforcer* the average payoff is $PG - c + m(b - h)$. Per assumption $m(b - h) > c$, so *Free-Riders* would earn a lower payoff and cannot invade the population. *Contributors*, however, can invade the population. If an *Enforcer* randomly changes her strategy and becomes a *Contributor* she will not pay the cost of enforcing the institution (i.e., the cost of giving a reward) but she will receive rewards. Assuming that she received m rewards, her payoff is given by $PG - c + mb$. Since the *Contributor's* payoff is higher than the *Enforcer's* payoff, the fraction of *Contributors* will increase. As more and more players become *Contributors* two things happen. First, the total amount of rewards given by all players decreases since the fraction of players who give rewards (i.e., *Enforcers*) decreases. The average number of rewards given to each player decreases. Secondly, over time *Enforcers* learn that *Contributors* do not reciprocate by returning rewards, so social distance between *Enforcers* and *Contributors* increases. As the network changes *Contributors* will be excluded from rewards, hence they now receive a lower payoff than *Enforcers* and *Contributor's* population share starts decreasing. Depending on whether an *Enforcer* or a *Free-Rider* has the highest payoff, *Contributors* will change their strategy to (CR) or (NN).

If every player is a *Contributor* the population can be invaded either by one *Free-Rider* or by two *Enforcers*. In a population of 100 percent *Contributors* each player's payoff is given by $PG - c$. A single player changing her strategy to *Free-Rider* would earn a higher payoff and so the fraction of *Free-Riders* would increase. Alternatively, it is possible that two players change their strategies to *Enforcer*. These two *Enforcers* contribute to the public good and give rewards to each other; their payoff is $PG - c + m(b - h)$ while the payoff of a typical *Contributor* is $PG - c$. Since *Enforcers* earn a higher payoff than *Contributors* the fraction of *Enforcers* will increase. In a similar way a population of 100 percent *Free-Riders* can be invaded by *Enforcers*.

Given that the state of the population will not converge to a pure state, how will the population state evolve? To answer this question we ran simulations for varying values of α and estimated average population shares of *Enforcers*, *Contributors* and *Free-Riders*. For each value of α, 100 simulations were run for $t = 600$ periods; the first 100 observations were discarded (to

avoid the influence of initial fluctuations). Figure 5.6 shows mean values and standard deviations of the population shares for different values of α.

We see that as α increases the share of *Enforcers* decreases (figure 5.6(a)). The share of *Contributors* increases until about $\alpha = 10$ percent and then decreases slightly but is relatively high (between 60 and 80 percent, see figure 5.6(b)). For *Free-Riders* it is noteworthy that their share increases as α increases beyond 10 percent and standard deviations increase also (figure 5.6(c)). The large standard deviations can be explained by looking at the representative simulation runs in figures 5.7 to 5.9.

The representative simulations were run for $t = 2,000$ periods; the simplices represent the population states (ignoring the time dimension) and the other figures show the evolution of the strategy shares over time. For very small values of α the share of *Contributors* is high (see figures 5.6(b) and 5.7(c)) while the shares of *Enforcers* and *Free-Riders* (figures 5.7(b) and 5.7(d)) are small but positive. Moreover, population shares are relatively stable. As the simplex (figure 5.7(a)) shows, the populations spends most of its time in the neighborhood of the lower right vertex, representing 100 percent *Contributors*. Although players still change their strategies the distribution of strategies remains roughly constant. There are periods in which *Contributors* have the highest payoff alternating with periods in which either *Enforcers* or *Free-Riders* have the highest payoff. If a well-connected *Enforcer* mutates and becomes a *Contributor*, this particular *Contributor* receives the highest payoff and will be imitated, leading to an increase in the share of *Contributors*. After a while, however, *Contributors* are excluded from rewards and have an incentive to change back to the *Enforcer* strategy. Since both *Enforcers* and *Contributors* contribute to the public good a stable and sustainable provision can be achieved. This slightly noisy equilibrium persists and is robust to mutations. Almost all players contribute to the public good although there are only very few players enforcing the institution. After a while (the first 200 periods) in which the share of *Enforcers* was high most players contribute to the public good and there is no need for much enforcement, so the share of *Enforcers* declines (figure 5.7(b)).[94]

For high values of α the population state evolves faster and different. It evolves faster because more players change their strategies within each period and it evolves different because the evolution of strategies is faster com-

94 A similar result is found in Huck and Kosfeld's model in which participation in neighborhood watch schemes breaks down if the primary aim is achieved, i.e., if burglaries get close to zero (Huck and Kosfeld, 2007).

pared to the evolution of the network. It becomes less likely that an *Enforcer* receives the highest payoff and gets imitated. The population state fluctuates between almost all players being *Contributors* and almost all players being *Free-Riders* (as can be seen in figures 5.8(c), 5.8(d), 5.9(c) and 5.9(d)). For short periods of time the share of *Enforcers* gets relatively large (see the spikes in figures 5.8(b) and 5.9(b)) but as α increases these fluctuations become less frequent. There will be only short periods of time in which most players contribute to the public good and a stable and sustainable provison of the public good will be impossible. Since our main concern in this chapter lies with the conditions for a stable and efficient provision of the public good, we summarize these conditions in Result 3.

Result 3 (Stable and Efficient Provision of the PG): A stable and almost efficient voluntary provision of the public good is achieved if α is small, meaning that social distances change faster than players' strategies. In such a situation the critical mass of players who behave as prescribed by the institution and give rewards to contributors is relatively small, but nonetheless the vast majority of players contribute to the public good.

Result 3 is illustrated in figure 5.7 where the share of *Enforcers* stays below 20 percent and contributions to the public good fluctuate between 85 and 100 percent.

5.6 Upshot of Chapter 5

We developed a public good game with rewards played on an endogenously changing network. The reward is considered to be the gain from receiving social approval when contributing to the public good, hence rewards are only given to contributors. Introducing rewards, however, does not solve the problem since rewards give rise to a second-order dilemma. If giving rewards is costly it is rational not to give rewards. In the standard model assuming random matching the population will converge to the *Free-Rider State*. The dilemma can be solved through assortative matching, i.e., a correlation between strategy and matching probability. Assortative matching decreases the payoff to *Free-Riders* and reduces the risk of being exploited. Depending on initial conditions the population will end up at either 100 percent *Free-Riders* or 100 percent *Enforcers*.

Assortative matching between *Enforcers* (players with strategy (CR)) is a necessary condition for the provision of the public good. Using reinforce-

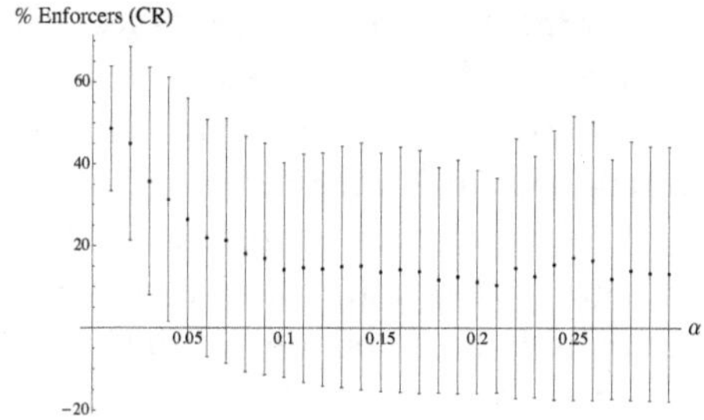

(a)

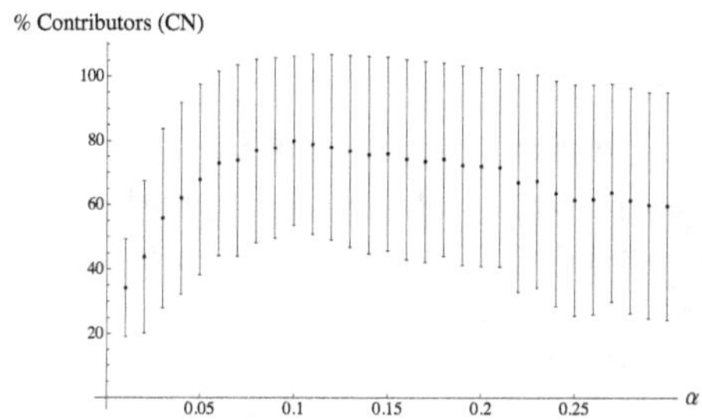

(b)

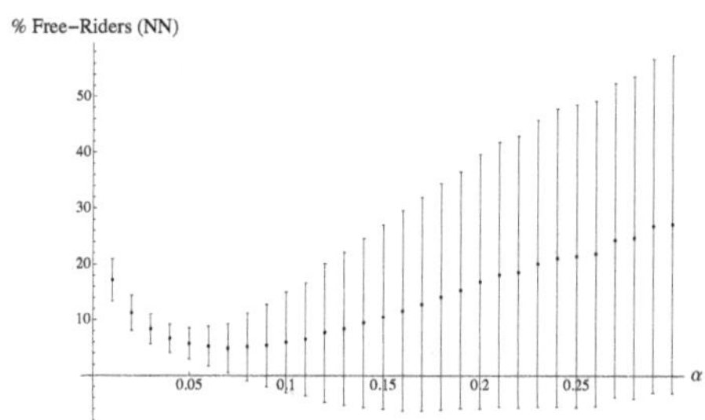

(c)

Figure 5.6: Statistical results: Mean values and standard deviations for *Enforcers* (top), *Contributors* (middle) and *Free-Riders* (bottom); $\eta = 1\%, m = 1, b = 1.3, h = 0.1, d = 0.9, n = 100$.

ment learning to model a stochastic dynamic network explains how assortative matching can arise. Without mutation the population will converge to one of the states in which all players employ the same strategy. The state the population will actually converge to depends on initial conditions and α. With faster updating of strategies (larger values of α) the provision of the public good becomes less likely because players change their strategies before the network has formed.

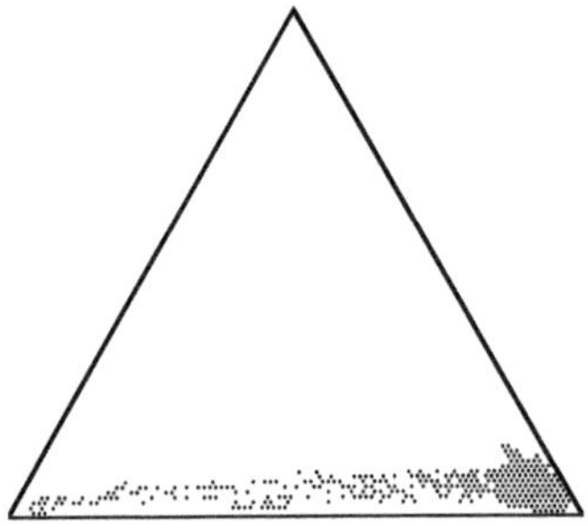

(a) Simplex, $\alpha = 0.05$.

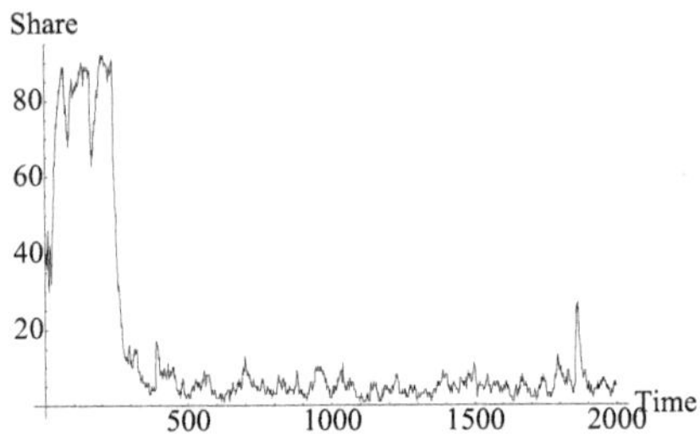

(b) Share of *Enforcers*.

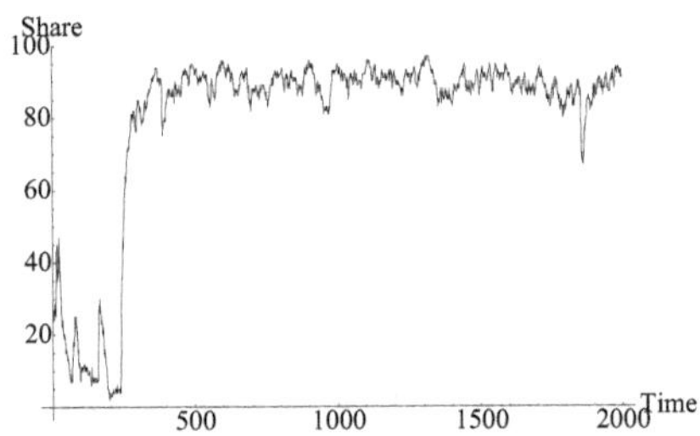

(c) Share of *Contributors*.

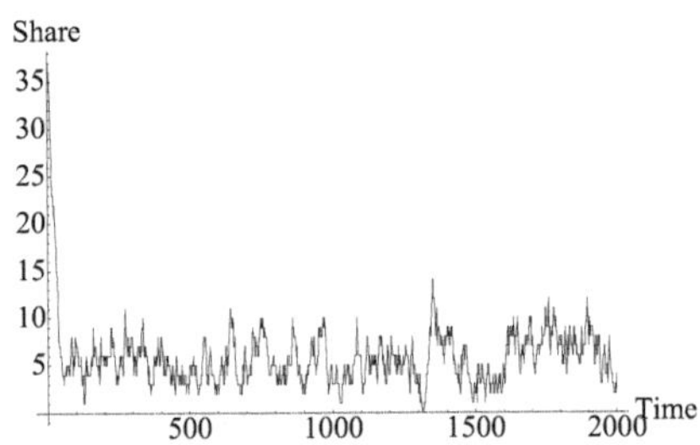

(d) Share of *Free-Riders*.

Figure 5.7: Representative run for $\alpha = 0.05$.

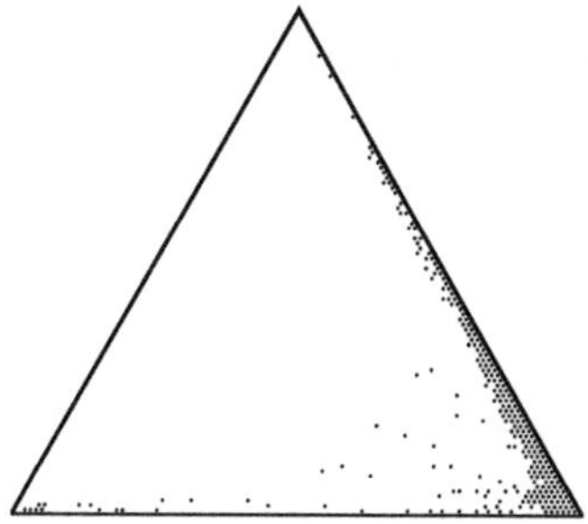

(a) Simplex, $\alpha = 0.15$.

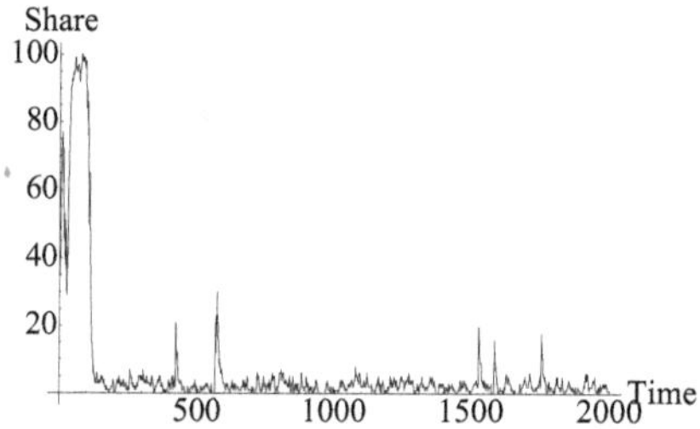

(b) Share of *Enforcers*.

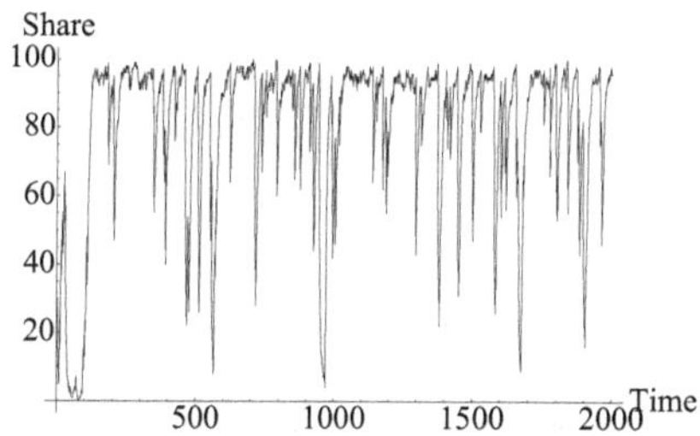

(c) Share of *Contributors*.

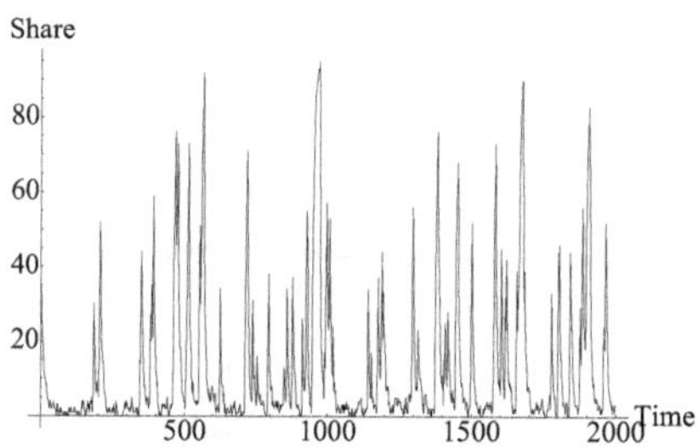

(d) Share of *Free-Riders*.

Figure 5.8: Representative run for $\alpha = 0.15$.

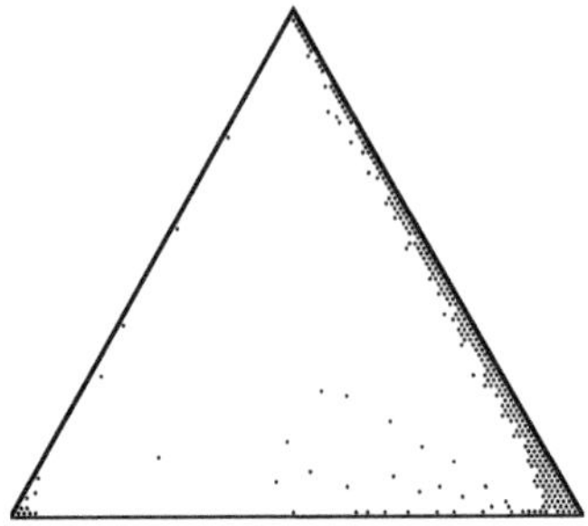

(a) Simplex, $\alpha = 0.30$.

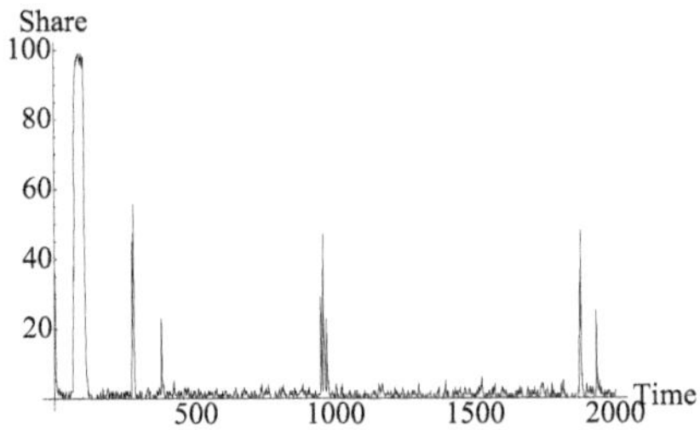

(b) Share of *Enforcers*.

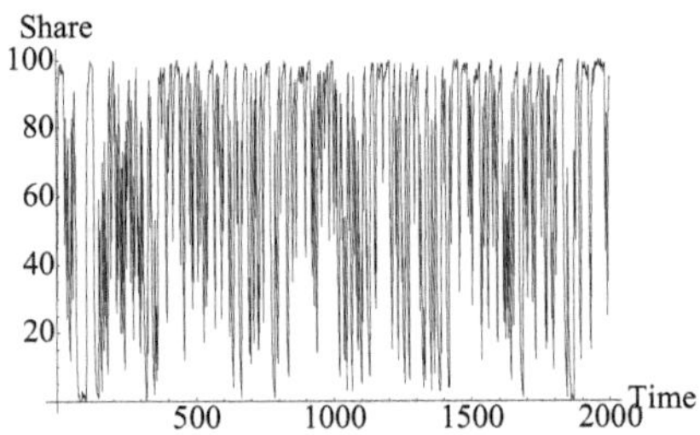

(c) Share of *Contributors*.

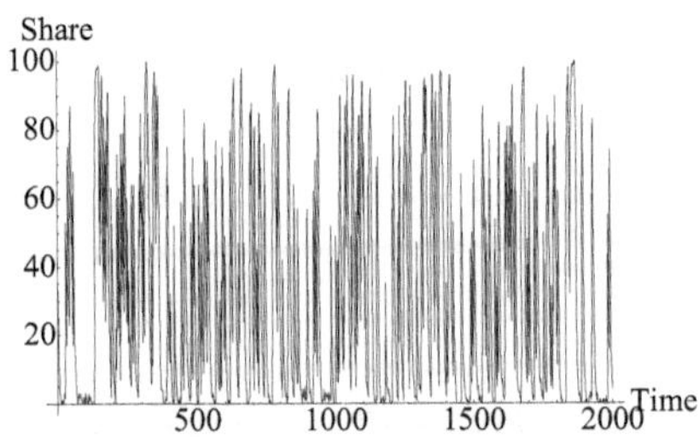

(d) Share of *Free-Riders*.

Figure 5.9: Representative run for $\alpha = 0.30$.

Introducing a small amount of noise changes the population dynamics. For low values of α (below 10 percent) the vast majority of the population will contribute to the public good but will not enforce the institution. The share of *Enforcers* and *Free-Riders* is small but positive. Although at the micro-level players still change their strategies, the state of the population remains roughly constant. Surprisingly, very high contribution levels are sustainable with a relatively small critical mass of players being *Enforcers* who give rewards, as institutionally prescibed. If players change their strategies more often (higher α) the population will fluctuate between being close to the *Contributing State* and the *Free-Rider State*. Occasionally, the share of *Enforcers* increases, but as α increases this becomes less frequent. There will be only short periods of time in which most players contribute to the public good, so the provision of the public good will be less stable or even impossible.

We find that if players do not change their strategies too fast, the social institution "give rewards to contributors" emerges from a population of selfish players and leads to the provision of the public good. In this case, the voluntary provision of the public good is almost efficient since the population state is close to the *Contributing State*, i.e., almost all players contribute to the public good. Players who do not behave according to the institutionally prescribed behavior will be sanctioned by exclusion from rewards. For exclusion to be effective, the evolution of the network has to be fast relative to the evolution of strategies. The social institution is enforced by a surprisingly small share of the community's members rather than by an external authority; and by enforcing the institution the community is able to self-organize and supply the public good.

The model presented in this chapter has significant implications not only for the provision of public goods but also for other dilemma problems, like collective action and team production. From the perspective of the leader of a social production community, our findings indicate that one can effectively increase contributions by allowing the community's members to give a reward by expressing social approval, even if only a relatively small number of members will actually give rewards. At this point we implicitely assume that all players' actions from the first stage of the game are observable, so that all players can distingush between contributing and non-contributing players (common knowledge of the *contribution profile*). Due to the availability of "credit files" and "history files" this is an appropriate assumption for open source communities. In team production it is also plausible that employees have information about each other's effort (for example Sol, 2010), but in

other dilemma problems this might be problematic. The crucial question that remains unanswered in this model concerns the role of information. Further work should address this issue and concentrate on information transmission between players.

Our findings contribute to the theoretical literature on the enforcement of social institutions. By dropping the assumption of random matching and modeling a population of players interacting on a dynamic network, our model is able to explain different outcomes. While with random matching Nash equilibrium and evolutionary stable equilibrium (ESS) coincide, this is not necessarily the case if the game is played in a network (see also Alexander, 2007).

In evolutionary models such as the one presented in this chapter, evolutionary pressure drives strategies with lower than average payoff to extinction. To increase the payoff to players who contribute to the public good, rewards are introduced. Five avenues for further research suggest themselves. First, the model could be modified and extended towards a more realistic model. Players could exchange two or more rewards and the size of the rewards could vary. This would have two counteracting effects on the speed at which the network evolves. The network would evolve faster if more rewards are exchanged, but if the size of the reward is smaller, reinforcement learning would be less strong leading to a slower evolution of the network. Another extension that suggests itself would be to run the model with players who are heterogeneous in terms of abilities. If ability is observable, players with higher ability would receive more rewards, eventually leading to self-selection. The third possibility for further work would be to broaden the scope and investigate the size dimension. This chapter's model showed that only a small fraction of *Enforcers* is enough to achieve an almost efficient provision of the public good. The literature on meso economics (Elsner, 2007; Elsner and Heinrich, 2009; Elsner et al., 2010) investigates the size dimension of this "carrier" or "meso group", which depends on the particular structure of the game. Further work could investigate how the size of the "meso group" changes in response to changes in payoffs or in response to other parameters of the model (speed of learning). The fourth direction for further research concerns the additivity of the payoff function. Additivity implies that there are no income effects so that demand depends only on relative prices and not on income. We acknowledge that this is a restrictive and unrealistic assumption. Further work should extend the model by relaxing this assumption. And fifthly, the model could be related to the be-

havioral economics literature. Chapter 6, experimentally investigating the effect of social approval on contributions to a public good, is an attempt into this direction and provides empirical support for the assumption that social approval increases contributions to a public good. But since social approval can be expressed in numerous different ways, a more thorough investigation of social approval in field and laboratory studies could greatly improve our understanding. Moreover, empirical investigations concerning the effect of rewards on interpersonal relations (as in van Dijk et al., 2002), and network formation more generally, would provide stronger empirical support for this chapter's model.

Chapter 6

An Experimental Analysis of Social Approval

The problem of motivating effort in social production communities is equivalent to a public good game, as we have argued in chapter 3. In chapter 4 we have argued that social approval is an important selective incentive for increasing contributions to the public good supplied by social production communities. The importance of social approval in relation to social production has not yet received adequate attention for the following reasons. In surveys in which the population consists of both contributors and non-contributors (Bitzer and Geishecker, 2010) factors relating to social approval are unobserved. And if explicitely asked about their motives contributors tend to downplay the importance of social approval due to norms of modesty, resulting in underreporting (Hertel et al., 2003; Franke and Shah, 2003). A thorough analysis of social approval is further complicated by the fact that social approval is closely intertwined with intrinsic motivation, team identity, and signaling. These two points, (i) the impossibility of identifying the importance of social approval in surveys and (ii) the interrelations between social approval, intrinsic motivation, team identity, and signaling make it difficult to identify the intrinsic effect of social approval directly. This chapter tries to fill this gap by presenting results from a laboratory experiment testing a simplified version of the model presented in the last chapter. In the simplified version subjects play eight rounds of the two-stage game described in section 5.4.1 with parameter values $n = 3$, $m = 2$, $h = 0$, and $\nu = 1.5$. The effect of changes in social distance is absent since the experiment relies on stranger matching and anonymity. This is necessary because without stranger matching and anonymity social approval would be of intrinsic and extrinsic value, and it would be impossible to separate both. A further difference is that while in chapter 5's model the decision to contribute

and the decision to give rewards are binary decisions, in the experiment subjects can contribute a part of their endowments and express social approval in various strength. The main aim of this experiment is to test whether subjects have a preference for the intrinsic value of social approval. In terms of chapter 5's model we test whether $b > 0$.

The experiment has two treatment effects. The first treatment effect concerns the exchange of social approval, and the second treatment effect concerns the information that subjects have about each other. The experiment isolates the intrinsic effect of social approval (described in detail in section 4.1) and investigates the effect of social approval on contributions in the laboratory. We find that individuals care about social approval even if receiving social approval does not lead to delayed rewards, and that the exchange of social approval induces higher contributions to the public good.

This is particularly relevant for our analysis because a closer inspection of the organization of social production (see sections 2.4 and 4.1) led us to the conclusion that there is a large number of channels through which social approval can be expressed almost costlessly, and that the strength of social approval is likely to be high. In the next section (6.1) we relate our experiment to the existing literature on experimental economics, public good games, and social approval. We relate social approval to our experiment in section 6.2 before we present the design of the experiment, derive theoretical predictions and formulate two hypothesis in section 6.3. In section 6.4 we discuss the results and derive implications before we summarize our findings and relate them to the rest of this thesis (section 6.5).

6.1 Experimental Economics

Experimental economics is a method which has recently gained much attention (Falk and Heckman, 2009), and on a methodological level there is still debate about the role of experiments (for a detailed discussion see Guala, 2005, and Bardsley et al., 2010). The aim of each experiment is to investigate the causal relation between two variables, the treatment variable and the outcome. An investigation of the causal relation is often complicated because other explanatory variables might be responsible for the observed outcome. By designing an artificial situation, the laboratory experiment makes it possible to control for the explanatory variables by keeping the environment constant. The environment includes all exogenous variables which are held

constant (e.g., group size, distribution of endowments, marginal per capita return). Usually, an experiment consists of two (or more) treatments. Between treatments the treatment variable is changed while the environment remains unchanged, making it possible to study the relation between treatment variable and outcome in isolation.

6.1.1 Experimental Economics and Public Good Games

The experiment which we present is a linear public good game. We introduced public good games and experiments in section 3.2.2, and detailed surveys of the experimental economics literature on public good games can be found in Ledyard (1995), Zelmer (2003), and Chaudhuri (2011). In linear public good games the Nash prediction is free-riding, i.e., no contributions to the public good. However, a general pattern which is observed in experiments is that contributions start around forty to sixty percent in the first round and decrease over time (Isaac et al., 1985; Andreoni, 1988b; Weimann, 1994). A plausible explanation for positive contributions is the existence of social preferences (Camerer and Fehr, 2004). Further experiments have shown that costly rewards and punishment induce higher contributions (Fehr and Gächter, 2000; Dickinson, 2001; Fehr and Gächter, 2002; Masclet et al., 2003), but nonmonetary rewards like social approval have rarely been investigated.

6.1.2 Experimental Economics and Social Approval

The first experiment relating social approval and public good games was done by Gächter and Fehr (1999). They conducted a ten-round public good game under partner matching and controlled for social distance by establishing a team identity through pre-play communication in selected treatments. Under the social approval treatments identities and contributions were revealed and subjects had to sit together and discuss their decisions after the tenth round. Since partner matching was used it is not clear if higher contributions in the first nine rounds are due to social approval or expectations of a common future. Although all treatments relied on partner matching, the expectation of a common future is likely to be stronger in treatments in which a strong team identity is established. By focusing on contributions in the last round, Gächter and Fehr isolate the intrinsic effect of social approval. They find that the opportunity to express social approval induces signifi-

cantly higher contributions in the last round if a team identity is established by allowing the subjects to communicate before the game. Without pre-play communication the effect of social approval was insignificant, indicating that the effect of social approval is inversely related to social distance. The absence of any significant effect of social approval in the treatments without team identity could also be due to the fact that social approval could only be expressed after the last round of the game. Allowing subjects to express social approval after each round would allow for subjects to learn that higher contributions are associated with higher social approval.

A similar public good experiment was conducted by Masclet et al. (2003) investigating the effect of monetary and nonmonetary punishment under stranger and partner matching. Nonmonetary punishment consisted of the opportunity to express disapproval after each round of the game, as opposed to Gächter and Fehr (1999) where social approval could only be exchanged at the end of the last round. Another difference is that while in Gächter and Fehr (1999) the exchange of social approval took place by face-to-face communication after the last round, in Masclet et al. (2003) the exchange of social approval happens after each round of the game through the assignment of points, where ten points correspond to most and zero points to least disapproval. Masclet et al. found the effect of monetary punishment to be stronger than the effect of nonmonetary punishment, and the effect of nonmonetary punishment to be stronger under partner than under stranger matching. Higher contributions under partner matching could support Gächter and Fehr's argument that the effect of social approval is higher if subjects are familiar with each other, but higher contributions could also be indicative of an extrinsic effect, i.e., expectations of a common future.

Rege and Telle (2004) present a non-repeated public good experiment with social approval. Each subject divided her endowment between two envelopes, one envelope representing private consumption, the other envelope representing contributions to the public good. In the social approval treatment subjects had to open the second envelope in front of all others, count the money, and write the sum on a blackboard. All other subjects were not allowed to express social approval verbally or directly, but Rege and Telle hypothesize that the mere suspicion that someone evaluates the observed behavior negatively is sufficient to induce higher contributions. And indeed, the experimental data confirms this hypothesis.

In other experiments (no public good games) the extrinsic effect is absent and the focus is on the instrinsic effect of social approval. Huberman et al.

(2004) show that in a rent-seeking game where there is a tradeoff between status and monetary gain, subjects are willing to trade off a monetary gain for an increase in status, even if this increase in status has no effect on monetary payoffs. Ellingsen and Johannesson (2008) document that the anticipation of feedback in form of an anonymous written message induces feelings of shame or pride and leads to higher offers in a dictator game. In contrast to Ellingsen and Johannesson (2008) and Gächter and Fehr (1999) we do not use written or verbal messages to express social approval. In our experiment subjects can assign between zero and ten stars in order to express social approval. This allows us to focus in the quantitative relation between contributions and social approval instead of focusing on the qualitative content of the messages.

Our experiment differs from the above contributions in at least two ways. First, our work combines real effort and social approval. Subjects have to exercise real effort in order to earn an endowment which they can contribute to a public good. In contrast to Gächter and Fehr (1999) and Masclet et al. (2003) subjects do not contribute part of a given endowment but part of an endowment that is the result of effort. We expect the effect of social approval to be stronger because how subjects reach their endowments matters for their decisions. If the endowment results from exercising real effort, subjects might feel that they deserve it more compared to a situation in which the endowment is assigned exogenously. Also, by choosing real effort our experiment is closer to social production communities, in which a public good is produced through individual effort, in contrast to public goods like charity to which individuals contribute part of their money. Second, our experiment is designed in such a way that the extrinsic effect of social approval is absent in all rounds of the game and we can focus on the intrinsic effect of social approval. In this respect our experiment is closest to the social approval, stranger matching treatment in Masclet et al. (2003). In Masclet et al., however, the emphasis is on disapproval while in experiment the emphasis is on approval. Our experiment relies exclusively on stranger matching, suggesting that social distance between subjects might be low. In contrast, Gächter and Fehr (1999) allow social distance to vary. We do not explore the aspect of social distance, rather we view experiments that do so as complementary to our own.

6.2 Social Approval in Our Experiment

Social approval have been discussed in depth in section 4.1. Here we give a brief review of the main argument before we relate our discussion of social approval to this experiment.[95]

6.2.1 Intrinsic and Extrinsic Value of Social Approval

In this experiment we test the hypothesis that the exchange of social approval induces higher contributions in public good games. Put bluntly, we argue that people care about what others think about them, and they care even more if others express their opinion. If our argument is right, social approval can be an inexpensive mechanism for the enforcement of institutions. More particular, our hypothesis is that people value social approval for its own sake. In order to test this hypothesis we have to distinguish between intrinsic and extrinsic value of social approval.

We will say that social approval has intrinsic value if it is desired for its own sake and independent from the consequences of receiving social approval, i.e., social approval will be valued even if it does not lead to higher material benefits in the future. Social approval has intrinsic value because social approval generates emotions like shame and pride, allows individuals to express their identity, and because it affects status. If higher material benefits in the future are the driving force behind people's desire for social approval, we will say that social approval has extrinsic value. The extrinsic value is often referred to as reputation. Reputation means that you are recognized for what you did in the past and this can be communicated to others (see section 4.1.2). Reputation can be considered to be a form of cheap-talk. It extends the time frame and audience increasing the instrumental value of social approval (Brennan and Pettit, 2004). If A tells B that C was such a nice host at last year's christmas party the extend of C's reputation is increased in time (from last year's christmas party until today) and audience (although B was not at the party she hears about it). Reputation signals competence and power, which in turn translate into higher future income (Huberman et al., 2004).

In the real world people are motivated by both the intrinsic and extrinsic value of social approval since most interactions are repeated. This dual

95 The reasons for discussing social approval again is to make this chapter self-contained and to relate social approval to our experiment.

character of social approval has been discussed in recent work on awards (Frey, 2006, 2007; Frey and Neckermann, 2008; Frey, 2010). Awards are a specific form of expressing social approval and serve as a signal for status. The signaling of status, Frey argues, satisfies the desire for social distinction (intrinsic value) and results in future monetary benefits (extrinsic value). In a more recent field experiment Kosfeld and Neckermann (forthcoming) clearly distinguish between intrinsic and extrinsic value of awards. They show that symbolic awards significantly increase performance in real-life work situations even if the awards do not lead to future monetary benefits. Kosfeld and Neckermann's field experiment is – to the best of our knowledge – the first experiment investigating the intrinsic value of symbolic awards and its effect on work performance. In contrast to Kosfeld and Neckermann (forthcoming) we test the motivational salience of symbolic awards in the laboratory and focus on contributions to a public good rather than work performance.

In our experiment we test the intrinsic value of social approval by designing a public good game where after contributions are made in the first stage and subjects exchange social approval in the second stage. The expression of social approval happens in the second stage of the game, it is anonyous and after the second stage the group's composition changes. There is no possibility to build up reputation and the experiment is designed as to ensure the absence of any strategic motives for seeking social approval.

While reputation is a strategic consideration with respect to increased future benefits, reciprocity can be another form of strategic behavior. In our experiment giving social approval is motivated by reciprocity if subjects respond to high contributions to the public good by expressing social approval. However, other considerations of reciprocity could also be at work. Subject A could express social approval for subject B because subject B expressed social approval for subject A in the period before. To rule out this second possibility we choose stranger matching. Consequently, the exchange of social approval has no effect on social distance and team identity in our experiment.

6.2.2 The Strength of Social Approval

In section 4.1.1.a we exposed several factors on which the strength of social approval depends on. In this and the following section we discuss these factor in relation to our experiment.

To be motivationally salient, the sincerity and exchange constraints must be fulfilled. Social approval has to be a sincere judgement and there cannot

be a straightforward exchange under offer. In our experiment judgements can only be based on others' contributions which are the result from individuals' real effort. Since all subjects are anonymously matched, the characteristics of the receiver are unknown, and the judgement cannot be based on any other characteristics, hence the sincerity constraint is fulfilled. In other words, subjects do not have a common future. If subject A assigned ten stars to subject B in period t, A cannot expect that B will reciprocate by assigning ten stars to A in period $t + 1$.

If social approval is expressed by the exchange of material objects, like awards, the overall effect will be a combination of the object's monetary value and its signaling value.[96] In social production communities most interactions are via web-based technologies and social approval is exchanged mostly in the form of written messages (see section 2.4.4). Since it is difficult to evaluate the content of a written message we take a different route by letting our subjects express social approval by assigning between zero and ten stars to each of their opponents' actions. Hence in our experiment we are concerned with the signaling value of stars.

For its effect to be strong, social approval has to be a qualified judgement. By providing information about subjects' contributions we ensure that subjects are in a position to give a qualified judgement since subjects are instructed about the effect of other's contributions of their own payoff. In other words, subjects know how their own payoff changes if others contribute more, making it possible to give a qualified judgement. The judgement will be more qualified, the more information the giver has about the person she judges. In social production communities it is not entirely clear, how much information contributors have about each other. We discuss this in the next section.

6.2.3 Information About Other Subjects

According to Brennan and Pettit (2004) social approval is given to a person because this person is good at something. How exactly "good" is defined depends on the frame of reference. Being absolutely ignorant about sports I

96 To avoid confusion: Signaling refers to actions taken not for the sake of their immediate results but to provide information for others. Here we use the term signaling to refer to the expression of judgement (approval or disapproval) in order to inform somebody else about how her behavior was perceived. In the literature on job market signaling (see section 4.1.2), we use the term signaling to refer to an individual's behavior which informs potential employers' about the individual's skills.

find it hard to evaluate a runner finishing a marathon in 2:55 hours. Seeing that all other runners took more than 3 hours I would probably acclaim the runner's performance, but if I would have known that that the runner's personal best is 2:40 hours my judgement would have been different. In the first case I have no information about the runner's ability, so I can only judge her performance relative to the other runners' performances. In the latter case I have knowledge about the runner so I can judge her performance relative to her ability.

It could be argued that in social production communities the effect of social approval is low because interactions over the internet are anonymous and ephemeral. In this respect social production communities resemble virtual teams (see section 2.3 and Jarvenpaa and Leidner, 1999). Members of virtual teams have no common past or future, they are decentralized and communicate using electronic media. In virtual teams personal trust and reputations are hard to develop because of their short-lived nature. Virtual teams produce a collective or public good, but for its members it is difficult to get to know the abilities of other team members. Contributions can only be judged on a team member's performance relative to the other team members' performances.[97]

However, there are aspects that allow contributors to assess each others' abilities in social production communities. Most interactions are repeated, so over time a reputation builds up. In fact, many social production communities use the internet to design mechanisms facilitating the exchange of social approval and allowing to build up a reputation. In Wikipedia it is possible to look at all activities of authors and assess their qualities, and in open source software each contributor's name is attached to her contributions, allowing to track contributions over time. At AllRecipes.com, an open source cookbook with thousands of contributors, each contributor's recipes can be judged using an assignment of zero to five stars as well as comments. Also, each contributor is assigned a "cooking level" and has the option to write a paragraph "about this cook". Hence, newbies to AllRecipes.com can eval-

97 A related aspect is the use of pseudonyms in the internet, effectively hiding users' real identities. Pseudonyms can be used as an insurance strategy, insuring against a possible risk of ridicule. The advantage of using a pseudonyms is that it might lead you to try out more courageous tasks. If you fail your reputation won't suffer because you are using a pseudonym. And if you are successful, you can reveal your identity (for a detailed discussion see Brennan and Pettit, 2004). We do not consider this aspect since in our experiment there are no courageous tasks to be solved nor are there any reputational effects due to stranger matching and anonymity, i.e it is impossible to build up a reputation.

uate a member's qualities based on the member's own assessment and the ratings assigned to her by others. In such settings the abilities of all contributors can, in principle, be assessed by others.

Taking into account both possibilities we test the effect of social approval on contributions to a public good under two treatments. In both treatments subjects have heterogeneous endowments which are a proxy for ability, and in both treatments social approval can be assigned after contributions to the public good are made. In treatment 1 subjects have no information about the endowments of others while in treatment 2 the distribution of endowments is public knowledge. We hypothesize that information about others' endowments increases contributions through strenghtening the effect of social approval because with more information being available, judgements will be more accurate. According to our hypothesis the strength of social approval will be higher in the second treatment, resulting in higher contributions.

6.3 Experimental Design

We design a linear public good experiment which is implemented with and without the option to express social approval. After earning an endowment subjects contribute to the public good (contribution stage) and exchange social approval (reward stage). According to our hypothesis subjects have a preference for social approval. If true, we will observe higher contributions to the public good in treatments in which social approval can be expressed.

In order to isolate the intrinsic value of social approval we run the experiment with stranger matching. Under the stranger matching protocol subjects are rematched after each round into new groups of three. Hence under stranger matching it is unlikely that the same two subjects will interact in two subsequent periods, and even if this is the case, they have no way of recognizing each other because all interactions are anonymous and identities are never revealed. Thus, the extrinsic effect of social approval is minimized.

In our experiment subjects' endowments are the result from an intelligence test which is made before each round of the game. Consequently, subjects will have heterogeneous endowments depending on the outcome of the intelligence test. Endowments are a proxy for ability. As argued in section 6.2.3, information about other subjects' abilities matters for the assignment of social approval. In our experiment we take this into account by running two treatments in which social approval can be assigned anonymously. In

treatment 1 only absolute contributions are observable. The distribution of endowments is unknown and social approval can only be assigned based on a subject's contribution relative to the other subjects' contributions. In treatment 2 relative contributions can be judged because all subjects' contributions and endowments are public knowledge.

In a team production experiment Dickinson (2001) reports on the use of monetary rewards and punishments to be given to the "best" and "worst" member of the team. In different treatments performance is measured by absolute contributions and contributions relative to endowment. Dickinson finds that the treatment with punishment and relative contributions was most effective. The paper by Dickinson (2001) differs in two important aspects from our experiment. First, in Dickinson (2001) heterogeneous endowments are assigned to subjects while in our experiment endowments are the product of real effort. And second, in Dickinson (2001) the experimenter assigned the monetary reward or punishment to the "best" or "worst" member of the team while in our experiment the subjects themselves decide how to allocate nonmonetary rewards in the form of social approval.

In our experiment social approval is visible to all group members. For subjects there is no option to abstain from giving social approval. Social approval is expressed by assigning between zero and ten stars to each opponent's performance. We use a positive framing by using stars (a symbol with a positive connotation) rather than points. Subjects are told that ten stars correspond to maximum social approval.

Following the existing literature on social approval (Holländer, 1990; Gächter and Fehr, 1999; Rege and Telle, 2004) we make the following two assumptions. First, we do not explicitely model the decision to express social approval but assume that the expression of social approval, i.e., the assignment of stars is an emotionally promted reaction. Holländer (1990), for example, argues that the expression of social approval is "not rationally calculated but, rather, promted by the stimulus-response mechanism of the human emotional system" (p. 1158). Second, we assume that high contributions go hand in hand with strong social approval. Subjects who make high (low) contributions will receive many (few) stars, i.e., we expect a positive correlation between contributions and stars. Since a subject's contribution will be compared to other subjects' contributions, we expect a negative relation between stars received and other subjects' contributions. For treatment 1, let ϕ_i^1 denote the number of stars received by subject i, and assume that

$\phi_i^1 = \phi_i^1(c_i, c_{-i})$ with $\frac{\partial \phi_i^1}{\partial c_i} > 0$ and $\frac{\partial \phi_i^1}{\partial c_{-i}} < 0$. The variables c_i and c_{-i} denote subject i's absolute contribution and the average contribution of the other players. Since in treatement 2 relative contributions are observable we write rc_i and rc_{-i} for subject i's relative contribution and the average relative contribution of the other players. The number of stars received in treatment 2 will then be given by $\phi_i^2 = \phi_i^2(rc_i, rc_{-i})$ with $\frac{\partial \phi_i^2}{\partial rc_i} > 0$ and $\frac{\partial \phi_i^2}{\partial rc_{-i}} < 0$.[98]

One objection could be that subjects will be lavish in their assignment of stars because it is costless. Introducing a small cost associated with every star that is assigned could solve this problem. We think that this is not necessary because of status effects. Subjects do not only care about how many stars they receive but care about how many stars they receive compared to their group members. The status effect, however, implies that a subject's utility from social approval is negatively related to the other subjects' contributions. Taken the number of stars received by subject i as given, subject i would maximize her utility from social approval by assigning no stars at all, which would imply that no stars are given at all. This, however, would only be the case if the decision to give social approval was strategic, which would contradict the first assumption.

6.3.1 Theoretical Predictions

Assuming a group size of n and $0 < \nu < 1 < n\nu$ economic theory, assuming that social approval does not matter, predicts free-riding (ν is the marginal per capita return). If players have no preference for social approval utility is given by the sum of public and private consumption.[99]

$$u_i = e_i - c_i + \nu \sum_{j=1}^{n} c_j \tag{6.1}$$

98 Empirical support for the signs of the derivatives can be found in a questionaire study (Gächter and Fehr, 1999). In this study the outcome of a hypothetical public good game was described, contributions and identities were revealed, and subjects had to indicate the strength of their emotions towards a specific contributor. A regularity that was found is that: "They expect that they receive more approval if they contribute more, and less approval if others contribute more" (p. 346).

99 As already mentioned in the preceeding chapter, additivity of the utility function is quite restrictive. In choosing this particular form of the utility function we follow Gächter and Fehr (1999). In a similar way, money and utility from status are additive in Huberman et al. (2004) while in most other experiments (Masclet et al., 2003; Rege and Telle, 2004; Kosfeld and Neckermann, forthcoming) no utility function is specified. One possibility to investigate preferences for social approval and money without assuming additivity would be along the lines of Neugebauer and Traub (2006) who investigate preferences for money and waiting time.

At the unique Nash equilibrium contributions are zero, $c_i = 0$, and each player's utility corresponds to her endowment, e_i. At the social optimum, however, each individuals contribution is given by $c_i = e_i$, and each player's utility is given by $\nu \sum_{j=1}^{n} e_i$.

According to our hypothesis players have a preference for social approval. Utility is given by the sum of social approval plus public and private consumption. In the model presented in chapter 5 the payoff from receiving social approval was given by the parameter b, and we assumed that $b > h$. In this experiment we assume that $h = 0$. Social approval can be expressed in various strength (the number of stars) so that the utility from receiving social approval depends on the number of stars received. For treatmemt 1 we denote the utility from social approval by $f(\phi_i, \phi_{-i})$ where ϕ_{-i} denotes the number of stars received by all other subjects but subject i. Following Gächter and Fehr (1999) we assume that $\frac{\partial f_i}{\partial \phi_i} > 0$, $\frac{\partial^2 f_i}{\partial \phi_i^2} \leq 0$ and $\frac{\partial f_i}{\partial \phi_{-i}} < 0$.[100] Total utility is given by equation 6.2.

$$u_i = \underbrace{e_i - c_i}_{\text{private c.}} + \underbrace{\nu \sum_{j=1}^{n} c_j}_{\text{public c.}} + \underbrace{f_i(\phi_i, \phi_{-i})}_{\text{social approval}} \tag{6.2}$$

Equation 6.2 mirrors 5.19. Since in the experiment everyone gives and receives social approval we can take equation 5.19, set $p(s_1|s_1) = 1$ and replace b by $f(\phi_i, \phi_{-i})$ to arrive at equation 6.2. Maximizing equation 6.2 with respect to c_i yields

$$1 - \nu = \frac{\partial f_i}{\partial \phi_i}\frac{\partial \phi_i}{\partial c_i} \tag{6.3}$$

as the first-order condition at an interior optimum.[101] Due to concavity of f_i the first-order condition is necessary and sufficient for the existence of a maximum. Here, $1 - \nu$ is the marginal loss in utility from contributing one additional unit to the public good; and $\frac{\partial f_i}{\partial \phi_i}\frac{\partial \phi_i}{\partial c_i}$ is the gain in social approval from contributing one additional unit to the public good. Players contribute

100 The sign of the second derivative is negative because quasi-concavity of f_i ensures that the optimum is unique.

101 The following two corner solutions can occur: If the effect of social approval is not sufficiently strong, meaning that $1 - \nu > \frac{\partial f_i}{\partial \phi_i}\frac{\partial \phi_i}{\partial c_i}$ (for $0 \leq c_i \leq e_i$) subjects will contribute nothing. If the effect of social approval is very strong, meaning that $1 - \nu < \frac{\partial f_i}{\partial \phi_i}\frac{\partial \phi_i}{\partial c_i}$ (for $0 \leq c_i \leq e_i$) subjects will contribute all their endowment.

more to the public good if the gain in social approval outweights loss from reduced monetary income.

In treatment 2 in which subjects can observe both contributions and endowments social approval is not a function of absolute but of relative contributions. Since the judgement is based on more information it is possible that subjects will perceive the same number of stars differently. For treatment 2 we denote the utility from social approval by $g_i = g_i(\phi_i, \phi_{-i})$ and assume that g behaves like f. The utility function and the first-order condition are then given by the following equations.

$$u_i = e_i - c_i + \nu \sum_{j=1}^{n} c_j + g_i\left(\phi_i, \phi_{-i}\right) \tag{6.4}$$

$$1 - \nu = \frac{\partial g_i}{\partial \phi_i} \frac{\partial \phi_i}{\partial r c_i} \tag{6.5}$$

6.3.2 The Three Treatments

We run three treatments which are visualized in table 6.1.

Treatment	social approval (first treatment effect)	information (second treatment effect)
T0	no	-
T1	yes	absolute contributions
T2	yes	contributions and endowments

Table 6.1: The three different treatments.

General features for all treatments: Our experiment is designed on the basis of linear public good experiments. In each session fifteen or eighteen individuals are randomly assigned in groups of size three. Each session consists of eight rounds. Each round subjects are asked to solve questions taken from an intelligence test. The test consists of ten questions and subjects are given fifteen seconds to answer each question, so that the intelligence test takes 150 seconds in total. When time is elapsed subjects are assigned an endowment depending on the ranking from the intelligence test. If two subjects' scores are identical, a fair coin is tossed to determine unique ranks. The subject with the highest score gets the highest endowment, the subject

with the second-highest score gets the second-highest endowment, and the subject with the lowest score gets the lowest endowment.

The distributions of endowments are depicted in table 6.2 and were generated in the following way. There is an urn containing eight different distributions of endowments. The distributions were generated by randomly drawing numbers from the interval $[3, 10]$. Drawing took place without replacement to ensure that no two subjects have identical endowments. In other words, the mapping from ranks to endowments is bijective. In all treatments the same eight distributions are used to ensure comparability across treatments. The distribution of endowments is identical across all groups within the same round but varies as we move from one round to the next. The rationale behind varying distributions between rounds is that it is not possible for subjects to learn something about the distribution, which is important in treatment 1.[102] Since each subject plays one round with an endowment drawn from each of the eight distributions the distributions are identical across sessions and treatments.

Period:	1	2	3	4	5	6	7	8
Rank 1	10	10	9	6	8	8	9	8
Rank 2	6	6	8	5	6	7	5	5
Rank 3	7	3	7	3	3	5	4	4
Total	23	19	24	14	17	20	18	17

Table 6.2: Assignment of endowments to subjects based on rank.

After taking part in the intelligence test and having been assigned an endowment, subjects have to decide how much to contribute to the public good, $0 \leq c_i \leq e_i$. After all subjects made their contributions the group's payoff is given by the quantity of the public good produced (see equation 6.6). After each round subjects were informed about the group's payoff. Subjects are rematched into new groups and the next round begins.

$$PG = 1.5 \times \sum_{i=1}^{3} c_i \tag{6.6}$$

Individual payoffs are given by

102 If subjects learned about the distribution of endowments they would assign social approval based on relative contributions instead of assigning social approval based on absolute contributions, blurring the distinction between treatments 1 and 2.

$$\pi_i = (e_i - c_i) + \frac{PG}{3} = (e_i - c_i) + \frac{1}{2}\sum_{j=1}^{3} c_j \quad (6.7)$$

The subjects' money earnings from the experiment are given by the sum of their payoffs multiplied by a constant.

Control Treatment: The game is played as described above. Subjects receive no information about other's endowments and the distribution of endowments is unknown. All subjects make their contributions simultaneously. After each round subjects are informed about contributions of their group's members but no social approval can be given.

Treatment 1: Same as Control Treatment but in addition subjects can evaluate the performance of their partners. After all contributions are made each subject can see the absolute contributions of her fellow group members, i.e., (c_i, c_j, c_k) is made public knowledge. The subjects' endowment levels remain private knowledge. Each subject signals approval by assigning between zero and ten stars to each other subject in her group. Decisions of social approval are made simultaneously by all members of the group. After all members of the group assigned social approval the results are displayed on the screen so that subjects could see their own "stars" as well as the "stars" assigned to the other to (anonymous) group members.[103]

Treatment 2: Same as Treatment 1 but instead of observing absolute contributions group members observe relative contributions. Both the subjects' endowments (e_i, e_j, e_k) and contributions (c_i, c_j, c_k) are made public knowledge and the distribution of endowments is public knowledge. Not the percentage is shown but the actual numbers for endowments and contributions. As in treatment 1, each subject signals approval by assigning between zero and ten stars to each other subject in her group.

6.3.3 Hypotheses

Our main hypothesis is that subjects have a preference for social approval. Denoting individual contributions in treatment i by $c(i)$ allows us to further specify our hypotheses.

Hypothesis 1: The exchange of social approval induces higher contributions, $c(0) < c(1)$ and $c(0) < c(2)$. If people care about the intrinsic value

103 A complete set of sample screens from the experiment can be found on the author's website, http://www.matthiasgreiff.net.

of social approval, we expect contributions to the public good to be be higher if the expression of social approval is allowed for. Hence we expect contributions in treatments 1 and 2 to be higher than in the control treatment.

Hypothesis 2: Contributions in treatment 2 will be higher than in treatment 1 because in treatment 2 more information is available so that contributions can be judged more accurately (see section 6.2.3). Compared to treatment 1, subjects have the additional information about endowments in treatment 2. This is particularly relevant for judging subjects who contributed very few tokens on an absolute scale but a high percentage of their endowment.

Hypothesis 2 requires some further explanation: In treatment 1 subjects do not know whether a small contribution resulted from a small endowment or from the subject behaving selfish. This uncertainty makes it difficult to evaluate the subject's small contribution. It is possible to compare the contribution to others contributions, which will result in an inaccurate judgement because the subject's endowment is not taken into account. The inaccurate judgement is a bad signal for social approval and could result in frustration. In treatment 2 we do not have this kind of uncertainty since both contributions and endowments can be observed. Since the additional information about subjects' endowments reduces uncertainty, we expect judgements to be more accurate and hence better signals for social approval in treatment 2.

6.4 Results

The experiment took place at the University of Bremen in October 2010 and was conducted using the z-Tree software (Fischbacher, 2007). We conducted 6 sessions, and in each session 15 or 18 students participated. In total, 102 students participated. Subjects came from different departments and were randomly assigned to a treatment. Subjects played 8 rounds of the game and in each round subjects were randomly and anonymously paired. Subjects' identities were never revealed to one another, and subjects were paid in private. Each subject received 5 euros as show-up fee plus her earnings in the experiment. During the experiment payoffs were denoted in tokens. At the end of the experiment one round was randomly selected and this round's payoffs, together with the show-up fee, determined the subjects' payments. The exchange rate between tokens and euros was 1:1 and was common knowledge.

The average payment (across treatments) was 12.80 euros and each session lasted about 90 minutes. We believe that earnings were sufficient to cover the opportunity costs of time for our subjects.

Upon arriving subjects were randomly assigned to a computer terminal and received a set of written instructions. The experimenter read the instructions aloud and presented an example to illustrate how payoffs are calculated. Subjects had the opportunity to ask questions both publicly and in private. Before the experiment started subjects had to answer six (T0) or seven (T1 and T2) control questions, testing whether they understood the experiment correctly. Although one subject answered only two questions correctly, the vast majority of subjects answered at least six questions correctly. The distribution of the number of questions answered correctly is left-skewed with mean = 6 and median = 6.255.[104] If dummy variables are included for individual control questions the effects of questions 1, 2, 4, and 5 are insignificant, the effects of questions 3 and 7 are negative and significant, and the effect of question 6 is positive and significant. However, it is unlikely that the answers to the control questions have a strong causal effect on contributions because after subjects answered the control questions, the correct answers were displayed on the screen in order to ensure that subjects understood the experiment.

Our main result is that the exchange of social approval increases contributions, supporting hypothesis 1. However, contributions in treatment 2 are not higher than contributions in treatment 1, hence the additional information about subjects' endowments does not increase contributions. The following two sections provide descriptive and statistical evidence from this experiment's results.

6.4.1 Descriptive Evidence

Figure 6.1 shows median contributions over all eight periods, and table 6.3 summarizes mean, median, and standard deviation of relative contributions for each period and for the pooled data from all periods. It is apparent from figure 6.1 that social approval is effective in raising contribution level. As expected, contributions are lowest in the control treatment (treatment 0), the median contribution declining from 40 to 13 percent. In treatments 1 and 2 in which subjects expressed social approval after observing contributions,

104 The control questions are included in the sample screens from the experiment which can be found on the author's website, http://www.matthiasgreiff.net.

		Period:								
Treatment:	Statistics:	1	2	3	4	5	6	7	8	Total
T0	median	0.40	0.20	0.25	0.20	0.17	0.20	0.00	0.13	0.30
11 groups	mean	0.39	0.31	0.26	0.33	0.33	0.29	0.28	0.24	0.21
33 subjects	std. dev.	0.32	0.35	0.24	0.37	0.39	0.33	0.37	0.32	0.34
T1	median	0.50	0.50	0.50	0.67	0.50	0.50	0.25	0.25	0.50
11 groups	mean	0.53	0.54	0.52	0.62	0.54	0.52	0.38	0.32	0.50
33 subjects	std. dev.	0.26	0.35	0.30	0.39	0.32	0.31	0.37	0.35	0.34
T2	median	0.50	0.42	0.40	0.40	0.35	0.34	0.16	0.06	0.38
12 groups	mean	0.49	0.45	0.43	0.45	0.44	0.34	0.35	0.34	0.41
36 subjects	std. dev.	0.28	0.40	0.33	0.43	0.40	0.33	0.40	0.39	0.37

Table 6.3: Relative contributions over time and in total.

median contributions are higher than median contributions in the control treatment in which social approval could not be expressed. Surprisingly, the highest median contributions are observed in treatment 1, where median contributions are above 50 percent in the first five periods and drop to 25 percent in the last period. Median contributions in treatment 2 are above 40 percent in the first four periods but then drop to 6 percent in the last period.

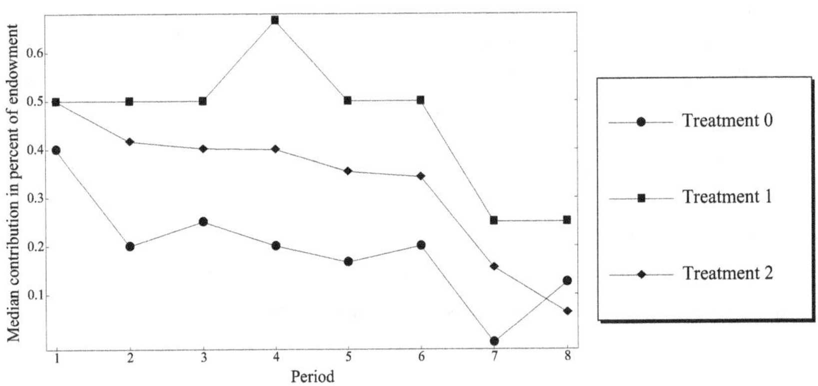

Figure 6.1: Median contributions over time.

Further, we observe that contributions decrease slightly at the end of the game. In treatments 0 and 1 the smallest average contribution is in the last period. In treatment 2 the lowest average contribution is in period 6 (33.8 percent), but is only slightly smaller than the last period's average contribution (34.0 percent). We believe that the endgame effect is rather small because we rely on stranger matching in our experiment.

In comparing contributions over time, another interesting finding is the increase in contributions in period four, which is observed in all treatments. This can be explained by looking at the group's aggregate endowment (table 6.2) which drops from 24 tokens (period three) to 14 tokens (period four). Subjects reduce their absolute contributions, but since the drop in endowment is larger, relative contributions increase.

The conclusion that we can draw from the descriptive evidence is formulated in the following two results. Result 1 is surprisingly clear and supports hypothesis 1, result 2 was unexpected and does not support hypothesis 2. In the next section we provide statistical evidence and discuss both results.

Result 1: The expression of social approval induces higher contributions to the public good. In both treatments in which social approval was expressed average contributions are significantly higher than in the control treatment. Hypothesis 1 is supported.

Result 2: The effect of social approval on contributions is stronger in treatment 1 compared to treatment 2. Giving subjects information about others' absolute contributions induces higher contributions than giving subjects information about others' absolute contributions and endowments. Hypothesis 2 is not supported.

To see if subjects assigned stars in accordance with our assumptions, we look at the correlations. Tables 6.4 and 6.5 depict the correlation between the number of stars received and a subject's contribution, as well as the correlation between the number of stars received and other subjects' average contribution. For treatment 1 absolute contributions are used and for treatment 2 relative contributions are used. The correlations provide evidence for the assumption that high (low) contributions receive much (little) social approval, but there is no clear-cut evidence for a negative relation between social approval received and others' contributions.

6.4.2 Statistical Tests for Treatment Effects

For a more detailed anaylsis of treatment effects we compare differences of means period by period. Since we have three treatments, three pairwise comparisons are possible. Table 6.6 depicts the differences of means (in the first line of each comparison) and the results of mean tests with individuals' relative contributions per period as observations. We performed both two-tailed t-tests and nonparametric Mann-Whitney tests. The results show that only treatment 1 is significantly different from the control treatment. Although contributions in treatment 2 are higher than in the control treatment, this effect is not significant. Using average contributions over all eight periods as observations (last column) shows that in all three comparisons the difference of means is significantly different from zero.

Tables 6.7 and 6.8 report the results from regressions analyses. Support for result 1 (social approval induces higher contributions in treatments 1 and 2) comes from regressions 1 to 4, all showing that the coefficients for the treatment dummies (Treatment 1 and Treatment 2) are positive and significant (all coefficients are significant at the one percent level). In regression 1 the magnitude of each coefficient of the treatment dummies represents the difference in absolute contributions compared to the control treatment. In regression 2 we use relative contributions as dependent variable. Since relative contributions are bounded between 0 and 1, we employ a logit transformation and use $\ln\left[rc_i/\left(1-rc_i\right)\right]$ as the dependent variable in regression 3. (Before the linearization zeros and ones were replaced by 0.001 and 0.999 respectively). In regression 4 we use standardized contributions (so-called z-scores) as dependent variable.[105] Regressions 3 and 4 arrive at similar results as regression 2. Besides the treatment effects we observe that, on average, subjects with higher endowments contribute absolutely more but relatively less.

T1	c_i	c_{-i}
ϕ_i	0.821	0.025

Table 6.4: Pearson product moment correlations between stars received and absolute contributions.

T2	rc_i	rc_{-i}
ϕ_i	0.871	-0.042

Table 6.5: Pearson product moment correlations between stars received and relative contributions.

105 The z-scores are computed as follows: z-score$_i = \frac{c_i - \bar{c}}{s.d.}$ where $\bar{c}$ is the mean and $s.d.$ is the standard deviation of absolute contributions.

Period:	1	2	3	4	5	6	7	8	Total
Comparisons									
T0 vs. T1	-0.147	-0.230	-0.260	-0.287	-0.208	-0.229	-0.099	-0.080	-0.193
t	-2.047	-2.693	-3.886	-3.065	-2.358	-2.937	-1.102	-0.970	-6.536
	(0.045)	(0.009)	(0.000)	(0.003)	(0.022)	(0.005)	(0.275)	(0.336)	(0.000)
Z	-2.094	-2.746	-3.545	-2.808	-2.511	-2.933	-1.284	-0.793	-6.482
	(0.036)	(0.006)	(0.000)	(0.005)	(0.012)	(0.003)	(0.199)	(0.428)	(0.000)
T0 vs. T2	-0.099	-0.144	-0.173	-0.116	-0.114	-0.050	-0.074	-0.101	-0.110
t	-1.355	-1.611	-2.501	-1.201	-1.192	-0.635	-0.803	-1.176	-3.610
	(0.180)	(0.112)	(0.015)	(0.234)	(0.237)	(0.528)	(0.425)	(0.244)	(0.000)
Z	-1.552	-1.29	-2.052	-0.851	-0.947	-0.565	-0.734	-0.763	-3.173
	(0.121)	(0.197)	(0.040)	(0.395)	(0.344)	(0.572)	(0.463)	(0.445)	(0.002)
T1 vs. T2	0.048	0.086	0.087	0.171	0.095	0.179	0.025	-0.021	0.084
t	0.731	0.966	1.147	1.742	1.086	2.336	0.275	-0.229	2.761
	(0.467)	(0.338)	(0.256)	(0.086)	(0.281)	(0.022)	(0.784)	(0.819)	(0.006)
Z	-0.706	-1.129	-1.229	-1.699	-1.226	-2.311	-0.472	-0.082	-2.838
	(0.480)	(0.259)	(0.219)	(0.089)	(0.22)	(0.021)	(0.637)	(0.935)	(0.005)

Table 6.6: Differences in mean contributions listed in the first line. Period-wise t-tests and Mann-Whitney tests for difference of means for each pair of treatments with subjects' relative contributions as the independent unit of observation. P-values in parentheses.

	1	2	3	4
Dependent variable	c_i	rc_i	$\ln\left[rc_i/\left(1-rc_i\right)\right]$	z-score
Constant	2.496***	0.743***	2.215***	0.012
	(8.823)	(11.690)	(3.517)	(0.095)
e_i	0.243***	-0.026***	-0.222***	0.107***
	(8.569)	(-5.597)	(-5.576)	(8.569)
Treatment 1	1.477***	0.219***	1.737***	0.649***
	(7.173)	(7.633)	(8.094)	(7.173)
Treatment 2	0.986***	0.133***	0.907***	0.433***
	(7.358)	(9.140)	(7.533)	(7.358)
Period	-0.157***	-0.027***	-0.223***	-0.069***
	(-7.132)	(-7.119)	(-6.789)	(-7.132)
K	-0.270***	-0.028***	-0.235**	-0.119***
	(-9.026)	(-3.743)	(-2.828)	(-9.026)
N	816	816	816	816
$\bar{R}^2$	0.139	0.085	0.076	0.139
F	27.23***	16.21***	14.52***	27.23***
AIC	1.502	-2.130	2.177	-0.142
χ^2	96.220***	103.661***	115.066***	118.407***

Table 6.7: Determinants of contributing behavior. OLS regressions with panel corrected standard errors; t-values are in parentheses. (K is the number of control questions answered correctly.) Significance codes: $0 \leq$ p-value < 0.001 : ***, $0.001 \leq$ p-value < 0.01: **, $0.01 \leq$ p-value < 0.05: *.

Also noteworthy is that the coefficient of the variable Period is negative and significant, confirming that contributions decline over time, which is known as end-game effect (Andreoni, 1988b). The end-game effect could be explained by learning or strategies. According to the learning hypothesis subjects learn about the game's payoffs as the game is played repeatedly. According to the strategy hypothesis, however, the decay in contributions is not the result of learning but the result of subjects forming multi-period strategies. One possible multi-period strategy could be "contribute half of the endowment if other subjects contributed at least half of their endowments in the period before." As the terminal period gets closer, subjects might re-

duce their contributions because they expect others to do the same. Does the end-game effect render our results invalid? Does the effect of social approval disappear after a few periods? We do not believe that this is the case in real life situations because in real life situations individuals have no information on what the terminal period is, i.e., the time horizon of the game is unknown. In social production communities it might be the case that a contributor unilaterally decides to leave the community, but others might not know when the contributor will leave. Such a situation corresponds to a repeated public good game where players have different time horizons with the information about the different time horizons being distributed asymmetrically. Gonzáles et al. (2005) have conducted an experimental analysis of such games. They found that asymmetric information about time horizons reduces the frequency of end-game effects. Hence we believe that the end-game effect does not render our results invalid.

According to hypothesis 2 we expect the effect from social approval on contributions to be stronger in treatment 2. Our data, however, cannot corroborate hypothesis 2. By looking at the coefficients of the treatment variables in regressions 1 to 4 (table 6.7), we see that the effect from social approval on contributions is larger in treatment 1 compared to treatment 2. Using Wald F-tests (H_0 : both coefficients have the same value), we can reject the null hypothesis at the one percent level (in all regressions). Hypothesis 2 is not supported but Result 2 is supported. We believe that this is because contributions are judged using different scales in treatment 1 and 2. In treatment 2 an obvious possibility is to assign social approval in proportion to relative contributions (e.g., 3 stars for a relative contribution of 30 percent and 6 stars for a contribution of 60 percent). In treatment 1 this scale could not be used since endowments were unknown and subjects assigned more stars than in treatment 2, suggesting an upward shift in the scale (e.g., 5 stars for a contribution of 30 percent and 8 stars for a contribution of 60 percent).[106] In his experiments Dickinson (2001) found support for what we formulated as hypothesis 2. The different outcomes of Dickinson's and our experiment can be rationalized in the same way. In Dickinson's experiment a reward was given to the subject with the highest contribution. The size of the reward was fixed and it was given by the experimenter (i.e., the scale was fixed). In our experiment the sizes of the rewards (i.e., the numbers of stars) could vary and the rewards were given by subjects themselves. Hence we believe

106 In treatment 1 the average number of stars received is 7.76, in treatment 2 it is 8.08.

that our second result (i.e. the rejection of hypothesis 2) is an artefact of our model, or more precisely, an artefact resulting from the way in which social approval was expressed. In general, we expect the effect of social approval to be stronger if more information is available due to the reasons described above (see Hypothesis 2).

Table 6.8 gives additional information on the relation between individual characteristics and contributing behavior. Regressions 5 to 8 are similar to regressions 1 to 4 but three independent variables – Male, Econ, Semester – are added. We see that, on average, male subjects contributed less. This effect is small but significant, and hence contradicts previous studies who find no evidence for gender effects (Bolton and Katok, 1995; Bolton et al., 1998; Zelmer, 2003).[107] Looking at the Econ dummy we see that the effect of studying economics is small and insignificant. The variable Semester corresponds to the number of semesters (half-year terms) that the subject has been enrolled. We find a small positive and significant effect on absolute contributions (in regression 5). We take Semester as a proxy for age. A possible interpretation for this effect is that older subjects have stronger social preferences.

For robustness reasons, we ran all regressions without the subject who answered only two control questions correctly (call her the "outlier") and arrive at similar results. Since the "outlier" participated in treatment 2 and contributed nothing in five periods of the game, the treatment effects are larger if the "outlier" is removed from the data. Also, the significance levels of the Wald F-tests (H_0: Treatment1 = Treatment2) are slightly higher but for all regressions they are significant at the five percent level.

6.4.3 Discussion and Implications

Our results emphasize the importance of nonmonetary rewards as incentives by providing an example of how higher contributions to a public good can be induced through the exchange of social approval. Positive contributions as well as changes in behavior in response to receiving social approval are both inconsistent with a subgame-perfect equilibrium in a noncooperative game where players maximize their monetary payoffs. Positive contributions can be explained by social preferences like altruism, inequality aversion, and reciprocity (see section 3.5.3). Social preferences can explain positive contributions in treatment 0, but they cannot explain the increase in contributions

107 One study even finds that male subjects contribute more than femal subjects (Brown-Kruse and Hummels, 1993).

	5	6	7	8
Dependent variable	c_i	c_i/e_i	$\ln\left[rc_i/\left(1-rc_i\right)\right]$	z-score
Constant	2.060***	0.708***	1.997***	-0.180
	(8.809)	(11.536)	(3.251)	(-1.753)
e_i	0.243***	-0.026***	-0.220***	0.107***
	(8.448)	(-5.374)	(-5.289)	(8.448)
Treatment 1	1.399***	0.211***	1.665***	0.615***
	(6.886)	(7.233)	(7.482)	(6.886)
Treatment 2	0.868***	0.124***	0.831***	0.382***
	(8.086)	(8.697)	(6.568)	(8.086)
Period	-0.157***	-0.027***	-0.222***	-0.069***
	(-7.120)	(-4.901)	(-6.755)	(-7.120)
K	-0.220***	-0.023**	-0.200*	-0.097***
	(-8.265)	(-3.129)	(-2.416)	(-8.265)
Male	-0.489***	-0.056**	-0.523**	-0.215***
	(-3.404)	(-3.064)	(-3.180)	(-3.404)
Econ	0.040	-0.013	-0.151	-0.0178
	(0.212)	(-0.522)	(-0.644)	(0.212)
Semester	0.067***	-0.007***	-0.054	0.029***
	(9.005)	(5.651)	(5.432)	(9.005)
N	816	816	816	816
$\bar{R}^2$	0.159	0.093	0.085	0.159
F	20.18***	11.45***	10.45***	20.18***
AIC	1.482	-2.135	2.172	-0.162
χ^2	118.225***	134.724***	150.624***	118.225***

Table 6.8: Determinants of contributing behavior including individuals' characteristics. OLS regressions with panel corrected standard errors; t-values are in parentheses. Significance codes: $0 \leq$ p-value < 0.001 : ***, $0.001 \leq$ p-value < 0.01: **, $0.01 \leq$ p-value < 0.05: *.

in treatments 1 and 2 where social approval was exchanged.[108] While models of social preferences assume that players only consider (the distribution of) monetary payoffs, our results show that in order to explain the observed behavior nonmonetary payoffs have to be taken into account. Moreover, the subjects' behavior in our experiment cannot be explained by signaling since any strategic considerations are absent.

The importance of nonmonetary incentives points to the question of how to integrate nonmonetary incentives into economic theory. An attempt into this direction is Kandel and Lazear's paper on peer pressure (1992). In discussing both guilt and shame they distinguish between internal and external peer pressure. In their model, however, the driving force for exercising peer pressure is strategic because peer pressure increases profitability. As Ellingsen and Johannesson (2007) correctly remark, "a satisfactory formal analysis of respect requires a signaling model, albeit one on which people care about others' beliefs directly, not merely the material consequences of those beliefs" (p. 144). For internal peer pressure the models by Andreoni (1990) and Brekke et al. (2003), described in chapter 3, are a step into this direction. For external peer pressure and social approval the model by Holländer (1990) remains to be mentioned. In his model, social approval takes the form of "a complex of sentiments" (p. 1159). Although his model is consistent with the data from our experiment, there is no consensus on how to model emotions analytically, as has also been pointed out by Masclet et al. (2003).

6.5 Upshot of Chapter 6

In social production communities social approval is cheap to give because of the existence of institutions for intense and open communication (e.g., fora, mailing lists, credit files, etc.). Monitoring of individual contributions is possible and even necessary in order to ensure compatibility and quality of contributions. The community represents a large and qualified audience whose

108 Recent results (Andreoni and Rao, forthcoming) have shown that communication can affect social preferences. Following this line of reasoning one could argue that the exchange of social approval strengthens social preferences and explain the treatment effects this way. For our experiment this explanation seems unplausible because in our experiment communication is the exchange of stars after subjects decided how much to contribute while in Andreoni and Rao (forthcoming) subjects communicate via written messages before a dictator game was played. Further, while in our experiment subjects were rematched every period, the dictator game in in Andreoni and Rao (forthcoming) was a repeated game with partner matching.

members are in the position to give a qualified judgement. Individuals have the possibility to seek social approval not too openly. We expect the social approval to be an important motive for explaining contributions to social production communities. However, it is difficult to empirically observe the importance of social approval because it is either unobservable or underreported due to norms of modesty. This led us to our experiment, which is designed in order to test the hypothesis that social approval induces higher contributions to a public good. More precisely, we are concerned with the intrinsic value of social approval, i.e., we test if social approval is valued even if it does not lead to higher payoffs in the future. This is different from the idea of reputation, according to which it makes sense to build up a reputation because high reputation will lead to higher payoffs in the future.

Our experiment is a linear public good game with real effort and stranger matching. In choosing real effort the subjects in our experiment are in a similar position than contributors in social production communities. In both cases contributions result from the expenditure of effort instead of giving a fraction of an exogenously given endowment to the public good. We choose stranger matching in order to avoid any reputation effect and isolate the intrinsic value of social approval. In each period subjects were randomly and anonymously paired and subject's identities were never revealed, making it impossible for subjects to build up a reputation. Each session consisted of a public good game which was played for eight periods. In treatment 1 subjects observed the absolute contributions of all other group members before they had to assign social approval (on a scale between zero and ten stars) to each group member. In treatment 2 subjects observed group members' endowments in addition to their contributions (more information).

The results are surprisingly clear and provide solid evidence for the hypothesis that the exchange of social approval induces higher contributions to the public good. In all periods contributions to the public good were higher in treatments 1 and 2 compared to a control treatment in which social approval could not be expressed. Contrary to our second hypothesis the effect of social approval was smaller in treatment 2 although individual contributions could be judged more accurately. Nonetheless, our experiment provides support for our claim that the exchange of social approval is important for inducing contributions in social production communities.

Chapter 7

Summary and Conclusions

In this last chapter we draw some conclusions from this research on social approval as an incentive for the voluntary provision of public goods, and the emergence, stability, and enforcement of institutions. We summarize the main results, derive some implications, and discuss possible directions for further research.

7.1 Summary

In this thesis we discussed the voluntary provision of public goods. The voluntary provision of public goods is puzzling because the cost of contributing to the public good is private while the benefit of the public good is available to everyone. This externality leads to a divergence of individually optimal behavior, free-riding, and socially optimal behavior, contributing. In our model, we assume that exclusion from the public good is not possible since in social production communities no effort is made to exclude free-riders. Rather, our explanation for the voluntary provision of public goods is centered around the existence of selective incentives. In particular, we focus on social approval as a nonmonetary selective incentive because in social production communities social approval is a reward that is omnipresent. The organization of social production communities as well as our experiment point to the importance of social approval as a reward, inducing higher contributions to public goods. The exchange of social approval explains why thousands of individuals collaboratively work on the Linux kernel and the Wikipedia encyclopedia, and why thousands of individuals write cooking recipes, make them publically available at AllRecipes.com, and comment on others' recipes.

The introduction of rewards transfers the dilemma to the second stage. "Giving rewards to contributors" can be understood as behavior prescribed by a social institution, and the corresponding problem which the community of players has to solve is the enforcement of the institution. In our model, this is achieved by reinforcement learning, in which players who do not behave as prescribed by the social institution are excluded from its benefits. We found that if the institution is enforced by exclusion, a critical mass of players will behave in accordance with the institutionally habituated behavior. Although this critical mass is actually relatively small, most players contribute to the public good and an almost efficient provision of the public good can be achieved.

As a particular example to illustrate the voluntary provision of public goods we have chosen the production of information and the instantiation of digital goods which are not protected by intellectual property rights. Information, culture, and software are all examples of digital goods since information, culture, and software can be stored, replicated and transmitted digitally. Digital goods can be copied at no cost, hence they are infinite expandable and nonrival. In our examples we neglect private companies which contribute to digital public goods and focus on digital goods that are supplied by groups of individuals operating outside the market. Such groups have been known under names like user-led innovation (innovation in physical products), user-generated content (information, culture), and open source (software). We summarized them under the term social production. In chapter 2 we provided terminology and defined some key concepts. Special attention is paid to the history, success, and organization of social production communities. As the history of open source illustrates, there was a long tradition of collaboration and sharing among software developers. The IT revolution boosted the power of social production communities which have increased both in number and size. With the IT revolution we observed a shift from small, geographically concentrated communities towards large, decentralized communities which voluntarily supply public goods. Many of the public goods compete with goods supplied by the private companies (e.g., Windows vs. Linux). Surprisingly often, the public good supplied by the social production community outcompetes the good supplied by the private company. This becomes obvious by looking at the market shares of several open source software applications like Linux (for server operating systems) and Apache (for web server software). The success of social production communities can be understood by answering two intertwined questions. First,

how do social production communities coordinate their activities so that a coherent product emerges out of the individual contributions? And second, what motivates individuals to contribute to social production communities? Our thesis focused on the second aspect, but since the effectiveness of different kinds of incentives depends on the organization of the community we discussed the organization of social production communities in chapter 2.

Chapter 3 provided the theoretical background by reviewing dilemma problems, of which the public good problem is a special case. Different solutions are discussed and it is argued that social production communities are self-organizing communities. Then, empirical studies on contributors and their motives are presented, and use value, intrinsic motivation, social preferences, and social approval are identified. These selective incentices are discussed from a theoretical perspective as well as in relation to social production communities in chapters 3 and 4. In chapter 3 use value, intrinsic motivation, and social preferences are discussed, and social approval is discussed in chapter 4. Taken together, these two chapters answered research questions 1 and 2. We found that several incentives coexist and argued that the most important incentives are use value, intrinsic motivation, social preferences, and social approval. These incentives are provided by the members of the community themselves. Out of these four incentives, social approval is of overarching importance because social approval is not only an incentive on its own but also increases intrinsic motivation and social preferences. Our main claim, derived in chapter 4, is that social approval represents an important selective incentive which has not been discussed thoroughly yet. In the organization and governance of social production communities there are various institutions facilitating intense and open communication so that social approval can be exchanged frequently and almost costlessly. In fact, many esteem services will be provided, resulting in the exchange of social approval which is visible to a large, qualified audience. The focus is on the quality of the contributions and discrimination is reduced to a minimum (e.g., the quality of the source code should speak for itself). Together with the high visibility this ensures that the motivational strength of social approval is high. Although social approval as an incentive has been identified before, it has not been analyzed in detail. In surveys in which the population consisted of both contributors and non-contributors factors relating to social approval are unobserved. If explicitly asked about their motives contributors tend to downplay the importance of social approval due to norms of modesty, resulting in underreporting (Hertel et al., 2003; Franke and Shah,

2003). A thorough analysis of social approval is further complicated by the fact that social approval is closely interwoven with intrinsic motivation, team identity, and signaling. However, a closer inspection of the organization of social production led us to the conclusion (i) that there is a large number of channels through which social approval can be expressed almost costlessly, (ii) that the exchange of esteem services is necessary in order to ensure the compatibility of different contributions and maintain the quality of contributions, and (iii) that, as a consequence, the strength of social approval is likely to be high. The results of chapter 4 suggest that social approval is a major incentive for an individual's decision to contribute to a social production community.

Social approval is discussed in chapter 4, where we distinguish between intrinsic and extrinsic value of social approval and focus on the intrinsic value of social approval. Social approval is a reward which changes the payoffs. But if rewards are costly to give the dilemma is not solved but merely shifted towards the second stage of the game in which players decide whether to give rewards or not. And if the game is extended into a supergame, cooperation is only one out of many possible outcomes. In an infinitely repeated public good game all players contributing can be a Nash equilibrium. This is possible, for example, if all players use a grim-trigger strategy, i.e., everyone contributes if everyone else contributes; and if one player defects cooperation breaks down. In the presence of small errors (trembling hands) this result is unstable and contributions will break down. In the infinitely repeated public good game strategies can become quite complex as the strategy space grows double-exponentially, hence, there is the need to restrict the number of possible strategies. As we have seen from Axelrod's and Lindgren and Nordahl's results, more complicated strategies are not necessarily better. For this reason we stick to simple strategies when analyzing an evolutionary game theory model of a public good game. The change towards evolutionary game theory implies that we are not looking for the optimal strategy, but rather for strategies which survive selectionary pressure in a population of players. After giving an introduction to evolutionary game theory we showed that under certain conditions ESS are a subset of NE, so that evolutionary game theory predicts no contributions to the public good.

In chapter 5 we set up a theoretical model. Our abstract, theoretical model represents the target system, the voluntary provision of public goods by social production communities, by virtue of a similarity relation between the

model and the target system. Since in many cases the target system is not fully understood, it makes sense to build a simplified model, abstracting from certain aspects of the target system, and investigating the properties of the model. The abstract, or idealized, model focuses on particular aspects and isolates social mechanisms which are assumed to be at work in the target system. A social mechanism singles out a causal relation between input and output variables. In the target system the social mechanism is embedded in a complex framework of interacting processes, hence, in the target system the social mechanism cannot be observed in isolation. The theoretical model, however, allows us to investigate the social mechanism while controlling other influences (e.g., keeping other variables constant or allowing them to change). The social mechanism that we isolate is the effect of social approval as a reward in a public good game played on a dynamic network. By changing payoffs and network structure social approval affects the share of contributors. By changing input variables, like speed of strategy updating, and observing output variables, like the distribution of strategies, we are in a position to investigate how the causal mechanism operates under various conditions. Of particular interest for us are the conditions for emergence and stability. In answering research question 3 our model shows that institutional emergence and stability are possible if players do not change their strategies too fast. And by showing that if social distance is taken into account, players who do not give rewards are excluded form the benefits of rewards, we answer research question 4 by showing that the institution is enforced by exclusion.

In order to achieve high levels of contribution to the public good, it is necessary that some players enforce the social institution by giving rewards to contributors (selective incentives), and that the exchange of rewards affects social distance (exclusion). The fact that the social institution is enforced does not imply that the behavior prescribed by the institution corresponds to an evolutionary stable strategy but implies that the prescribed behavior is dynamically stable (see also pp. 279-281, Alexander, 2007). Evolutionary stable strategies are strategies that cannot be driven out by any other strategy. In repeated population games the space of possible strategies is very large, this is why we restricted our analysis to three simple and plausible strategies. This restriction is justified by the following two reasons. First, as the number of complete strategies grows double-exponentially with each repetition of the game (see section 4.3), an examination of the complete strategy space would be too tedious and purposeless since many of the strategies are too compli-

cated or senseless. Support for this claim is derived from Axelrod's tournaments showing the success of Tit-For-Tat, a strategy which is both simple and sensible. Second, even if we would analyze the complete strategy space and characterize the evolutionary stable strategies, this would not give us a reasonable prediction of actual human behavior since decision problems in the real world are far more complex compared to the simple game considered in chapter 5. Human beings are boundedly rational, hence we cannot expect them to actually find the evolutionary stable strategy because of lack of information, fundamental uncertainty, or limited cognitive abilities and computational capabilities (relative to the cognitive abilities and computational capabilities of homo oeconomicus).[109] By using the notion of dynamically stable strategies rather than evolutionary stable strategies we do not expect our players to play Nash equilibrium strategies. What we require from a dynamically stable strategy is that the strategy stays dominant in a population of competing strategies over a long period of time. To survive selectionary pressure the dynamically stable strategy must achieve (over the long-run) a higher payoff than competing strategies, but it must not necessarily be the optimal strategy, for reasons mentioned above. The dynamically stable strategy can be interpreted as a moral principle, a heuristic or a social institution that prescribes a behavior maximizing the long-run payoff. Interpreted as a social institution a dynamically stable strategy illustrates the instrumental character of institutions as a problem-solving device.

A crucial lesson that can be learned from the model is the importance of selective incentives and the enforcement of institutions. At the first stage of the game a dilemma exists since free-riding is the dominant strategy. The introduction of rewards transfers the dilemma to the second stage. The second-stage dilemma concerns the enforcement of the institution and is solved through exclusion. The claim that institutions are enforced by exclusion provides the answer to research question 4. Exclusion is achieved by introducing social distance between players, modeled as a dynamic social network. The exchange of rewards changes social distance, and, if the decision to give rewards is based on both contributions and social distance, free-riders will be excluded from rewards. As a result, rewards represent a selective incen-

109 Two other points are worth mentioning here: (i) It is possible that no Nash equilibrium (and hence no evolutionary stable equilibrium) exists in games with infinite strategies. (ii) Also, it has been shown that there are games for which the existence of a Nash equilibrium can be proved but the Nash equilibrium is non-computable, i.e., it cannot be determined even by hyper-rational players or the fastest computers (Prasad, 1991, 1997).

tive given only to contributors. Although the public good is nonexcludable, an efficient provision of the public good can be achieved by transferring the dilemma to the second stage in which rewards are excludable. The crucial role of the network points to the importance of interpersonal relations, such as social distance, the absence of which has been criticized recently (Gui and Sugden, eds, 2005). Incorporating social networks into economic theory the importance of interpersonal relations is taken into account. By introducing social approval as a nonmonetary reward and social distance as a dynamic network the model is able to predict the voluntary provision of public goods by social production communities in particular, and self-organizing communities in general. In conjunction with the rest of the thesis the formal model presents a contribution for a better understanding of the importance of nonmonetary incentives and interpersonal relations for the solution of social dilemma problems and the enforcement of institutions.

Chapter 6 presents the results from a laboratory experiment and provides the answer to research question 5. The experiment tests the hypothesis that social approval is valued on its own, i.e., it tests whether subjects have a preference for the intrinsic value of social approval. On the one hand, the experiment corroborates the claim that social approval is of overarching importance in social production communities, developed in chapter 4. On the other hand, the experiment is a test of a simplified version of the model developed in chapter 5. In this simplified version the effect from changes in social distance is absent, and the focus is not on emergence, stability, and enforcement of institutions but on social approval as an nonmonetary incentive. Although it is commonplace that people care about social approval, a detailed investigation of social approval is reasonable for the following reasons. First, the motivational strength of social approval depends on various factors, like the form in which social approval is expressed, how it is perceived, and the organizational context. A thorough understanding of these factors allows us to see the importance of social approval in social production communities. Our experiment is a step into this direction by comparing the effect of social approval in two different treatments which differ in the amount of information subjects have about others. Second, an experimental investigation of the effect of social approval on contributions to a public good provides empirical evidence. We compare two different treatments in which subjects anonymously assign social approval based on information about others' absolute and relative contributions. Strategic aspects are absent and we investigate the hypothesis that social approval is valued on its

own. We found that contributions to the public good increased substantially in both treatments in which social approval could be exchanged, compared to a control treatment in which social approval could not be exchanged. Surprisingly, we found that the effect of social approval was greater in treatment 1 than in treatment 2. In treatments 1 and 2 subjects had information about others absolute contributions but in treatment 2 subjects had additional information about others' endowments. The additional information, however, did not increase but decrease the effect of social approval. In the light of these findings, our experiment can be considered to be exploratory work, testing the effect of social approval under different conditions.

7.2 Implications and Directions for Further Research

The central question now is, what does all this imply for the voluntary provision of public goods, social institutions, and economic organization in general? Because we have discussed the specific implications from our game-theoretical model and our experiment at the end of chapters 5 and 6, we confine this section to the discussion of some more general implications.

On a practical level our thesis shows how communities may be able to self-organize and solve social dilemmas without resorting to an external agent. This was also shown by Ostrom (1990) who investigated self-organizing communities from a historical perspective. Our research, in contrast, focuses on social approval as an incentive, presents a theoretical model, and investigates social approval empirically. Two main implications can be drawn for leaders of social production communities.

The first implication concerns the *availability of information* about contributions. Social approval is a reward given to someone because of her contribution. It depends on the quality of the contribution. This implies that it must be possible to associate individual contributors with their contributions and points to the importance of listing contributors' names and contributions in the source code itself, in credit files, or on websites. The aforementioned institutions ensure that the identity and effort of each contributor is revealed in social production communities. For the judgement not only the quality of the contribution but also the information about the contributor's characteristics matter, as has been shown in the experiment. Further work should investigate what kind of information about the contributor's characteristics makes the judgement most effective.

The second implication concerns contributions to the public good. The challenge facing leaders of social production communities is to motivate members to sustain and increase their contributions. We found that social approval significantly increases contributions to a public good. Acknowledging the importance of social approval means that leaders can effectively increase contributions by facilitating the exchange of social approval. This implies that the success of social production communities depends, at least partly, on the *availability of channels in which social approval can be expressed*. Through establishing mailing lists, discussion groups, etc., members of the community are given the opportunity to discuss their contributions with peers. Of course this requires availability of information about contributions. What is important here is that the discussion is open and that there is no discrimination (focus on content). It also implies that there must be some rules defining acceptable behavior within the discussion, and that these rules have to be enforced.

The importance of these two crucial factors, the availability of information about contributions and the possibility to express social approval, is not confined to social production communities. In team production settings, for example, it is plausible to assume that employees have more information about each others' effort than the employer. Hence, the availability of information about contributors and the availability of channels in which social approval can be expressed can also help solving other public good and collective action problems, like team production, neighborhood watch schemes, fund raising, protests, and strike movements. Solving collective action problems is of major importance because such problems are ubiquitous and embedded in any decision (Elsner and Heinrich, 2009; Elsner et al., 2010).

Regarding economic organization in general, it is important to acknowledge the *feedback from the organization of production on the effectiveness of incentives*. In social production intrinsic motivation is high because the work environment induces feelings of self-determination, mastery, and development, which are reinforced by the exchange of social approval. Social approval is an incentive which is contractually unenforceable and represents an externality which cannot be internalized. However, social approval and other nonmonetary incentives clearly affect performance. A notable strand of research into this direction is Frey (2010), providing evidence for a positive effect of awards, a nonmonetary incentive which signals social approval, on performance. Further research should investigate the interrelation between monetary and nonmonetary incentives. Especially relevant here is Crowding-Out,

i.e., the negative effect of larger monetary incentives on performance. In open source projects, for example, it could come to Crowding-Out if private companies hire developers from open source communities. This suggests that nonmonetary incentives like, social approval and awards, can be used in employee-employer relationships. Here the goal is to design work environments which take into account nonmonetary incentives because nonmonetary incentives that are sensitive to employees' preferences for social approval can be beneficial from the employer's perspective. In general, further research on nonmonetary incentives and Crowding-Out will lead to a better understanding of human motivation with the goal of designing more efficient incentive schemes minimizing Crowding-Out and increasing the motivational salience of nonmonetary rewards.

Further practical implications relate social production to property rights, innovation, and industry structure. Since a detailed discussion of these implications could fill a book on its own, we confine ourselves and provide only sketches.

While our discussion was restricted to the internal mechanisms of social production communities, investigating *the relation between social production communities and private companies* is an important area for future research. The role of property rights will play a crucial role in this dicsussion. From a public policy perspective, property rights are used to ensure that socially beneficial activities are also commercially beneficial so that they will be pursued by private campanies. Social production communities, however, pursue socially beneficial activities without relying on property rights. In fact, strong property rights might actually reduce the activity of social production communities.

"Closed" production by private companies and "open" production by social production communities are two competing ways of supplying information and digital goods which are a main source for innovation. The strength and weaknesses of both forms of production should be taken into account when considering policy issues. This becomes especially important when thinking about dynamic efficiency and recombinant growth where today's output is used as tomorrow's input. Dynamic efficiency is concerned with the impact of short run concerns on innovation, i.e., the improvement in efficiency over time. Both "open" and "closed" production might increase dynamic efficiency, but using different channels.

At first it seems that "open" production comes without any disadvantages. Unfortunately, this is not the case since "open" production competes

with "closed" production, thus reducing private companies' profits and their incentives to innovate. The impact of "open" development on private companies' incentives to innovate and on innovative activity in general are difficult to anticipate. Whether the Schumpeterian entrepreneur will thrive in "open" or "closed" production remains an empirical question and will differ between industries. In industries where innovation is capital intensive, the "closed" production model might result in higher innovative activity because property rights ensure a private return to the innovator. On the other hand, strong property rights can constrain innovation, especially when later innovations rely on earlier innovations. If value added chains are fragmented, property rights will be dispersed and multiple parties hold overlapping property rights to the components necessary to constitute a larger innovation. In such situations transaction costs will be high, which can constrain innovation.

Actually, the question is not whether "open" or "closed" production will result in higher innovative activity, but about the relation between the optimal division of labor between social production communities and private companies. Which goods are more efficiently supplied by social production communities, and which goods are more efficiently supplied by private companies? When supplying the same good (e.g., Linux and Microsoft Windows) there is competition between "open" and "closed" production, but if they supply complementary goods they can exist in a symbiotic relation. Many examples (e.g., mountain bike, turntablism) illustrate that this is the case when social production communities supply information by modifying existing products, and private companies use the information and mass manufacture the product. In this case, social production is more efficient in producing new ideas while private companies are more efficient in manufacturing the physical good. At the end, this question is concerned with the boundaries of the firm, and it is not unreasonable to expect that this boundary will shift in response to the growth of social production.

Closely related to the impact of social production on the speed of innovation is the impact of social production on industry structure. A first step into this direction has been done by Bitzer and Schröder (2003, 2005) who provide theoretical and empirical support for positive effects on product quality and speed of innovation resulting from increased competition in the software industry. Unfortunately, the impact of user-generated content is still controversial. Enthusiasts argue that the increased amount of information supplied by user-generated content will result in better decisions, but sceptics claim

that it could lead to an information overload (Benkler, 2006). This, however, will be the subject of further research.

On a theoretical level this thesis contributes to the literature on *evolutionary games played on dynamic networks*. The main implication is that interpersonal relations can change the outcome of the game. Modeling interpersonal relations and their changes as a dynamic social network thus makes a difference by making the model more realistic and increasing its predictive power. With respect to our theoretical model (chapter 5) we see that if exclusion from the public good is not possible, the introduction of rewards can transfer the problem to another stage. At this second stage players compete for rewards. Since rewards are excludable, exclusion can be an efficient mechanism to overcome the dilemma and achieve the voluntary provision of public goods.

The topic of this thesis, social approval and the voluntary provision of public goods, lies at the intersection of two research areas: evolutionary game theory and experimental economics. In both research areas there exist various *directions for further research*. Additionally, the model from chapter 5 could be brought to the data by conducting a social network analysis examining interaction patterns on social production communities.

One possible avenue for further research concerns different *extensions of the game-theoretic model* presented in chapter 5. First, the model could be extended by introducing players who are heterogeneous with respect to ability. This has already been suggested at the end of chapter 5. Second, we could extend the strategy space and allow players to use mixed strategies, as in Jun and Sethi (2009). With mixed strategies, we expect players to change their strategies less fast, dampening fluctuations in the state of the population. And thirdly, we could run the model with different learning rules for partner selection. Here the question is whether the model is robust to the choice of the learning rule. Preliminary results from simulations in which we substituted Arthur's learning rule (Arthur, 1990, 1991) for reinforcement learning confirm our results.

Another possible avenue for further research is the *difference between unstructured and structured populations* in evolutionary game theory. If played in an unstructured population our model fails to predict the voluntary provision of the public good, regardless of the size of the reward. Substituting the dynamic network for random matching allows us to explicitly model the structure of the population. Since now the game is played in a structured population our model is able to explain both the structure of the network and the provision of the public good. Further research should aim at a de-

tailed discussion of how the assumption of a structured population changes the predictive power of the model, for example, how different learning rules generate different neighborhood structures. The discussion of structured versus unstructured populations should not be confined to public good games but should focus on games in general.

In order to study the effect of social approval empirically *further experiments* are an obvious and promising avenue for further research. Notably here is Frey's recent work on awards (Frey, 2006, 2007; Frey and Neckermann, 2008; Frey, 2010), but awards are only a formalized way of expressing social approval. Future work should investigate *different forms of expressing social approval* (e.g., gestures, facial expressions, verbal and written messages) and compare the effects of different forms of expressing social approval. One possibility to extend our experiment would be to isolate the status effect, i.e., the effect of social comparison. In our experiment subjects had information about the amount of social approval others' received, resulting in social comparison. In different treatments one could compare the effect of social approval if the distribution of social approval is public knowledge, so that each subject knows each others' social approval, to the effect of social approval if subjects have information only about their own social approval, so that social comparison is impossible. These two treatments would correspond to two extreme cases in which all information about the distribution of social approval is available, and no information about others' contributions is available. Inbetween, there are cases in which only some information about the distribution of social approval (e.g., the mean or median, or minimum and maximum) is available. Such a modified version of our experiment would investigate how different social comparisons affect behavior and would provide implications for how different ways of presenting social approval can effectively be used to increase contributions to public goods.

In this thesis we discussed different components of a larger research program including the voluntary provision of public goods and the enforcement of institutions. We chose social production as an example, illustrating the importance of social approval as a selective incentive. The experiment which we presented confirmed the importance of social approval as an incentive, but, as the theoretical model revealed, the existence of selective incentives is necessary but not sufficient. If the exchange of social rewards is understood as an institution, it becomes clear that the institution has to be enforced by exclusion. The results presented in this thesis are only small steps for towards

a better understanding of the voluntary provision of public goods and the enforcement of institutions. More work is needed.

Bibliography

Akerlof, George A., "Labor Contracts as Partial Gift Exchange," *The Quarterly Journal of Economics*, 1982, *97* (4), 543–569.

_ and Rachel E. Kranton, "Economics and Identity," *The Quarterly Journal of Economics*, August 2000, *115* (3), 715–753.

_ and _ , "Identity and the Economics of Organizations," *Journal of Economic Perspectives*, 2005, *19* (1), 9–32.

Albert, Max, "Product Quality in a Simple OLG Model of Scientific Competition," *MAGKS Joint Discussion Paper Series in Economics*, 2008.

_ , "Methodology and Scientific Competition," *Episteme*, 2011, *8* (2).

Alchian, Armen A. and Harold Demsetz, "Production, Information Costs, and Economic Organization," *American Economic Review*, 1972, *62* (5), 777–795.

Alexander, Jason McKenzie, *The Structural Evolution of Morality*, Cambridge University Press, 2007.

Allen, Robert C., "Collective Invention," *Journal of Economic Behavior and Organization*, 1983, *4* (1), 1–24.

Andreoni, James, "Privately Provided Public Goods in a Large Economy: The Limits of Altruism," *Journal of Public Economics*, 1988, *35* (1), 57–73.

_ , "Why Free Ride? Strategies and Learning in Public Good Games," *Journal of Public Economics*, 1988, *37* (3), 291–304.

_ , "Giving with Impure Altruism: Applications to Charity and Ricardian Equivalence," *The Journal of Political Economy*, 1989, *97* (6), 1447–1458.

_ , "Impure Altruism and Donations to Public Goods: A Theory of Warm-Glow Giving," *The Economic Journal*, 1990, *100* (401), 464–477.

_ and Justin Rao, "The Power of Asking: How Communication Affects Selfishness, Empathy, and Altruism," *Journal of Public Economics*, forthcoming.

_ , William Harbaugh, and Lise Vesterlund, "The Carrot or the Stick: Rewards, Punishments and Cooperation," *American Economic Review*, 2003, *93* (3), 893–902.

Ariely, Dan, Anat Bracha, and Stephan Meier, "Doing Good or Doing Well? Image Motivation and Monetary Incentives in Behaving Prosocially," *American Economic Review*, 2009, *99* (1), 544–555.

_ , Uri Gneezy, George Loewenstein, and Nina Mazar, "Large Stakes and Big Mistakes," *Review of Economic Studies*, 2009, *76* (2), 451–469.

Arrow, Kenneth J., "Economic Welfare and the Allocation of Resources for Innovation," Technical Report P-1856-RC, RAND Cooperation 1959.

_ , "Rawls's Principle of Just Saving," *The Swedish Journal of Economics*, 1973, *75* (4), 323–335.

Arthur, W. Brian, "Competing Technologies, Increasing Returns, and Lock-In by Historical Events," *The Economic Journal*, 1989, *99*, 116–131.

_ , "A Learning Algorithm That Mimics Human Learning," Technical Report, Santa Fe Institute 1990.

_ , "Designing Economic Agents that Act like Human Agents: A Behavioral Approach to Bounded Rationality," *American Economic Review*, 1991, *81* (2), 353–359.

_ , Yu. M. Ermoliev, and Yu. M. Kaniovski, "Path-Dependent Processes and the Emergence of Macro-Structure," *European Journal of Operational Research*, 1987, *30*, 294–303.

Asundi, Jai, Rick Kazman, and V. S. Arunachalam, "Understanding Change Contribution Patterns in Open Source and Commercial Software Projects," 2005. Center for the Analysis of Property Rights and Innovation (CAPRI) Working Paper 05-05.

Aumann, Robert and R. Myerson, "Endogeneous Formation of Links Between Players and Coalitions: An Application of the Shapley Value," in Alvin E. Roth, ed., *The Shapley Value*, Cambridge University Press, 1988.

Axelrod, Robert, *The Evolution of Cooperation*, Basic Books, 1984.

_ , *The Evolution of Cooperation*, revised ed., Basic Books, 2006.

Bala, Venkatesh and Sanjeev Goyal, "A Non-Cooperative Model of Network Formation," *Econometrica*, 2000, *68* (5), 1181–1229.

Bardsley, Nicholas, Robin Cubitt, Graham Loomes, Peter Moffatt, Chris Starmer, and Robert Sugden, *Experimental Economics – Rethinking the Rules*, Princeton University Press, 2010.

Bates, Jeff and Mark Stone, "Communicating Many to Many," in Chris Di-Bona, ed., *Open Sources 2.0: The Continuing Evolution*, O'Reilly Media, 2006.

Becker, Gary S., "A Theory of Social Interactions," *The Journal of Political Economy*, 1974, *82* (6), 1063–1093.

Bénabou, Roland and Jean Tirole, "Self-Confidence and Social Interactions," *NBER Working Paper No. 7585*, 2000.

_ and _ , "Self-Confidence And Personal Motivation," *The Quarterly Journal of Economics*, 2002, *117* (3), 871–915.

_ and _ , "Intrinsic and Extrinsic Motivation," *The Review of Economic Studies*, 2003, *70* (3), 489–520.

Benkler, Yochai, "Coase's Penguin, or, Linux and The Nature of the Firm," *Yale Law Journal*, December 2003, *112* (3), 369–446.

_ , *The Wealth of Networks*, Yale University Press, 2006.

_ and Helen Nissenbaum, "Commons-based Peer Production and Virtue," *The Journal of Political Philosophy*, 2006, *14* (4), 394–419.

Bitzer, Jürgen and Ingo Geishecker, "Who Contributes Voluntarily to OSS? An Investigation Among German IT Employees," *Research Policy*, 2010, *39*, 165–172.

_ and Phillip J.H. Schröder, "Competition and Innovation in a Technology Setting Software Duopoly," *DIW Discussion Paper 363*, 2003.

_ and _ , "The Impact of Entry and Competition by Open Source Software on Innovation Activity," *International Business Section Working Paper 2005-12*, 2005.

_ , Wolfram Schrettl, and Phillip J.H. Schröder, "Intrinsic Motivation in Open Source Software Development," *Journal of Comparative Economics*, 2007, *35* (1), 160–169.

Blättel-Mink, Birgit and Kai-Uwe Hellmann, eds, *Prosumer Revisited*, VS Verlag für Sozialwissenschaften, 2010.

Blinder, Alan S. and Don S. Choi, "A Shred of Evidence on Theories of Wage Stickiness," *The Quarterly Journal of Economics*, 1990, *105* (4), 1003–1016.

Bolton, Gary E. and Axel Ockenfels, "ERC: A Theory of Equity, Reciprocity, and Competition," *American Economic Review*, 2000, *90* (1), 166–193.

_ and Elena Katok, "An Experimental Test for Gender Differences in Beneficent Behavior," *Economic Letters*, 1995, *48* (3-4), 287–292.

_ , _ , and Rami Zwick, "Dictator Game Giving: Rules of Fairness Versus Acts of Kindness," *International Journal of Game Theory*, 1998, *27* (2), 269–299.

Bonacich, Phillip and Thomas M. Liggett, "Asymptotics of a Matrix Valued Markov Chain Arising in Sociology," *Stochastic Processes and their Applications*, 2003, *104* (1), 155–171.

Bowles, Samuel, *Microeconomics – Behavior, Institutions, and Evolution*, Princeton University Press, 2004.

Bravo, Giangiacomo, "Voluntary Contribution to Public Goods in Mutual-Help Forums: Reciprocity or Group Attachment?," *Socio-Economic Review*, 2010, *8* (4), 709–733.

Brekke, Kjell Arne, Snorre Kverndokk, and Karine Nyborg, "An Economic Model of Moral Motivation," *Journal of Public Economics*, 2003, *87* (9-10), 1967–1983.

Brennan, Geoffrey, *Democracy and Decisions: The Pure Theory of Electoral Preference*, Cambridge University Press, 1993.

_ and Phillip Pettit, "The Hidden Economy of Esteem," *Economics and Philosophy*, 2000, *16* (1), 77–98.

_ and _ , "Esteem, Identifiability and the Internet," *Analyse & Kritik*, 2004, *26* (1), 139–157.

Brenner, Thomas, "Agent Learning Representation: Advice on Modelling Economic Learning," in Leigh Tesfatsion and Kenneth L. Judd, eds., *Handbook of Computational Economics*, Vol. 2, Elsevier, 2006, chapter 18.

Brost, Marc and Wolfgang Uchatius, "Ein Laufrad für Deutschland," *Die Zeit*, 2009, *16. April*, 19–20.

Brown-Kruse, Jamie and David Hummels, "Gender Effects in Laboratory Public Goods Contribution," *Journal of Economic Behavior and Organization*, 1993, 22 (3), 255–267.

Bünstorf, Guido, "Designing Clunkers: Demand-Side Innovation and the Early History of the Mountain Bike," in J. Stan Metcalfe and Uwe Cantner,

eds., *Change, Transformation and Development*, Physica-Verlag, 2003, pp. 53–70.

Bush, Paul D., "The Theory of Institutional Change," *Journal of Economic Issues*, 1987, *21* (3), 1075–1116.

_ and Marc R. Tool, "The Evolutionary Principles of American Neoinstitutionalist Economics," in Kurt Dopfer, ed., *Evolutionary Economics: Program and Scope*, Kluwer Academic Publishers, 2001.

Camerer, Colin and Ernst Fehr, "Measuring Social Norms and Preferences Usong Experimental Games: A Guide for Social Scientists," in Joseph Henrich, Robert Boyd, Samuel Bowles, Colin Camerer, Ernst Fehr, and Herbert Gintis, eds., *Foundations of Human Sociality*, Oxford University Press, 2004, chapter 3, pp. 55–95.

Charness, Gary and Matthew Rabin, "Understanding Social Preferences with Simple Tests," *The Quarterly Journal of Economics*, 2002, *117* (3), 817–869.

Chaudhuri, Ananish, "Sustaining Cooperation in Laboratory Public Goods Experiments: A Selective Survey of the Literature," *Experimental Economics*, 2011, *14* (1), 47–83.

Chesbrough, Henry, *Open Innovation: The New Imperative for Creating and Profiting from Technology*, McGraw-Hill, 2003.

Coase, Ronald H., "The Problem of Social Cost," *Journal of Law and Economics*, 1960, *3* (1), 1–44.

Cohen, Wesley M. and Daniel A. Levinthal, "Absorptive Capacity: A New Perspective on Learning and Innovation," *Administrative Science Quarterly*, 1999, *35* (1), 128–152.

Croson, Rachel, "Theories of Commitment, Altruism and Reciprocity: Evidence from Linear Public Good Games," *Economic Inquiry*, 2007, *45* (2), 199–216.

Crowne, Douglas P. and David Marlowe, "A New Scale of Social Desirability Independent of Psychopathology," *Journal of Consulting Psychology*, 1960, *24* (4), 349–354.

David, Paul A., "Clio and the Economics of QWERTY," *American Economic Review*, 1985, *75* (2), 332–337.

de Condorcet, Marquis, *Essai sur l'application de l'analyse à la probabilité des décisions rendues à la pluralité des voix*, Paris, 1785.

Deci, Edward L., *Intrinsic Motivation*, Plenum Press, 1975.

_ and Richard M. Ryan, *Intrinsic Motivation and Self-Determination in Human Behavior*, Plenum Press, 1985.

Demange, Gabrielle and Myrna Wooders, eds, *Group Formation in Economics: Networks, Clubs, and Coalitions*, Cambridge University Press, 2005.

Dempsey, Bert J., Debra Weiss, Paul Jones, and Jane Greenberg, "A Quantitative Profile of a Community of Open Source Linux Developers," Technical Report, School of Information and Library Science, University of Noth Carolina at Chapel Hill 1999.

Deshpande, Amit and Dirk Riehle, "The Total Growth of Open Source," in "Proceedings of the Fourth Conference on Open Source Systems" Springer Verlag 2008.

DeSilva, Hannelore, Christoph Hauert, Arne Traulsen, and Karl Sigmund, "Freedom, Enforcement, and the Social Dilemma of Strong Altruism," *Journal of Evolutionary Economics*, 2010, *20* (2), 203–217.

Deutsch, Francine M. and Donna M. Lamberti, "Does Social Approval Increase Helping?," *Personality and Social PSychology Bulletin*, 1986, *12* (2), 149–157.

Dewey, John, *The Public and its Problems*, Henry Holt Co., 1927.

DiBona, Chris, Danese Cooper, and Mark Stone, eds, *Open Sources 2.0: The Continuing Evolution*, O'Reilly Media, 2006.

Dickinson, David L., "The Carrot vs. the Stick in Work Team Motivation," *Experimental Economics*, 2001, *4* (1), 107–124.

Dopfer, Kurt, ed., *Evolutionary Economics: Program and Scope*, Kluwer Academic Publishers, 2001.

Douglas, Mary and Baron Isherwood, *The World of Goods - Towards an Anthropology of Consumption*, Allen Lane, 1978.

Dugar, Subhasish, "Nonmonetary Sanctions and Rewards in an Experimental Coordination Game," *Journal of Economic Behavior and Organization*, 2010, *73* (3), 377–386.

Dur, Robert and Joeri Sol, "Social interaction, co-worker altruism, and incentives," *Games and Economic Behavior*, 2010, *69* (2), 293–301.

Durrett, Richard and Simon A. Levin, "The Importance of Being Discrete (and Spatial)," *Theoretical Population Biology*, 1994, *46* (3), 363–394.

Easterlin, Richard A., "Income and Happiness: Towards a Unified Theory," *The Economic Journal*, 2001, *111* (473), 465–484.

Eckel, Catherine C. and Philip J. Grossman, "Managing Diversity by Creating Team Identity," *Journal of Economic Behavior and Organization*, 2005, *58* (3), 371–392.

Ellingsen, Tore and Magnus Johannesson, "Paying Respect," *Journal of Economic Perspectives*, 2007, *21* (4), 135–149.

_ and _ , "Anticipated Verbal Feedback Induces Altruistic Behavior," *Evolution and Human Behavior*, 2008, *29* (2), 100–105.

Elsner, Wolfram, "The New Economy: Complexity, Coordination and a Hybrid Governance Approach," *International Journal of Social Economics*, 2004, *31*, 1029–1049.

_ , "Real-World Economics Today: The New Complexity, Co-ordination, and Policy," *Review of Social Economy*, 2005, *63* (1), 19–53.

_ , "Why Meso? On Aggregation and Emergence, and Why and How the Meso Level is Essential in Social Economics," *Forum for Social Economics*, 2007, *36*, 1–16.

_ , "The Process and a Simple Logic of 'Meso'. Emergence and the Co-Evolution of Institutions and Group Size," *Journal of Evolutionary Economics*, 2010, *20* (3), 445–477.

_ , "The Theory of Institutional Change Revisited, After (About) 25 Years," 2011. paper presented at the Annual Meeting of the Association for Evolutionary Economics, January 2011.

_ and Torsten Heinrich, "A Simple Theory of 'Meso'. On the Co-Evolution of Institutions and Platform-Size - With an Application to Varieties of Capitalism and 'Medium-Sized' Countries," *The Journal of Socio-Economics*, 2009, *38* (5), 843–858.

_ and _ , "Towards 'Meso'-Economics. On the Co-Evolution of Institutionalized Coordination, 'Platform' Size, and Performance," in Stefan Mann, ed., *Sectors Matter – Exploring Mesoeconomics*, Springer Verlag, forthcoming.

_ , Gero Hocker, and Henning Schwardt, "Simplistic vs. Complex Organization: Markets, Hierarchies, and Networks in an Organizational Triangle," *Journal of Economic Issues*, 2010, *44* (1), 1–29.

_ , Matthias Greiff, Torsten Heinrich, and Henning Schwardt, *Microeconomics of Interactive Economies – Evolutionary and Institutional Perspectives* (draft available online at www.iino.de/elsner), Edward Elgar, forthcoming.

Elster, Jon, *Sour Grapes - Studies in the Subversion of Rationality*, Cambridge University Press, 1983.

Eshel, Ilan, Larry Samuelson, and Avner Shaked, "Altruists, Egosists, and Hooligans in a Local Interaction Model," *American Economic Review*, 1998, *88* (1), 157–179.

Espejo, Roman, ed., *User-Generated Content (At Issue)*, Greenhaven Press, 2007.

Falk, Armin and James J. Heckman, "Lab Experiments Are a Major Source of Knowledge in the Social Sciences," *Science*, 2009, *326* (5952), 535–538.

_ , Ernst Fehr, and Urs Fischbacher, "On the Nature of Fair Behavior," *Economic Inquiry*, 2003, *41* (4), 20–26.

_ , _ , and _ , "Testing Theories of Fairness – Intentions Matter," *Games and Economic Behavior*, 2008, *62* (1), 287–303.

Faulkner, Phil and Jochen Runde, "On the Identity of Technological Objects and User Innovations in Function," *Academy of Management Review*, 2009, *34* (3), 442–462.

Fehr, Ernst and Armin Falk, "Psychological Foundations of Incentives," *European Economic Review*, 2002, *46* (4-5), 687–724.

_ and Klaus M. Schmidt, "A Theory of Fairness, Competition, and Cooperation," *The Quarterly Journal of Economics*, 1999, *114* (3), 817–868.

_ and Simon Gächter, "Cooperation and Punishment in Public Goods Experiments," *American Economic Review*, 2000, *90* (4), 980–994.

_ and _ , "Altruistic Punishment in Humans," *Nature*, 2002, *415*, 137–140.

_ , _ , and Georg Kirchsteiger, "Reciprocity as a Contract Enforcement Device - Experimental Evidence," *Econometrica*, 1997, *65* (4), 833–860.

Fischbacher, Urs, Simon Gächter, and Ernst Fehr, "Are People Conditionally Cooperative? Evidence from a Public Goods Experiment," *Economic Letters*, 2001, *71* (3), 397–404.

Fischbacher, Urs, "z-Tree: Zurich Toolbox for Ready-made Economic Experiments," *Experimental Economics*, 2007, *10* (2), 171–178.

Fiske, Susan, Daniel T. Gilbert, and Gardner Lindzey, eds, *Handbook of Social Psychology*, 5th ed., Vol. 2, Wiley, 2010.

Foster, Dean and Peyton Young, "Stochastic Evolutionary Game Dynamics," *Theoretical Population Biology*, 1990, *38* (2), 219–232.

Frank, Robert H., *Choosing the Right Pond – Human Behavior and the Quest for Status*, Oxford University Press, 1985.

Franke, Nikolaus and Sonali Shah, "How Communities Support Innovative Activities: An Exploration of Assistance and Sharing Among End-Users," *Research Policy*, 2003, *23* (1), 157–178.

Freeman, Richard B., "Working for Nothing: The Supply of Volunteer Labor," *Journal of Labor Economics*, 1997, *15* (1), S140–S166.

Frey, Bruno S., "Giving and Receiving Awards," *Perspectives on Psychological Science*, 2006, *1* (4), 377–388.

_ , "Awards as compensation," *European Management Review*, 2007, *4* (1), 6–14.

_ , "Geld oder Anerkennung? Zur Ökonomik der Auszeichnungen," *Perspektiven der Wirtschaftspolitik*, 2010, *11* (1), 1–15.

_ and Reto Jegen, "Motivation Crowding Theory," *Journal of Economic Surveys*, 2001, *15* (1), 589–611.

_ and Stephan Meier, "Social Comparison and Pro-social Behavior: Testing "Conditional Cooperation" in a Field Experiment," *American Economic Review*, 2004, *94* (5), 1717–1722.

_ and Susanne Neckermann, "Awards: A View from Psychological Economics," *Journal of Psychology*, 2008, *216* (4), 198–208.

Friedman, James W., "A Non-Cooperative Equilibrium for Supergames," *Review of Economic Studies*, 1971, *38* (1), 1–12.

Gächter, Simon and Ernst Fehr, "Collective Action as a Social Exchange," *Journal of Economic Behavior and Organization*, 1999, *39* (4), 341–369.

Gaertner, Wulf, *A Primer in Social Choice Theory (Revised Edition)*, Oxford University Press, 2009.

Gibbons, Robert, "An Introduction to Applicable Game Theory," *The Journal of Economic Perspectives*, 1997, *11* (1), 127–149.

Gigerenzer, Gerd and Reinhard Selten, eds, *Bounded Rationality: The Adaptive Toolbox*, MIT Press, 2001.

Giles, Jim, "Internet Encyclopedias go Head to Head," *Nature*, 2005, *438* (7070), 900–901.

Gonzáles, Luis G., Werner Güth, and M. Vittoria Levati, "When does the game end? Public goods experiments with non-definite and non-commonly known time horizons," *Economic Letters*, 2005, *88* (2), 221–226.

Gordon, Robert J., "Foundations of the Goldilocks Economy: Supply-Shocks and the Time-Varying NAIRU," *Brookings Papers on Economic Activity*, 1998, (2), 297–346.

Granovetter, Mark S., "The Strength of Weak Ties," *American Journal of Sociology*, 1973, *78* (6), 1360–1380.

Guala, Francesco, *The Methodology of Experimental Economics*, Cambridge University Press, 2005.

Gui, Benedetto and Robert Sugden, eds, *Economics and Social Interaction: Accounting for Interpersonal Relations*, Cambridge University Press, 2005.

Hamilton, William D., "The Genetical Evolution of Social Behaviour I," *Journal of Theoretical Biology*, 1964a, *7* (1), 1–16.

_ , "The Genetical Evolution of Social Behaviour II," *Journal of Theoretical Biology*, 1964b, *7* (1), 17–52.

Hanaki, Nobuyuki, Alexander Peterhansl, Peter S. Dodd, and Duncan J. Watts, "Cooperation in Evolving Social Networks," *Management Science*, 2007, *53* (7), 1036–1050.

Hardin, Garrett, "The Tragedy of the Commons," *Science*, 1968, *162* (3859), 1243–1248.

Hargreaves Heap, Shaun P., *Rationality in Economics*, Blackwell Publishers, 1989.

_ , "Expressive Rationality: Is Self-Worth Just Another Kind of Preference?," in Uskali Mäki, ed., *The Economic World View, Studies in the Ontology of Economics*, Cambridge University Press, 2001, pp. 98–113.

_ and Yanis Varoufakis, *Game Theory: A Critical Introduction (Second Edition)*, Routledge, 2004.

Harhoff, Dietmar, Joachim Henkel, and Eric von Hippel, "Profiting from Voluntary Information Spillovers: How Users Benefit by Freely Revealing their Innovations," *Research Policy*, 2003, *32* (10), 1753–1769.

Helpman, Elhanan, ed., *General Purpose Technologies and Economic Growth*, MIT Press, 1998.

Hennig-Schmidt, Heike, Bettina Rockenbach, and Abdolkarim Sadrieh, "In Search Of Workers' Real Effort Reciprocity - A Field and a Laboratory Experiment," *Journal of The European Economic Association*, 2010, *8* (4), 817–837.

Henrich, Joseph, Robert Boyd, Samuel Bowles, Colin Camerer, Ernst Fehr, and Herbert Gintis, eds, *Foundations of Human Sociality – Economic Experiments and Ethnographic Evidence from Fifteen Small-Scale Societies*, Oxford University Press, 2004.

Herrnstein, R.J., "On the Law of Effect," *Journal of the Experimental Analysis of Behavior*, 1970, *13*, 243–266.

Hertel, Guido, Sven Niedner, and Stefanie Herrmann, "Motivation of Software Developers in Open Source Projects: An Internet-Based Survey of Contributors to the Linux Kernel," *Research Policy*, 2003, *32* (7), 1159–1177.

Hobbes, Thomas, *Leviathan oder Stoff, Form und Gewalt eines kirchlichen und bürgerlichen Staates*, 14 ed., Suhrkamp, 1984.

Hogg, Michael A. and Graham M. Vaughan, *Social Psychology*, 5 ed., Prentice Hall, 2008.

Holländer, Heinz, "A Social Exchange Approch to Voluntary Cooperation," *American Economic Review*, 1990, *80* (5), 1157–1167.

Holler, Manfred J. and Gerhard Illing, *Einführung in die Spieltheorie*, 7 ed., Springer, 2009.

Holmström, Bength, "Managerial Incentive Problems - A Dynamic Perspective," *Review of Economic Studies*, 1999, *66* (1), 169–182.

Holt, Charles A. and Susan K. Laury, "Theoretical Explanations of Treatment Effects in Voluntary Contribution Experiments," in Charles R. Plott and Vernon L. Smith, eds., *Handbook of Experimental Economics Results*, Vol. 1 of *Handbooks in Economics*, North-Holland, 2008.

Howe, Jeff, *Crowdsourcing: Why the Power of the Crowd Is Driving the Future of Business*, Crown Business, 2008.

Huberman, Bernardo A., *The Laws of the Web*, MIT Press, 2001.

_ , Christoph H. Loch, and Ayse Öncüler, "Status As a Valued Resource," *Social Psychology Quarterly*, 2004, *67* (1), 103–114.

Huck, Steffen and Michael Kosfeld, "The Dynamics of Neighborhood Watch and Norm Enforcement," *The Economic Journal*, 2007, *117* (516), 270–286.

Iannacci, Federico, "The Social Epistemology of Open Source Software." PhD dissertation, London School of Economics 2005.

Ichiishi, T., A. Neyman, and Y. Tauman, eds, *Game Theory and Applications*, San Diego: Academic Press, 1990.

Imhof, Lorens A., Drew Fudenberg, and Martin A. Nowak, "Tit-For-Tat or Win-Stay, Lose-Shift?," *Journal of Theoretical Biology*, 2007, *247* (3), 574–580.

Isaac, R. Mark, Kenneth F. McCue, and Charles R. Plott, "Public Goods Provision in an Experimental Environment," *Journal of Public Economics*, 1985, *26* (1), 51–74.

Jackson, Matthew O., "A Survey of Network Formation Models: Stability and Efficiency," in Gabrielle Demange and Myrna Wooders, eds., *Group Formation in Economics: Networks, Clubs, and Coalitions*, Cambridge University Press, 2005.

_ , *Social and Economic Networks*, Princeton University Press, 2008.

_ and Alison Watts, "The Evolution of Social and Economic Networks," *Journal of Economic Theory*, 2002, *106* (2), 265–295.

_ and Asher Wolinsky, "A Strategic Model of Social and Economic Networks," *Journal of Economic Theory*, 1996, *71* (1), 44–74.

Jarvenpaa, Sirkka L. and Dorothy E. Leidner, "Communication and Trust in Global Virtual Teams," *Organization Science*, 1999, *10* (6), 791–815.

Jennings, Fred B., "How Efficiency/Equity Tradeoffs Resolve Through Horizon Effects," *Journal of Economic Issues*, 2005, *39* (2), 365–373.

_ , "Toward a Horizonal Theory of Justice: Efficiency, Equity, Rights and Capabilities in a Free Market Economy," *Forum for Social Economics*, 2010, *39* (1), 77–87.

Jorgensen, Dale W., Kevin J. Stiroh, Robert J. Gordon, and Daniel E. Sichel, "Raising the Speed Limit: U.S. Economic Growth in the Information Age," *Brookings Papers on Economic Activity*, 2000, (1), 125–235.

Jovanovic, Boyan and Peter L. Rousseau, *Handbook of Economic Growth*, Vol. 1B, Elsevier, 2005.

Jun, Tackseung and Rajiv Sethi, "Reciprocity in Evolving Social Networks," *Journal of Evolutionary Economics*, 2009, *119* (3), 379–396.

Kagel, John H. and Alvin E. Roth, eds, *Handbook of Experimental Economics*, Princeton University Press, 1995.

Kahneman, Daniel and Jack L. Knetsch, "Valuing Public Goods: The Purchase of Moral Satisfaction," *Journal of Environmental Economics*, 1992, 22 (1), 57–50.

Kalai, Ehud, "Bounded Rationality and Complexity in Repeated Games," in "Game Theory and Applications," San Diego: Academic Press, 1990.

Kandel, Eugene and Edward P. Lazear, "Peer Pressure and Partnerships," *The Journal of Political Economy*, 1992, *100* (4), 801–817.

Kandori, Michihiro, George J. Mailath, and Rafael Rob, "Learning, Mutation, and Long Run Equilibria in Games," *Econometrica*, 1993, *61* (1), 29–56.

Katz, Michael L. and Carl Shapiro, "Technology Adoption in the Presence of Network Externalities," *The Journal of Political Economy*, 1986, *94* (4), 822–841.

Katzenbach, Jon R. and Douglas K. Smith, *The Wisdom of Teams: Creating the High Performance Organization*, Harper-Collins, New York, 1994.

Kaul, Inge, Isabelle Grunberg, and Marc Stern, eds, *Global Public Goods*, Oxford University Press, 1999.

Kollock, P., *Communities in Cyberspace*, Routledge, 1998.

Kosfeld, Michael and Susanne Neckermann, "Getting More Work for Nothing? Symbolic Awards and Worker Performance," *American Economic Journal: Microeconomics*, forthcoming.

Kramer, Roderick M. and Tom R. Tyler, eds, *Trust in Organizations: Frontiers of Theory and Research*, Sage Publications, 1996.

Kreps, David M. and Robert Wilson, "Reputation and Imperfect Information," *Journal of Economic Theory*, 1982, *27* (2), 253–279.

_ , Paul R. Milgrom, John Roberts, and Robert Wilson, "Rational Cooperation in the Finitely Repeated Prisoners' Dilemma," *Journal of Economic Theory*, 1982, *27* (2), 245–252.

Kube, Sebastian, Michel André Maréchal, and Clemens Puppe, "The Currency of Reciprocity – Gift-Exchange in the Workplace," *mimeo*, 2010.

Langlois, Richard N., "Modularity in Technology and Organization," *Journal of Economic Behavior and Organization*, 37 2002, *49* (1), 19.

Leadbeater, Charles, *We-Think*, second edition ed., Profile Books, 2009.

Ledyard, John O., "Public Goods: A Survey of Experimental Research," in John H. Kagel and Alvin E. Roth, eds., *Handbook of Experimental Economics*, Princeton University Press, 1995.

Lerner, Josh and Jean Tirole, "The Open Source Movement: Key Research Questions," *European Economic Review*, 2001, *45* (4-4), 819–826.

_ and _ , "Some Simple Economics of Open Source," *Journal of Industrial Economics*, 2002, *50* (2), 197–234.

_ , Parag A. Pathak, and Jean Tirole, "The Dynamics of Open-Source Contributors," *American Economic Review*, May 2006, *96* (2), 114–118.

Lindgren, Kristian and Mats G. Nordahl, "Evolutionary Dynamics of Spatial Games," *Physica D*, 1994, *75* (1-3), 292–309.

Lipsey, Richard G., Kenneth I. Carlaw, and Clifford T. Bekar, *Economic Transformations Economic Transformations - General Purpose Technologies and Long-Term Economic Growth*, Oxford University Press, 2005.

Ljungberg, Jan, "Open Source Movement as a Model for Organising," *European Journal of Information Systems*, 2000, *9* (4), 208–216.

Luce, Duncan, *Individual Choice and Behavior*, John Wiley Sons, 1959.

_ and Howard Raiffa, *Games and Decisions: Introduction and Critical Survey*, John Wiley Sons, 1957.

Lutterbeck, Bernd, Matthias Bärwolf, and Robert A. Gehring, eds, *Open Source Jahrbuch 2007: Zwischen Softwareentwicklung und Gesellschaftsmodell*, Lehmanns, 2007.

Mann, Stefan, ed., *Sectors Matter – Exploring Mesoeconomics*, Springer Verlag, 2012.

Manzini, Paola, Abdolkarim Sadrieh, and Nicolaas J. Vriend, "On Smiles, Winks and Handshakes as Coordination Devices," *The Economic Journal*, 2009, *119s*, 826–854.

March, James G., "Variable Risk Preferences and Adaptive Aspirations," *Journal of Economic Behavior and Organization*, 1988, *9* (1), 5–24.

Mas-Colell, Andreu, Michael D. Whinston, and Jerry R. Green, *Microeconomic Theory*, Oxford University Press, 1995.

Masclet, David, Charles Noussair, Steven Tucker, and Marie-Claire Villeval, "Monetary and Nonmonetary Punishment in the Voluntary Contributions Mechanism," *American Economic Review*, 2003, *93* (1), 366–380.

Mauss, Marcel, *The Gift - Forms and Functions of Exchange in Archaic Societies*, Cohen and West, 1954.

Maynard Smith, John, "The Theory of Games and the Evolution of Animal Conflicts," *Journal of Theoretical Biology*, 1974, *47* (1), 209–221.

_ and G. R. Price, "The Logic of Animal Conflict," *Nature*, 1973, *246* (5427), 15–18.

Menges, Roland and Stefan Traub, "An Experimental Study on the Gap Between Willingness to Pay and Willingness to Donate for Green Electricity," *FinanzArchiv / Public Finance Analysis*, 2009, *65* (3), 335–357.

Metcalfe, John Stan and Uwe Cantner, eds, *Change, Transformation and Development*, Physica-Verlag, 2003.

Meyerson, Debra, K. E. Weick, and R. M. Kramer, "Swift Trust and Temporary Groups," in R. M. Kramer and T. R. Tyler, eds., *Trust in Organizations: Frontiers of Theory and Research*, Sage Publications, 1996, pp. 166–195.

Milgrom, Paul R. and John Roberts, *Economics, Organizations, and Management*, Prentice Hall, 1992.

Mossholder, Kevin W., Randall P. Settoon, and Stephane C. Henagan, "A Relational Perspective on Turnover: Examining Structural, Attitudinal, and Behavioral Predictors," *Academy of Management Journal*, 2005, *48* (4), 607–618.

Myerson, Roger, *Game Theory: Analysis of Conflict*, Harvard University Press, 1991.

Neugebauer, Tibor and Stefan Traub, "Public Good and Private Good Valuation for Waiting Time Reduction – A Laboratory Study," 2006. Working Paper.

Newell, Allen and Herbert A. Simon, *Human Problem Solving*, Prentice Hall, 1972.

Neyman, Abraham and Daijiro Okada, "Two-Person Repeated Games with Finite Automata," *International Journal of Game Theory*, 2000, *29* (3), 309–325.

Nielsen, Ivy K., Steve M. Jex, and Gary A. Adams, "Development and Validation of Scores on a Two-Dimensional Workplace Friendship Scale," *Educational and Psychological Measurement*, 2000, *60*, 628–643.

Nowak, Martin A. and Robert M. May, "The Spatial Dilemmas of Evolution," *International Journal of Bifurcation and Chaos*, 1993, *3* (1), 35–78.

Nowak, Martin and Karl Sigmund, "A Strategy of Win-Stay, Lose-Shift that Outperforms Tit-For-Tat in the Prisoner's Dilemma Game," *Nature*, 1993, *364*, 56–58.

Oates, Kerris and Margo Wilson, "Nominal Kinship Cues Facilitate Altruism," *Proceedings of the Royal Society B*, January 2002, *269* (1487), 105–109.

OECD, "Participative Web: User-Created Content," Technical Report, Organisation for Economic Co-operation and Development 2007.

Offer, Avner, "Between the Gift and the Market: the Economy of Regard," *Economic History Review*, 1997, *50* (3), 450–476.

Ogawa, Susumu, "Does Sticky Information Affect the Locus of Innovation?," *Research Policy*, 1998, *26* (7-8), 777–790.

Okada, Daijiro and Abraham Neyman, "Growing Strategy Sets in Repeated Games," Working Paper, 2003.

Olson, Mancur, *The Logic of Collective Action*, Harvard University Press, 1965.

Ortega Soto, José Felipe, "Wikipedia: A Quantitative Analysis." PhD dissertation, Departamento de Sistemas Telemáticos y Computación, Universidad Rey Juan Carlos, Móstoles, Madrid 2009.

Osterloh, Margit, Sandra Rota, and Marc von Wartburg, "Open Source – New Rules in Software Development," 2001. Working Paper, University of Zurich.

Ostrom, Elinor, *Governing the Commons: The Evolution of Institutions for Collective Action*, Cambridge University Press, 1990.

– , James Walker, and Roy Gardner, "Covenants With and Without a Sword: Self-Governance is Possible," *American Political Science Review*, 1992, *86* (2), 404–417.

Peitz, Martin and Patrick Waelbroeck, "Piracy of Digital Products: A Critical Review of the Theoretical Literature," *Information Economics and Policy*, 2006, *18* (4), 449–476.

Plott, Charles R. and Vernon L. Smith, eds, *Handbook of Experimental Economics Results*, Vol. 1 of *Handbooks in Economics*, North-Holland, 2008.

Powell, Walter W., "Neither Market Nor Hierarchy," *Research in Organizational Behavior*, 1990, *12*, 295–336.

Prasad, Kislaya, "Computability and Randomness of Nash equilibrium in Infinite Games," *Journal of Mathematical Economics*, 1991, *20* (5), 429–442.

_ , "On the Computability of Nash Equilibria," *Journal of Economic Dynamics and Control*, 1997, *21* (6), 943–953.

Price, James L. and Charles W. Mueller, "A Causal Model of Turnover for Nurses," *Academy of Management Journal*, 1981, *24* (3), 543–565.

Quah, Danny, "Technology Dissemination and Economic Growth: Some Lessons for the New Economy," Technical Report 522, Centre for Economic Performance, LSE 2001.

_ , "Matching Demand and Supply in a Weightless Economy: Market-Driven Creativity With and Without IPRs," Technical Report 534, Centre for Economic Performance, LSE 2002.

_ , "Digital Goods and the New Economy," Technical Report 563, Centre for Economic Performance, LSE 2003.

Quintas, Paul and Ken Guy, "Collaborative, pre-competitive RD and the Firm," *Research Policy*, 1995, *24* (3), 325–348.

Rabin, Matthew, "Incorporating Fairness Into Game Theory and Economics," *American Economic Review*, 1993, *83* (5), 1281–1302.

Rand, David G., Anna Dreber, Tore Ellingsen, Drew Fudenberg, and Martin A. Nowak, "Positive Interactions Promote Public Cooperation," *Science*, September 2009, *325* (5945), 1272–1275.

Ray, Debraj, "Nonpaternalistic Intergenerational Altruism," *Journal of Economic Theory*, 1987, *41* (1), 112–132.

Raymond, Eric S., *The Cathedral and the Bazaar: Musings On Linux And Open Source By An Accidental Revolutionary (second edition)*, O'Reilly Media, 2001.

Rege, Mari and Kjetil Telle, "The Impact of Social Approval and Framing on Cooperation in Public Good Situations," *Journal of Public Economics*, 2004, *88* (12), 2801–2816.

Rheingold, Howard, *Smart Mobs: The Next Social Revolution*, Basic Books, New York, 2002.

Roth, Alvin E. and Ido Erev, "Learning in Extensive-Form Games: Experimental Data and Simple Dynamic Models in the Intermediate Term," *Games and Economic Behavior*, 1995, *8*, 164–212.

Rubinstein, Ariel, "Equilibrium in Supergames with the Overtaking Criterion," *Journal of Economic Theory*, 1979, *21* (1), 1–9.

Sacchetti, Silvia and Roger Sugden, "The Organization of Production and its Publics: Mental Proximity, Market and Hierarchies," *Review of Social Economy*, 2009, *67* (3), 289–311.

Samuelson, Paul A., "The Pure Theory of Public Expenditure," *Review of Economic Studies*, 1954, *36* (4), 387–389.

Satow, Kay L., "Social Approval and Helping," *Journal of Experimental Social Psychology*, 1975, *11* (6), 501–509.

Sauermann, Heinz and Reinhard Selten, "Anspruchsanpassungstheorie der Unternehmung," *Zeitschrift für die gesamte Staatswissenschaft*, 1962, *118*, 577–597.

Schor, Juliet B. and Douglas B. Holt, eds, *The Consumer Society Reader*, The New Press, 2000.

Schotter, Andrew, *The Economic Theory of Social Institutions*, Cambridge University Press, 1981.

Schumpeter, Joseph A., *The Theory of Economic Development*, Harvard University Press, 1934.

Sefton, Martin, Robert Shupp, and James Walker, "The Effect of Rewards and Sanctions in Provision of Public Goods," *Economic Inquiry*, 2007, *45* (4), 671–690.

Selten, Reinhard, "Reexamination of the Perfectness Concept for Equilibrium Points in Extensive Games," *International Journal of Game Theory*, 1975, *4* (1), 25–55.

– , "Aspiration Adaptation Theory," *Journal of Mathematical Psychology*, 1998, *42* (2), 191–214.

_ and Peter Hammerstein, "Gaps in Harley's Argument on Evolutionary Stable Learning Rules and in the Logic of Tit-For-Tat," *Behavioral and Brain Sciences*, 1984, *7* (1), 115–116.

Sennett, Richard, *Handwerk*, Berlin Verlag, 2008.

Shah, Sanoli K., "Sources and Patterns of Innovation in a Consumer Products Field: Innovations in Sporting Equipment," *Massachusetts Institute of Technology, Sloan School Working Paper 4105*, 2000.

_ , "Open Beyond Software," in Danese Cooper, Chris DiBona, and Mark Stone, eds., *Open Sources 2.0: The Continuing Evolution*, O'Reilly Media, 2006, pp. 339–360.

Shapiro, Carl and Hal R. Varian, *Information Rules*, Harvard Business School Press, 1999.

Siegel, Sidney, "Level of Aspiration and Decision Making," *Psychological Review*, 1957, *64* (4), 252–262.

Sigmund, Karl, Christoph Hauert, and Martin A. Nowak, "Reward and Punishment," *Proceedings of the National Academy of Sciences*, 2001, *98* (19), 10757–10762.

Simon, Herbert A., "On a Class of Skew Distribution Functions," *Biometrika*, 1955, *42* (3/4), 425–440.

_ , *Models of Man: Social and Rational*, John Wiley Sons, 1957.

_ , "The Architecture of Complexity," *Proceedings of the American Philosophical Society*, 1962, *106* (6), 467–482.

Skyrms, Brian, *Evolution of the Social Contract*, Cambridge University Press, 1996.

_ and Robin Pemantle, "A Dynamic Model of Social Network Formation," *Proceedings of the National Academy of Sciences*, 2000, *97* (16), 9340–9346.

Sol, Joeri, "Peer Evaluation: Incentives and Co-Worker Relations," *Tinbergen Institute Discussion Paper 055/1*, 2010.

Spence, Michael, "Job Market Signaling," *The Quarterly Journal of Economics*, 1973, *87* (3), 355–374.

Spiekermann, Kai, "Sort out your Neighborhood," *Synthese*, 2008, *168* (2), 273–294.

Stark, Oded and Doris A. Behrens, "An Evolutionary Edge of Knowing Less (or: On the 'Curse' of Global Information)," *Journal of Evolutionary Economics*, 2010, *20* (1), 77–94.

Stephan, Paula E., "The Economics of Science," *Journal of Economic Literature*, 1996, *34* (3), 1199–1235.

Stiglitz, Joseph E., "Knowledge As a Global Public Good," in Inge Kaul, Isabelle Grunberg, and Marc Stern, eds., *Global Public Goods*, Oxford University Press, 1999.

Surowiecki, James, *The Wisdom of Crowds: Why the Many Are Smarter Than the Few and How Collective Wisdom Shapes Business, Economies, Societies and Nations*, Doubleday, Garden City, NY, 2004.

Sydow, Jörg and Guido Möllering, *Produktion in Netzwerken - Make, Buy Cooperate (2. Auflage)*, Verlag Vahlen, München, 2009.

Tapscott, Don and Anthony D. Williams, *Wikinomics*, Portfolio Hardcover, 2008.

Taylor, Peter D. and Leo B. Jonker, "Evolutionary Stable Strategies and Game Dynamics," *Mathematical Biosciences*, 1978, *16* (76-83), 145–156.

Tißler, Jan, "Offener Umgang, stetiger Dialog und Anerkennung sind die Schlüssel," *t3n Open Source Web*, 2009, (16), 68–69.

Titmuss, Richard M., *The Gift Relationship*, London: Allen and Unwin, 1970.

Torvalds, Linus and David Diamond, *Just for Fun: The Story of an Accidential Revolutionary*, Harper, 2001.

Trivers, Robert L., "The Evolution of Reciprocal Altruism," *Quarterly Review of Biology*, 1971, *46* (1), 35–57.

van Dijk, Frans, Joep Sonnemans, and Frans van Winden, "Social Ties in a Public Good Experiment," *Journal of Public Economics*, 2002, *85* (2), 275–299.

van Wendel de Joode, Ruben, "Understanding Open Source Communities – An Organizational Perspective." PhD dissertation, Technische Universiteit Delft 2005.

van Winden, Frans, Frans van Dijk, and Joep Sonnemans, "Intrinsic Motivation in a Public Good Environment," in Charles R. Plott and Vernon L. Smith, eds., *Handbook of Experimental Economics Results*, Vol. 1 of *Handbooks in Economics*, North-Holland, 2008, chapter 89, pp. 836–845.

Varian, Hal R. and Carl Shapiro, "Linux Adoption in the Public Sector," in Bernd Lutterbeck, Matthias Bärwolf, and Robert A. Gehring, eds., *Open Source Jahrbuch 2007*, Lehmanns, 2007.

Veblen, Thorstein, "Conspiciuous Consumption," in Juliet B. Schor and Douglas B. Holt, eds., *The Consumer Society Reader*, W.W. Norton & Company, 2000, pp. 187–204.

Veblen, Thorstein B., *The Theory of The Leisure Class*, Dover Publication, 1994 (1899).

Vignolo, Thierry, "Imitation and Selective Matching in Reputational Games," *Journal of Evolutionary Economics*, 2010, *20* (3), 395–412.

von Hippel, Eric, *The Sources of Innovation*, Oxford University Press, 1988.

_ , *Democratizing Innovation*, MIT Press, 2005.

_ and Georg von Krogh, "Free Revealing and the Private-Collective Model for Innovation Incentives," *R&D Management*, 2006, *36* (3), 291–302.

von Neumann, John and Oskar Morgenstern, *Theory of Games and Economic Behavior*, Princeton University Press, 1944.

Weber, Steven, *The Success of Open Source*, Harvard University Press, 2004.

Weibull, Jörgen, *Evolutionary Game Theory*, paperback ed., MIT Press, 1997.

Weimann, Joachim, "Individual Behavior in a Free-Riding Experiment," *Journal of Public Economics*, 1994, *54* (2), 185–200.

Weitzman, Martin L., "Recombinant Growth," *The Quarterly Journal of Economics*, 1998, *113* (2), 331–360.

West, Stuart A., Andy Gardner, and Ashleigh S. Griffin, "Quick Guide: Altruism," *Current Biology*, 2006, *16* (13), 482–483.

Wichmann, Thorsten, *FLOSS Final Report Part 2. Firms' Open Source Activities: Motivations and Policy Implications*, Berlecon Research GmbH, Berlin, 2002.

Wilkinson, Dennis M. and Bernardo A. Huberman, "Cooperation and Quality in Wikipedia," in "Proceedings of the 2007 International Symposium on Wikis" 2007, pp. 157–164.

Yule, G. Udny, "A Mathematical Theory of Evolution, Based on the Conclusions of Dr. J. C. Willis, F.R.S.," *Philosophical Transactions of the Royal Society (B)*, 1925, *213*, 21–87.

Zeitlyn, David, "Gift Economies in the Development of Open Source Software: Anthropological Reflections," *Research Policy*, 2003, *32* (7), 1287–1291.

Zelmer, Jennifer, "Linear Public Goods Experiments: A Meta-Analysis," *Experimental Economics*, 2003, *6* (3), 299–310.

Appendix A: Websites

In the following we list all websites and their URLs used throughout research for this thesis. All websites were last accessed in January 2011. The URLs were mentioned in the text as footnote on their first occurence. The first entry is the name of the organization or individual maintaning the website, the second entry is the website's title. If the title is inappropriate it is replaced by a descriptive phrase. The third entry is the website's URL.

Adelstein, Tom / Linux Journal	Linux in Government: Open Source Innovation within the DoD http://www.linuxjournal.com/article/7644
AllRecipes	AllRecipes Homepage http://www.allrecipes.com
The Apache Software Foundation	The Apache Software Foundation Homepage http://apache.org
The Apache Software Foundation	Foundation Project http://apache.org/foundation/
The Apache Software Foundation	How the ASF works http://apache.org/foundation/how-it-works.html
Creative Commons	Licenses http://creativecommons.org/about/-licenses/
Daffara, Carlo	Estimating the Number of Active and Stable FLOSS Projects http://robertogaloppini.net/2007/08/23/-estimating-the-number-of-active-and-stable-floss-projects/

The Debian Project	Debian – The Universal Operating System http://www.debian.org/
The Debian Project	Debian Voting Information http://www.debian.org/vote/
The Debian Project	Debian's Organizational Structure http://www.debian.org/intro/-organization/
European Patent Office	EPO - European Patent Office Homepage http://www.epo.org/
European Patent Office	EPO - Häufig gestellte Fragen (FAQ) http://www.epo.org/metanav/help/-faq_de.html#a4
Facebook	Facebook Homepage http://www.facebook.com
GoLatex	Kann man Tabellen im Querformat darstellen? http://www.golatex.de/kann-man-tabellen-im-querformat-darstellen-t2003.html
LastFM	LastFM Homepage http://www.last.fm
Linux Onine	The Linux Homepage at Linux Online http://www.linux.org
Linux Online	About the Linux Operating System http://www.linux.org/info
Linux Online	Linux Online – User Groups Germany http://www.linux.org/groups/-germany.html
Linux V-Server	Hall of Fame http://linux-vserver.org/Hall_of_Fame
München	LiMux – Die IT Revolution http://www.muenchen.de/Rathaus/dir/-limux/english/147197/index.html
MySpace	MySpace Homepage http://www.myspace.com
Netcraft Ltd.	Netcraft SSL Survey http://news.netcraft.com/ssl-survey/ and https://ssl.netcraft.com/ssl-sample-report/

Netcraft Ltd.	Web Server Survey Archive http://news.netcraft.com/archives/-category/web-server-survey/
The Open Source Initiative	Mission http://opensource.org
The Open Source Initiative	Open Source Licenses http://opensource.org/licenses/
Python Software Foundation	Python Programming Language – Official Website http://python.org
The R-Project	The R-Project for Statistical Computing http://www.r-project.com
Theo de Raadt	Email exchange between NetBSD and Theo de Raadt http://www.theos.com/deraadt/coremail/
Stallman, Richard	Philosophy of the GNU Project http://www.gnu.org/philosophy/-philosophy.html
W3Schools	Browser Statistics http://www.w3schools.com/browsers/-browsers_stats.asp
Wallen, Jack / TechRepublic	U.S. Department of Defense officially adopts open source http://blogs.techrepublic.com.com/-opensource/?p=347
The Wikimedia Foundation	Wikimedia Traffic Analysis Report http://stats.wikimedia.org/-archive/squid_reports/2010-10/-SquidReportOperatingSystems.htm
Wikipedia	Wikipedia Homepage http://www.wikipedia.org
Wikipedia	Wikipedia's Linux entry http://en.wikipedia.org/wiki/Linux
Wikipedia	Wikipedia User Page Woohookitty http://en.wikipedia.org/wiki/-User:Woohookitty

Wikipedia	Wikipedia User Page Woohookitty Awards http://en.wikipedia.org/wiki/-User:Woohookitty/Awards
YouTube	YouTube Homepage http://www.youtube.com
Zuckerman, Ethan	Samuel Bowles Introduces Kudunomics http://www.ethanzuckerman.com/blog/-2009/11/17/samuel-bowles-introduces--kudunomics/2010

Institutional and Socio-Economics

Edited by Wolfram Elsner,
Wilfred Dolfsma, Arne Heise,
Helge Peukert and Werner Schönig

Volumes 1-9 are available at Centaurus Verlags- GmbH & Co. KG, Herbolzheim. Please send your order to them.

Band 1 Adelheid Biesecker / Klaus Grenzdörffer / Holger Heide (Hrsg.): Neue Bewertungen in der Ökonomie. 1995.

Band 2 Adelheid Biesecker / Klaus Grenzdörffer (Hrsg.): Kooperation, Netzwerk, Selbstorganisation. Elemente demokratischen Wirtschaftens. 1996.

Band 3 Sabine Wolf: Ökonomie und Geschlechterverhältnisse. Zu den Möglichkeiten und Grenzen der Einbindung des Geschlechterverhältnisses in die ökonomische Theorie. 1997.

Band 4 Adelheid Biesecker / Klaus Grenzdörffer / Christina Vocke (Hrsg.): Neue institutionelle Arrangements für eine zeitgemäße Wohlfahrt. 1997.

Band 5 Stefan Kesting: Diskurs und Macht. 1999.

Band 6 Adelheid Biesecker / Wolfram Elsner / Klaus Grenzdörffer (Hrsg.): Ökonomie der Betroffenen und Mitwirkenden. Erweiterte Stakeholder-Prozesse. 1998.

Band 7 Adelheid Biesecker / Wolfram Elsner / Klaus Grenzdörffer (Hrsg.): Vielfalt und Interaktion sozioökonomischer Kulturen. Modernität oder Zukunftsfähigkeit. 2000.

Band 8 Adelheid Biesecker / Wolfram Elsner / Klaus Grenzdörffer (Hrsg.): Ökonomische Be-Wertungen in gesellschaftlichen Prozessen. Markt – Macht – Diskurs. 2002.

Band 9 Jens Rose: Weiterbildung peripher Beschäftigter im Arbeitskräfte- und Wissenspool. Auf dem Weg zu einer FlexStAbility. 2001.

Band 10 Andreas Hirt: Konstitutionelle Ökonomik und Kommunikatives Handeln. Ein Beitrag zur ökonomischen Institutionentheorie. 2002.

Band 11 Adelheid Biesecker / Wolfram Elsner / Klaus Grenzdörffer (Hrsg.): Kooperation und interaktives Lernen in der Ökonomie. 2002.

Band 12 Volker Wellhöner: Ökonomik – Physik – Mathematik. Die Allgemeine Gleichgewichtstheorie im interdisziplinären Kontext. 2002.

Band 13 Changhoon Lee: Kritik der neoklassischen Umweltökonomik. Über die (Un-)Möglichkeit einer pareto-effizienten Umweltsteuer. 2004.

Band 14 Wolfram Elsner / Adelheid Biesecker (Hrsg.): Neuartige Netzwerke und nachhaltige Entwicklung. Komplexität und Koordination in Industrie, Stadt und Region. 2003.

Band 15 Adelheid Biesecker / Wolfram Elsner (Hrsg.): Erhalten durch Gestalten. Nachdenken über eine (re)produktive Ökonomie. 2004.

Band 16 Sebastian Berger: Europäischer Institutionalismus. Die Kernkonzepte Open System Approach (OSA) und Circular Cumulative Causation (CCC) und ihre Bedeutung für die moderne evolutorisch-institutionelle Ökonomik. Unter besonderer Berücksichtigung der Werke von N. Georgescu-Roegen, K. W. Kapp, A. Lowe, G. Myrdal und K. Polanyi. 2007.

Band 17 Matthias Greiff: Social Approval as an Incentive. The Voluntary Provision of Public Goods in Social Production Communities. 2011.

www.peterlang.de

Peter Lang · Internationaler Verlag der Wissenschaften

Władysław Welfe (ed.)

Knowledge-based Economies

Models and Methods

Frankfurt am Main, Berlin, Bern, Bruxelles, New York, Oxford, Wien, 2009.
216 pp.
ISBN 978-3-631-57981-7 · pb. € 43,80*

Growth of new market economies is associated with rapid expansion of knowledge capital. It leads to the emergence of knowledge-based economies. As the literature broadly uses international cross-section samples to study the role of knowledge capital, we tried to recapitulate on the results of this research. However, our main aim was to show how they can be applied to analyse the growth of single economies and develop scenarios for the next 20 to 30 years. Extended production functions with endogenous TFP determined by knowledge capital generate potential output that may considerably differ from effective output. This calls for constructing complete models, addressing both final demand and total supplies. Their suggested structure is presented using the annual long-term macro-econometric models W8D of Polish economy.

Content: The role of knowledge capital in economic growth and the modelling of its effects within macro-econometric models · Explaining and measuring the extended production function and total factor productivity by analyzing the impacts of R&D and human capital

FSC
www.fsc.org
MIX
Papier | Fördert
gute Waldnutzung
FSC® C083411

Kolibri 360 GmbH
Ferdinand-Jühlke-Straße 7
99095 Erfurt, Deutschland
produktsicherheit@kolibri360.de